CARL ROGERS ON PERSONAL POWER

Also by Carl Rogers

CARL ROGERS ON PERSONAL POWER

Carl R. Rogers, Ph. D.

CONSTABLE LONDON

First published in Great Britain 1978
by Constable and Company Limited
3 The Lanchesters, 162 Fulham Palace Road
London W6 9ER
Copyright © 1977, 1978 by Carl Rogers
ISBN 0 09 462090 3
Reprinted 1979, 1982, 1985, 1986, 1989
1992,1994, 1996, 1998

A CIP catalogue record for this book
is available from the British Library

ACKNOWLEDGMENTS

Grateful acknowledgment is made for permission to use the following material.

Cassette No. 7, Personal Adjustment Series: Used by permission of Instructional Dynamics, Inc.

"Mike": Used by permission of AAP Tape Library, American Academy of Psychotherapists, 1040 Woodcock Road, Orlando, Florida 32803.

"Because That's My Way": Used by permission of Great Plains National Television.

"Follow-Up of a Counseling Case Treated by the Non-Directive Method" by A. W. Coombs: *Journal of Clinical Psychology,* Vol. 1, April 1945, pp. 147–154. Used by permission.

"Project Freedom" by J. B. Carr: From *English Journal,* Copyright © 1964 by the National Council of Teachers of English. Reprinted by permission of the author and the publisher.

Excerpt from *Pedagogy of the Oppressed* by Paulo Freire: © 1970 by Paulo Freire. Used by permission of The Seabury Press.

"The Politics of Group Process" by Judith L. Henderson: Used by permission of the author. First published in *Rough Times,* Jan./Feb. 1974.

Excerpts from "The Steel Shutter": This film is available for rental through the Center for Studies of The Person, 1125 Torrey Pines Road, La Jolla, California 92037.

"Intercultural Communication Groups" by Binnie Kristal-Andersson: *Invandrar Rapport,* Vol. 3 No. 7, 1975. Boras, Sweden. Used by permission of the author.

"The Actualizing Tendency in Relation to 'Motives' and to Consciousness" by Carl Rogers: First published in 1963 Nebraska Symposium on Motivation, University of Nebraska Press.

Contents

CONTENTS

A special
note

I have been greatly perplexed by the pronoun problem, or, more exactly, the "he-she" issue. I am totally in sympathy with the view that women are subtly demeaned by the use of the masculine pronoun when speaking in general of a member of the human species. On the other hand I enjoy forceful writing, and a "himself/herself" in the middle of a sentence often destroys its impact. I do not believe a satisfactory solution will be found until someone comes up with an acceptable set of nonsexual pronouns.

I have chosen to deal with the problem in this way: In one chapter all general references to members of our species are put in feminine terms—in the next chapter masculine. Thus the first chapter uses feminine pronouns where the reference is general, the second chapter uses masculine pronouns for the same purpose, alternating similarly throughout the book. It is the best solution I could find to serve both of my purposes, an equalitarian aim and a desire for forcefulness.

—Carl Rogers

Introduction

Some months ago a strange thing happened to me. I think it was the nearest I have ever come to having a psychic experience. I was intent on some work I was doing at my desk, when suddenly there flashed into my mind a complete sentence: "I walk softly through life." I was puzzled by the intrusion, but since it had nothing to do with the work at hand I shrugged it off. A bit later the peculiar nature of this "flash" struck me, and I began to speculate about it.

All sorts of associations crowded in. As a boy I'd read hundreds of books about frontiersmen and Indians, men who could glide noiselessly through the forest without stepping on a dead twig or disturbing the foliage. No one knew their whereabouts until they had reached their destination and accomplished their purpose, whether they were on an errand of mercy or a warlike mission. I realized my professional life had had that same quality. I haven't wanted to make a fuss about where I am going until I have arrived. I have avoided noisy confrontations whenever possible. When I was told, early in my career, that it was absolutely impossible for a psychologist to carry on psychotherapy, because this was the province of the psychiatrist, I made no attempt to meet the issue head-on. Instead, I first used the term treatment interviews to describe what we were doing.

Later the label counseling seemed more acceptable. Only after years of experience, and the amassing of a considerable body of research by me and my colleagues, did I openly speak of the fact —by then obvious—that we were doing psychotherapy. I had walked softly through life, making relatively little noise until I had arrived at my destination—and it was too late to stop me. I do have a stubborn streak.

One disadvantage of this way of proceeding is that I have not always realized the full significance of the pathway that I, and an increasing number of others, have taken. It is only in recent years that I have come to recognize how "radical" and "revolutionary" our work has been. I use those terms in their original, not their popular, meanings. Our work has "gone to the root of" many of the concepts and values of our culture and has brought about "a complete or marked change" in many principles and procedures. Most notably it has altered the thinking about power and control in relationships between persons. That is what this book is about.

So you will find in these pages many men and women who are walking softly through life—and creating a revolution as they do so. The book tells of homes and schools and industries and interfaces between races and cultures, all of which have been drastically changed by persons who trust their own power, do not feel a need to have "power over," and who are willing to foster and facilitate the latent strength in the other person. It tells of specific instances—a family relationship, a workshop, a day camp, a group of Catholics and Protestants from Belfast—where ordinary ways of proceeding have been turned upside down by a basic trust in the constructive potential of the person.

As Gertrude Stein said of Paris, "It is not what Paris gives you; it is what she does not take away." This can be paraphrased to become a definition of the person-centered approach, the value-laden concept central to this book. "It is not that this approach gives power to the person; it never takes it away." That such a seemingly innocent base can be so truly revolutionary in its implications may seem surprising. It is, however, the central theme of what I have written.

I have endeavored to give examples—both anecdotal and research—to illustrate the force of the person-centered approach. Such a way changes the very nature of psychotherapy, of marriage, of education, of administration, even of politics.

These changes indicate that a quiet revolution is already under way. They point to a future of a very different nature, built around a new type of self-empowered person who is emerging.

Part I

A quiet revolution: the impact of a person-centered approach

Chapter 1 | The politics of the helping professions

Three years ago I was first asked about the politics of the client-centered approach to psychotherapy. I replied that there was no politics in client-centered therapy, an answer which was greeted with a loud guffaw. When I asked my questioner to explain, he replied, "I spent three years of graduate school learning to be an expert in clinical psychology. I learned to make accurate diagnostic judgments. I learned the various techniques of altering the subject's attitudes and behavior. I learned subtle modes of manipulation, under the labels of interpretation and guidance. Then I began to read your material, which upset everything I had learned. You were saying that the power rests not in my mind but in his organism. You completely reversed the relationship of power and control which had been built up in me over three years. And then you say there is no politics in the client-centered approach!"

This was the beginning—perhaps a late beginning—of my education regarding the politics of interpersonal relationships. The more I thought and read, and the more I sensed the present-day concern with power and control, the more new facets I experienced in my relationships in therapy, in intensive groups, in families, and among friends. Gradually I realized my experience ran parallel to the old story of the uneducated man and his first exposure to a course in literature. "You know," he told his friends later, "I've found out I've been speaking prose all my life and never knew it." In similar vein I could now say "I've been practicing and teaching politics all my professional life and never realized it fully until now." So I am no longer surprised when Farson, in an appraisal of my work, says, "Carl Rogers is not known for his politics. People are more likely to associate his name with widely acclaimed innovations in counseling technique, personality theory, philosophy of science, psychotherapy research, encounter groups, student-centered teaching. . . . But in recent years, I have come to think of him more as a political figure, a man whose cumulative effect on society has made him one of the . . . social revolutionaries of our time."[1] It is not just that I am a slow learner, that I have only recently realized my political impact. It is partly that a new concept has been in the process of construction in our language. It is not just a new label. It brings together a cluster of meanings into a powerful new concept.

The use of the word "politics" in such contexts as "the politics of the family," "the politics of therapy," "sexual politics," "the politics of experience" is new. I have not found any dictionary definition that even suggests the way in which the word is currently utilized. The *American Heritage Dictionary* still gives definitions only of this sort: **politics:** "The methods or tactics involved in managing a state or government."[2]

Yet the word has acquired a new set of meanings. Politics, in present-day psychological and social usage, has to do with *power and control:* with the extent to which persons desire, attempt to obtain, possess, share, or surrender power and control over others and/or themselves. It has to do with *the maneuvers, the strategies and tactics, witting or unwitting,* by which such power and control over one's own life and others' lives is sought and gained—or shared or relinquished. It has to do with the *locus of decision-making power:* who makes the decisions which, consciously or unconsciously, regulate or control the thoughts, feelings, or behavior of others or oneself. It has to do with the *effects of these decisions and these strategies,* whether proceeding from an individual or a group, whether aimed at gaining or relinquishing control upon the person himself, upon others, and upon the various systems of society and its institutions. In sum it is the process of gaining, using, sharing or relinquishing power, control, decision-making. It is the process of the highly complex interactions and effects of these elements as they exist in relationships between persons, between a person and a group, or between groups.

This new construct has had a powerful influence on me. It has caused me to take a fresh look at my professional life work. I've had a role in initiating the person-centered approach. This view developed first in counseling and psychotherapy, where it was known as client-centered, meaning a person seeking help was not treated as a dependent patient but as a responsible client. Extended to education, it was called student-centered teaching. As it has moved into a wide variety of fields, far from its point of origin—intensive groups, marriage, family relationships, administration, minority groups, interracial, intercultural, and even international relationships—it seems best to adopt as broad a term as possible: person-centered.

It is the psychological dynamics of this approach that has interested me—how it is seen by and how it affects the individual. I have been interested in observing this approach from a scientific and empirical point of view; what conditions make it possible for a person to change and develop, and what are the specific effects or outcomes of these conditions. But I have never given careful consideration to the interpersonal politics set in motion by such an approach. Now I begin to see the revolutionary nature of those political forces. I have found myself compelled to reassess and reevaluate all my work. I wish to ask what are the *political* effects (in the new sense of political) of all that I, and my many colleagues throughout the world, have done and are doing.

What is the impact of a client-centered point of view on the issues of power and control in individual psychotherapy? We shall explore the politics of various approaches to helping people, whether through one-to-one therapy, or through encounter or other intensive groups. We shall confront openly a subject not often discussed: the issue of power and control in the so-called helping professions.

In 1940 I began to try to change what I would now call the politics of therapy. Describing an emerging trend, I said, "This newer approach differs from the older one in that it has a genuinely different goal. It aims directly toward the greater independence and integration of the individual rather than hoping that such results will accrue if the counselor assists in solving the problem. The individual and not the problem is the focus. The aim is not to solve one particular problem but to assist the individual to *grow,* so that he can cope with the present problem and with later problems in a better integrated fashion. If he can gain enough integration to handle one problem in more independent, more responsible, less confused, better organized ways, then he will also handle new problems in that manner.

"If this seems a little vague, it may be made more specific. . . . It relies much more heavily on the individual drive toward growth, health, and adjustment. Therapy is not a matter of doing something *to* the individual, or of inducing him to do something about himself. It is instead a matter of freeing him for normal growth and development, of removing obstacles so that he can again move forward."[3]

When they were enunciated first in 1940, great furor was aroused by these statements. I had described various counseling techniques much in use at that time—such as suggestions, advice, persuasion, and interpretation—and had pointed out that these rested on two basic assumptions: that "the counselor knows best," and that he can find techniques by which to move his client most efficiently to the counselor-chosen goal.

I see now that I had dealt a double-edged political blow. I had said that most counselors saw themselves as competent to control the lives of their clients. And I had advanced the view that it was preferable simply to free the client to become an independent, self-directing person. I was making it clear that if they agreed with me, it would mean the complete disruption and reversal of their personal control in their counseling relationships.

Over the years, the point of view I advanced so tentatively in 1940 became enlarged, deepened, and reinforced, both by clinical experience and research. It became known as client-centered psychotherapy, and in the intervening years it has been buttressed by more empirical studies than any other therapeutic approach.

From the perspective of politics, power, and control, person-centered therapy is based on a premise which at first seemed risky and uncertain: a view of man as at core a trustworthy organism. This base has over the years been strengthened by experience with troubled individuals, psychotic persons, small intensive groups, students in classes, and staff groups. It has become more and more firmly established as a basic stance, though each person must learn it step by step for himself, to be convinced of its soundness. I have recently described it as "the gradually formed and tested hypothesis that the individual has within himself vast resources for self-understanding, for altering his self-concept, his attitudes, and his self-directed behavior —and that these resources can be tapped if only a definable climate of facilitative psychological attitudes can be provided."[4]

Is there any basis for this premise other than wishful thinking and the experience of a few people? I believe so. Biologists, neurophysiologists, and other scientists, including psychologists, have evidence that adds up to one conclusion. There is in every organism, at whatever level, an underlying flow of movement toward constructive fulfillment of its inherent possibilities. There is a natural tendency toward complete development in man. The term that has most often been used for this is the actualizing tendency, and it is present in all living organisms. It is the foundation on which the person-centered approach is built.

The actualizing tendency can of course be thwarted, but it cannot be destroyed without destroying the organism. I remember that in my boyhood the potato bin in which we stored our winter supply of potatoes was in the basement, several feet below a small basement window. The conditions were unfavorable, but the potatoes would begin to sprout—pale white sprouts, so unlike the healthy green shoots they sent up when planted in the soil in the spring. But these sad, spindly sprouts would grow two or three feet in length as they reached toward the distant light of the window. They were, in their bizarre, futile growth, a sort of desperate expression of the directional tendency I have been describing. They would never become a plant, never mature, never fulfill their real potentiality. But under the most adverse circumstances they were striving to become. Life would not give up, even if it could not flourish. In dealing with clients whose lives have been terribly warped, in working with men and women on the back wards of state hospitals, I often think of those potato sprouts. So unfavorable have been the conditions in which these people have developed that their lives often seem abnormal, twisted, scarcely human. Yet the directional tendency in them is to be trusted. The clue to understanding their behavior is that they are striving, in the only ways available to them, to move toward growth, toward becoming. To us the results may seem bizarre and futile, but they are life's desperate attempt to become itself. It is this potent tendency which is the underlying basis of client-centered therapy and all that has grown out of it.

It is obvious that even this premise of client-centered therapy, without going further, has enormous political implications. Our educational system, our industrial and military organizations, and many other aspects of our culture take the view that the nature of the individual is such that he cannot be trusted—that he must be guided, instructed, rewarded, punished, and controlled by those who are wiser or higher in status. To be sure, we give lip service to a democratic philosophy in which all power is vested in the people, but this philosophy is "honored more in the breach than in the observance." Hence simply describing the fundamental premise of client-centered therapy is to make a challenging political statement.

What psychological climate makes possible the release of the individual's capacity for understanding and managing his life? There are three conditions for this growth-promoting climate, whether it is in the therapist and client relationship or parent and child, leader and group, teacher and students, administrator and staff—in fact, in any situation in which the development of the person is a goal.

The first has to do with genuineness, realness—congruence. The more the therapist is herself in the relationship, putting up no professional front or personal facade, the greater is the likelihood that the client will change and grow in a constructive manner. It means that the therapist is openly being the feelings and attitudes that are flowing within at the moment. The term transparent catches the flavor of this element—the therapist makes herself transparent to the client; the client can see right through what the therapist *is* in the relationship; the client experiences no holding back on the part of the therapist. As for the therapist, what she is experiencing is available to awareness, can be lived in the relationship, and can be communicated if appropriate. Thus there is a close matching, or congruence, between what is being experienced at the gut level, what is present in awareness, and what is expressed to the client.

What does this mean in practical terms? It means that when the client is in pain or distress, the therapist is likely to be experiencing warmth or compassion or understanding. But at other times in the relationship she may be experiencing boredom or anger or even fear of a destructive client. The more the therapist can be aware of—and can become and express these feelings, whether positive or negative—the more likely she is to be helpful to the client. It is the *feelings* and *attitudes* that are helpful when expressed, not opinions or judgments about the other. Thus the therapist cannot *know* that the client is a boring conversationalist or a demanding bastard or a beautiful person. All these are debatable points. The therapist can only be congruent and helpful in expressing the feelings she *owns*. To the extent that the therapist experiences, owns, knows, expresses what is going on within—to that extent she is likely to facilitate growth in the client.

From the perspective of interpersonal politics, this first element of the relationship—congruence—gives a maximum space to *be*—for the client and for the therapist. The therapist is saying, in effect, "Here I am, as I am." There is no hint of any kind of control over the client's response to her way of being. To the contrary, finding that the therapist is permitting herself to be as she is, the client tends to discover that same freedom.

The second attitude of importance in creating a climate for change is acceptance, or caring or prizing—unconditional positive regard. It means that when the therapist is experiencing a positive, acceptant attitude toward whatever the client *is* at that moment, therapeutic movement or change is more likely. It involves the therapist's willingness for the client to be whatever feeling is going on at that moment—confusion, resentment, fear, anger, courage, love, or pride. It is a nonpossessive caring. The therapist prizes the client in a total rather than a conditional way. This resembles the love the parent sometimes feels toward an infant. Research indicates that the more this attitude is experienced by the therapist, the greater the probability that therapy will be successful.

It is not, of course, possible to feel such an unconditional caring all of the time. A therapist who is real will often have very different feelings, negative feelings toward the client. Hence it is not to be regarded as a "should," that the therapist *should* have an unconditional positive regard for the client. It is simply a fact that unless this is a reasonably frequent ingredient in the relationship, constructive client change is less likely.

What of the interpersonal politics of such an attitude? It is a powerful factor, but it is in no way manipulative or controlling in the relationship. There is no judgment or evaluation involved. Power over her own life is left completely in the hands of the client. It provides a nurturant atmosphere but not a forcing one.

The third facilitative aspect of the relationship is empathic understanding. This means that the therapist senses accurately the feelings and personal meanings that are being experienced by the client and communicates this understanding to the client. At its best the therapist is so much inside the private world of the other that she can clarify not only the meanings of which the client is aware but even those just below the level of awareness. When she responds at such a level the client's reaction is of this sort: "Perhaps that *is* what I've been trying to say. I haven't realized it, but yes, that's how I *do* feel!" This third element of the relationship is perhaps the most easily improved through even brief training. Therapists can *learn,* quite quickly, to be better, more sensitive listeners, more empathic. It is in part a skill as well as an attitude. To become more genuine or more caring, however, the therapist must change experientially, and this is a slower and more complex process.

Being empathic involves a choice on the part of the therapist as to what she will pay attention to, namely the inner world of the client as that individual perceives it. Thus it does change the interpersonal politics of the relationship. It in no way, however, exercises control over the client. On the contrary it assists the client in gaining a clearer understanding of, and hence a greater control over, her own world and her own behavior.

You may well ask why a person seeking help changes for the better when she is involved in a relationship with a therapist that contains these elements. Over the years I have come to see more and more clearly that the process of change in the client is a reciprocal of the attitudes of the therapist.

As the client finds the therapist listening acceptantly to her feelings, she becomes able to listen acceptantly to herself—to hear and accept the anger, the fear, the tenderness, the courage that is being experienced. As the client finds the therapist prizing and valuing even the hidden and awful aspects which have been expressed, she experiences a prizing and liking of herself. As the therapist is experienced as being real, the client is able to drop façades, to more openly *be* the experiencing within.

Politically, by listening to the feelings within, the client reduces the power others have had in inculcating guilts and fears and inhibitions, and is slowly extending the understanding of, and control over, self. As the client is more acceptant of self, the possibility of being in command of self becomes greater and greater. The client possesses herself to a degree that has never occurred before. The sense of power is growing. As the client becomes more self-aware, more self-acceptant, less defensive and more open, she finds at last some of the freedom to grow and change in the directions natural to the human organism. Life is now in her hands, to be lived as an individual.

I tried years ago to describe the process of change as it is inwardly experienced by the client in a person-centered therapy with a male therapist:

"I'm afraid of the therapist. I want help, but I don't know whether to trust him. He might see things which I don't know in myself—frightening and bad elements. He seems not to be judging me, but I'm sure he is. I can't tell him what really concerns me, but I can tell him about some past experiences that are related to my concern. He seems to understand those, so I can reveal a bit more of myself.

"But now that I've shared with him some of this bad side of me, he despises me. I'm sure of it, but it's strange I can find little evidence of it. Do you suppose that what I've told him isn't so bad? Is it possible that I need not be ashamed of it as a part of me? I no longer feel that he despises me. It makes me feel that I want to go further, exploring *me,* perhaps expressing more of myself. I find him a sort of companion as I do this—he seems really to understand.

"But now I'm getting frightened again, and this time deeply

frightened. I didn't realize that exploring the unknown recesses of myself would make me feel feelings I've never experienced before. It's very strange because in one way these aren't new feelings. I sense that they've always been there. But they seem so bad and disturbing I've never dared to let them flow in me. And now as I live these feelings in the hours with him, I feel terribly shaky, as though my world is falling apart. It used to be sure and firm. Now it is loose, permeable and vulnerable. It isn't pleasant to feel things I've always been frightened of before. It's his fault. Yet curiously I'm eager to see him and I feel more safe when I'm with him.

"I don't know who I am any more, but sometimes when I *feel* things I seem solid and real for a moment. I'm troubled by the contradictions I find in myself—I act one way and feel another—I think one thing and feel another. It is very disconcerting. It's also sometimes adventurous and exhilarating to be trying to discover who I am. Sometimes I catch myself feeling that perhaps the person I am is worth being, whatever that means.

"I'm beginning to find it very satisfying, though often painful, to share just what it is I'm feeling at this moment. You know, it is really helpful to try to listen to myself, to hear what is going on in me. I'm not so frightened any more of what *is* going on in me. It seems pretty trustworthy. I use some of my hours with him to dig deep into myself to know what I *am* feeling. It's scary work, but I want to *know*. And I do trust him most of the time, and that helps. I feel pretty vulnerable and raw, but I know he doesn't want to hurt me, and I even believe he cares. It occurs to me as I try to let myself down and down, deep into myself, that maybe if I could sense what is going on in me, and could realize its meaning, I would know who I am, and I would also know what to do. At least I feel this knowing sometimes with him.

"I can even tell him just how I'm feeling toward him at any given moment, and instead of this killing the relationship, as I used to fear, it seems to deepen it. Do you suppose I could be

13

my feelings with other people also? Perhaps that wouldn't be too dangerous either.

"You know, I feel as if I'm floating along on the current of life, very adventurously, being me. I get defeated sometimes, I get hurt sometimes, but I'm learning that those experiences are not fatal. I don't *know* exactly *who* I am, but I can feel my reactions at any given moment, and they seem to work out pretty well as a basis for my behavior from moment to moment. Maybe this is what it *means* to be *me*. But of course I can only do this because I feel safe in the relationship with my therapist. Or could I be myself this way outside of this relationship? I wonder. I wonder. Perhaps I could."[5]

The politics of the client-centered approach is a conscious renunciation and avoidance by the therapist of all control over, or decision-making for, the client. It is the facilitation of self-ownership by the client and the strategies by which this can be achieved; the placing of the locus of decision-making and the responsibility for the effects of these decisions. It is politically centered in the client.

Client-centered therapy has forever changed the politics of psychotherapy by the recording and publishing of transcribed therapeutic interviews. The mysterious, unknowable operations of the therapist are now wide open for all to see. This has let a breath of fresh air and common sense pervade the therapeutic world. The individual is able at least to choose a school of therapy that appears congenial to him. And where, at first, only client-centered interviews were available for discussion and criticism, there are now available on tape recordings expert therapists of a variety of orientations.[6]

Tom Hanna summarizes well the effect of this, and places a person-centered psychotherapy in a broader context. "Humanistic psychology has served to demystify the nature of therapy. Both the theory and the practice of therapeutic change should be made public, so that this knowledge can be be shared in common by both the patient and the therapist. . . . It is not a matter of the therapist following the old authoritarian medical model of keeping the patient in the dark as a patriarch might treat a child. . . . It is a matter of the habituated, unhappy individual regaining self-control and self-maintenance of his own wholeness and health.

"Of course, this is a most 'unprofessional' procedure, for it gives away the authority, the secrecy and the unquestionability of the professional healer and therapist. And it gives these things away to the patient. The center of the therapeutic action is not, therefore, considered to be within the therapist's decisions but within the patient's decisions."[7]

It is hardly necessary to say that the person-centered view drastically alters the therapist-patient relationship, as previously conceived. The therapist becomes the "midwife" of change, not its originator. She places the final authority in the hands of the client, whether in small things such as the correctness of a therapist response, or large decisions like the course of one's life direction. The locus of evaluation, of decision, rests clearly in the client's hands.

A person-centered approach is based on the premise that the human being is basically a trustworthy organism, capable of evaluating the outer and inner situation, understanding herself in its context, making constructive choices as to the next steps in life, and acting on those choices.

A facilitative person can aid in releasing these capacities when relating as a real person to the other, owning and expressing her own feelings; when experiencing a nonpossessive caring and love for the other; and when acceptantly understanding the inner world of the other. When this approach is made to an individual or a group, it is discovered that, over time, the choices made, the directions pursued, the actions taken are increasingly constructive personally and tend toward a more realistic social harmony with others.

So familiar has this humanistic, person-centered concept become—more familiar in the realm of the intellect than in actual practice—that we sometimes forget what a blow it struck at the views then current. It has taken me years to recognize that the violent opposition to a client-centered therapy sprang not only from its newness, and the fact that it came from a psychologist rather than a psychiatrist, but primarily because it struck such an outrageous blow to the therapist's *power.* It was in its *politics* that it was most threatening.

Freud shows his degree of distrust of the basic nature of man when he says, speaking of the need for super-ego control: "Our mind, that precious instrument by whose means we maintain ourselves alive, is no peacefully self-contained unity. It is rather to be compared with a modern State in which a mob, eager for enjoyment and destruction, has to be held down forcibly by a prudent superior class."[8]

To the end of his days, Freud still felt that if man's basic nature were released, nothing but destruction could be expected. The need for control of this beast within man was a matter of the greatest urgency. "The core of our being, then, is formed by the obscure id. . . . The one and only endeavor of these instincts is toward satisfaction. . . . But an immediate and regardless satisfaction of instinct, such as the id demands, would often enough lead to perilous conflicts with the external world and to extinction. . . . The id obeys the inexorable pleasure principle . . . and it remains a question of the greatest theoretical importance, and one that has not yet been answered, when and how it is ever possible for the pleasure principle to be overcome."[9]

As for the question of power and control in the everyday world, Freud took a very authoritarian stance: "The great majority of people have a strong need for authority which they can admire, to which they can submit, and which dominates and sometimes even ill-treats them. We have learned from the psychology of the individual whence comes this need of the masses. It is the longing for the father that lives in each of us from his childhood days."[10]

Freud's view of groups is equally pessimistic and startling. It would almost seem that Hitler must have studied and adopted these views: "A group is extraordinarily credulous and open to influence, it has no critical faculty, and the improbable does not exist for it. . . . Inclined as it itself is to all extremes, a group can only be excited by an excessive stimulus. Anyone who wishes to produce an effect upon it needs no logical adjustment in his arguments; he must paint in the most forcible colors, he must exaggerate, and he must repeat the same thing again and again. . . . It respects force and can only be slightly influenced by kindness, which it regards merely as a form of weakness. . . . It wants to be ruled and oppressed, and to fear its masters. . . . And, finally, groups have never thirsted after truth. They demand illusions, and cannot do without them. They constantly give what is unreal precedence over what is real; they are almost as strongly influenced by what is untrue as by what is true. They have an evident tendency not to distinguish between the two. . . . A group is an obedient herd, which could never live without a master. It has such a thirst for obedience that it submits instinctively to anyone who appoints himself as its master."[11]

For a therapist who was guided by Freud's thinking, client-centered views such as the following must have seemed not only heretical but highly dangerous: that the human organism is, at its deepest level, trustworthy; that man's basic nature is not something to be feared, but to be released in responsible self-expression; that small groups (in therapy or in classrooms) can responsibly and sensitively build constructive interpersonal relationships and choose wise individual and group goals; that all of the foregoing will be achieved if a facilitative person assists by creating a climate of realness, understanding and caring. Now that I review again Freud's views I can better understand why I was solemnly warned at the Menninger Clinic, around 1950, about the results of my views. I was told I would produce a dangerous psychopath because there would be no one to control her innately destructive core.

Over the years, Freudian analysts have softened their views of the politics of therapy. Along with Gestalt therapists, Jungians, rational emotive therapists, advocates of transactional analysis, and many other new therapies, they now take a middle-of-the-road view. The expert is at times definitely the authority (as in the Gestalt therapist dealing with the person in the "hot seat"), but there is also a recognition of the right of the individual to be responsible for himself. There has been no attempt to rationalize these contradictions. These therapists take a paternalistic stance, or follow the medical model, believing that at times control is best vested in the therapist, at other times (to be decided by the therapist) control and responsibility are best placed in the client's, or patient's, hands.

One approach which has been very definite in the politics of relationships is behaviorism. Its clear purpose is outlined in Skinner's famous *Walden II*.[12] For the good of the person (individually or collectively), an elitist technocracy of behaviorists sets the goals that will make the person happy and productive. It then shapes her behavior by operant conditioning (with or without the "subject's" knowledge) to achieve those goals. One's behavior is, after all, *completely* determined by environment, and this might better be planned so as to make one happy, socialized, and moral. Who it is that sets the environment for the *planners* so that their completely determined behavior causes them to operate as such a wise and good elite is a question always deftly avoided. Nevertheless it is assumed that their goals will be constructively social, and the shaping of behavior will be for the good of the person as well as society.

Yet at times, when applied to aberrant behavior, this approach seems a little startling. In "Criminals Can Be Brainwashed—Now," McConnell says: "We'd assume that a felony was clear evidence that the criminal had somehow acquired a full-blown social neurosis and needed to be cured, not punished. We'd send him to a rehabilitation center where he'd undergo positive brainwashing until we were quite sure he had become a law-abiding citizen who would not again commit an antisocial act. We'd probably have to restructure his entire personality."[13] McConnell seems completely oblivious to the political implications of what he is saying. Clearly psychologists who believe as he does would be the first to be subsidized and employed by a dictator, who would be very happy to have them "cure" various "felonies" that threatened the state.

In fairness to behaviorists it should be said that many of them have come to adopt a greatly changed view of the politics of relationships. In the commune Twin Oaks, patterned initially after Walden II, the residents often choose for themselves which behaviors they wish to change, and select the rewards which will be most reinforcing. Clearly this is completely opposed to the politics of the strict behaviorist, since it is self-initiated, self-evaluated change. It is not the environment shaping the individual's behavior, but the individual choosing to shape the environment for her own personal development.

Some behaviorists have gone even further. Several recent books depart completely from the basic Skinnerian view. Rather than controlling the individual, they are helping the person learn to achieve her own betterment. The title of the latest book to come to my attention is sufficient in itself to show that its philosophy is far removed from that of Walden II. The title is *Self-Control: Power to the Person!*[14] In its politics this is the reverse of strict behaviorism.

The foregoing paragraphs may give the impression that therapists, in the interpersonal politics of their therapies, are gradually drifting toward a more humanistic view, and may not actually differ very much from each other in the pattern of their relationships. Nothing could be further from the truth, as is dramatically illustrated by a landmark study by Raskin,[15] begun more than a decade ago but only recently appearing in published form.

Raskin took six recorded interviews, conducted by six widely known and experienced therapists, each from a different school of thought. Each therapist approved a selected segment of his interview as being representative of his way of working. These segments were rated by eighty-three therapists, who classified themselves as belonging to twelve different therapeutic orientations. The segments were rated on many variables drawn from differing therapeutic theories and practices. Looked at politically, those who rated high on such variables as "therapist-directed" or "systematically reinforces" are clearly therapists whose behavior is controlling, and who make important choices for the client. Those who rate high on such variables as "warm and giving," "equalitarian," and "empathic" obviously leave power and choice in the hands of the client.

When these eighty-three therapists used the same variables to give their picture of the "ideal" therapist, there was very substantial agreement, and the outstanding characteristics were all *non*-controlling. In other words they *desire* to behave in ways that treat the client as an autonomous person.

Yet in practice the picture is very different. Of the six expert therapists rated, only two—the client-centered and experiential therapists—showed any great similarity to the ideal therapist. The other four—including the rational emotive, the psychoanalytic, the Jungian—correlated negatively with the ideal, some sharply so. In other words, in *practice* four of the six were more opposite to than like the ideal therapist as perceived by the eighty-three practicing therapists. The politics of the therapeutic relationship thus not only differs sharply from therapist to therapist, but in the same therapist may show a sharp difference between the professed ideal of the group and the way she actually behaves.

Most procedures in psychotherapy may be placed on a scale having to do with power and control. At one end of the scale stand orthodox Freudians and orthodox behaviorists, believing in a politics of authoritarian or elitist control of persons "for their own good," either to produce better adjustment to the status quo or happiness or contentment or productivity or all of these. In the middle are most of the contemporary schools of psychotherapy, confused, ambiguous, or paternalistic in the politics of their relationships (though they may be very clear regarding their therapeutic strategies). At the other end of the scale is the client-centered, experiential, person-centered approach, consistently stressing the capacity and autonomy of the person, her right to choose the directions she will move in her behavior, and her ultimate responsibility for herself in the therapeutic relationship, with the therapist's person playing a real but primarily catalytic part in that relationship.[16]

This same scale can be applied to the interpersonal relationships in intensive groups. These are so multiform—T-groups, encounter groups, sensitivity training, sensory awareness groups, Gestalt groups, and the like—that generalization is well-nigh impossible. The outstanding fact is that different group leaders vary enormously in the way of relating. Some are highly authoritarian and directive. Others make maximum use of exercises and games to reach goals they have chosen. Others feel little responsibility toward group members: "I do my thing and you do your thing." Others, including me, endeavor to be facilitative, but in no way controlling.[17] Each leader should probably be considered as an individual if we are to assess the politics of her approach.

One new approach appears to be sweeping the country. This is the Erhard Seminars Training, founded by Werner Erhard, and better know as "est." It is the extreme of the leader-dominated type of group. Members are held to an absolute discipline, subjected to long hours of ridicule and abuse. All their beliefs are "bullshit," and they themselves are "assholes." This leads to such confusion that eventually the unquestioned authority of the leader is established. The final damning statement is that "You are nothing but a goddamn machine! And you can't be anything but what you are." Then comes the optimistic revelation that "if you accept the nature of your mind . . . and take responsibility for having created all the . . . mechanisms it comprises, then in effect you have freely chosen to do everything you have ever done and to be precisely what you are. In that instant you become exactly what you always wanted to be!"[18]

A great many of the group experience conversion-type experiences and feel their lives have been greatly changed for the better. From the point of view of interpersonal politics, two things impress me. One is the leader's assumption of absolute control. Though some resent this, the majority who surrender to the will of the leader indicates what a large proportion of persons desires to be dependent on a guru. The second point is that in Erhard's voluminous speeches, where he describes in many ways the outcomes of his work, he never once refers to the authoritarian *process* by which these changes are brought about. As in all authoritarian approaches, the end justifies the means. In the person-centered approach, the *process* is all-important, and the changes are only partially predictable.

While est is an extreme example, there is much political significance in the increasing use of games and exercises in all types of intensive groups. There must by now be hundreds of such exercises, and many who are active in the intensive group movement use them constantly.

There are many varieties of the fantasy trip. "I'm going to play some music, and I want each of you to have a fantasy while you listen. Then we can each share our fantasies with the others." There are also many exercises involving touching. Here is one that involves both touching and feedback. "One at a time, go around the circle. Touch each person, look in his eyes, and tell him what you feel about him." And of course this one: "We will speak only of our feelings in the here and now, with no references to the past or to the outside world."

The politics of these exercises depend very much on how they are used. If the leader describes the game and its purpose, asks the members if they wish to participate, permits individuals to opt out if they desire, it is clearly not a coercive move. On the other hand, if the leader declares "Now we will all . . ." the impact is very different indeed. There is no doubt that in general the use of exercises or games makes the group leader-centered rather than member-centered.

I rarely use such exercises. I prefer to start an encounter

group with some brief statement such as, "This is our group. We're going to be spending about fifteen hours together, and we can make of this experience what we wish." Then I listen, attentively and acceptantly, to whatever is expressed. I dislike using any procedure that is planned. But sometimes I have tried to use an exercise. In one apathetic group I suggested that we try to get out of our doldrums by doing as other groups had done: forming an inner circle and an outer one, with the person in the outer circle prepared to speak up for the real feelings of the individual in front of him. The group paid absolutely no attention to the suggestion and went on as though it had never been made. But within an hour, one man picked up the central aspect of this device and used it, saying, "I want to speak for John and say what I believe he is *actually* feeling." At least a dozen times in the next day or two, others used it—but in their own spontaneous ways, not as a crude or stiff device.[19] This shows how *knowledge* of different exercises can feed into the realness and spontaneity that is the essence of a person-centered group.

Here is an example that indicates the efficacy of the person-centered approach. Diabasis is a center for dealing with acutely schizophrenic young persons that was established by John W. Perry, M.D., a respected Jungian analyst. Diabasis is a Greek word meaning "crossing over."

Perry had had twenty-five years of experience in dealing with psychotics in various settings. He had become increasingly convinced that most schizophrenic episodes were actually a chaotic but vital attempt at growth and self-healing, and that if such an "Individual" (he dropped the term patient) were treated as a person and provided with a close and trusting relationship, she could, in a relatively short time, live through this crisis and emerge stronger and healthier.[20]

Dr. Perry and Dr. Howard Levine, another Jungian analyst,

23

set up Diabasis to implement this view more fully than could be done in a psychiatric hospital. The first step was to select a staff. Paper credentials were disregarded. The criteria for selection consisted of attitudes. They chose people, mostly young, who showed in their training seminars an ability to relate to withdrawn individuals who were preoccupied with events in their inner worlds. Many of these young volunteers were members of the counter-culture. They knew what it was to be alienated. Often they had been on drug trips—good and bad. They were not frightened by bizarre thoughts or behavior.

The home that housed Diabasis had room for only six Individuals, plus volunteers and minimal house staff. It "is a non-authoritarian, non-judgmental milieu in which each individual (staff as well as client) is allowed to express himself in whatever modes he chooses, emotionally, artistically, and physically. Clients at every point of their psychosis are regarded as being in a 'legitimate' state and are not compelled . . . to conform to 'rational' modes of behavior."[21] Instead the psychotic individual is accepted in two important ways. He is accepted by everyone in the house as going through a stressful period of growth during which he needs understanding and companionship.

Of equal importance is the special relationship with one staff person, who thoroughly invests herself in building a trusting closeness with the troubled person. Whenever possible the Individual selects this special person with whom to work. Dr. Perry describes well the reason for this special staff member. "The inner journey or renewal process tends to remain scattered, fragmented, and incoherent until the point at which the individual begins to open up to another person enough to entrust to him his inner experience as it unfolds. When this happens the content of his symbolic experience becomes more intensified, and thereupon apparently moves ahead in a more progressive fashion toward its conclusion. It is often surprising how 'psychotic' and yet at the same time coherent the patient's communication can be, providing he feels related to the therapist."[22]

The same point is made by a young man who worked for two years at Diabasis, first as a volunteer, recently on the paid staff. He says: "We feel that what is called madness can best be understood as a journey of exploration and discovery, regulated by the psyche, in which the various elements of the personality can be reorganized in a more fruitful and self-fulfilling way. This process can only occur, however, in an environment in which these altered states of consciousness are respected as valid ways of being, rather than being derided as 'crazy' and of no value."[23]

The contrast with the medical model of treatment of psychosis could scarcely be greater. Under the medical model, this individual is first of all a patient rather than a person. She is diagnosed, and either explicitly or implicitly is given to know that she has an "illness," a craziness, which is to be eliminated by heavy medication or shock therapy, or even restraint if necessary, until her "illness" is eradicated. It is clear that there is something "wrong" with her state, and she must somehow be brought around into a "right" state. "In the traditional settings there is massive use of medication and behavioral restraint in the early phase of the treatment to *suppress* the psychotic material. There is no attempt to see the material as useful to the individual involved. Thus, after *control* of the psychosis has been established, no efforts are made to integrate the material into the ongoing life of the individual."[24] It is a politics of suppression and control by professional power, and it has a very poor record, as indicated by the "revolving door" syndrome of psychiatric hospitals.

In Diabasis, as in any person-centered therapy, the politics is completely reversed. As Perry says, "The philosophy of therapy is, in this case, not one of imposing order from above downwards by a regimen of strict management, but rather it is a more fluid one of sensitively following the Individual's concerns as they evolve through the process in order to catalyze it. Then a democratic structure of the ward community is the appropriate form, in which ordering and integrating are expected to emerge from the spontaneous concerns and feelings and insights of both resident Individuals and staff together."[25] This means that the Individual provides the leads, points the directions she needs to go. Empathically, the therapist and the other house staff act as companions in following those leads, without sacrificing their own feelings or their own personhood. "The non-rational concerns of the client are given a full hearing and, to the best of the staff's ability (which increases with experience) are empathically understood, as a necessary and deeply meaningful inner journey."[26] The nurses take their cues from the Individual and these closer staff companions. The psychiatrist aids in helping them all understand the directions they are taking, but in no sense directs the process. Essential power and control thus flow upward from the psychotic person and her needs, to the dedicated house staff, to the nurses and psychiatrists. It is a complete reversal of traditional hierarchical, psychiatric treatment.

This focus on the person is evident in the highly equalitarian atmosphere. Staff and Individuals eat together, dress as they desire. The casual visitor would have no way of knowing who was client and who was staff.

This whole atmosphere has permeated the organization as well. From the first the administration of Diabasis became the province of the whole staff rather than of a director. The power, responsibility, and decision-making are shared by all. "Democracy can be recognized as a state of psychic development in which the ordering and ruling principle is realized as belonging essentially within the psychic life of the individual. . . . The social structure and culture established in the therapeutic milieu should be a reflection of this natural need, a fitting external expression of what is happening in depth."[27] In person-centered therapy, the traditional organization, with power flowing down from the top, becomes totally inappropriate and ridiculous.

The immediate result of this whole program on the psychotic individual is dramatic. "What has been most remarkable and beyond all of our expectations, is that individuals in acutely psychotic turmoils very rapidly settle down and become clear and coherent, usually within a period of a few days to a week, and without the use of medication. Thus severely disturbed behavior becomes manageable when staff relate with feeling to the individual's emotional state."[28]

Although the history of this unique place is brief, the outcomes appear to be good. One indication is that four former clients (Individuals) are already on the staff of a conceptually similar small institution. They are now able to use their own past experience to help others. The cost is far less than in the usual facility. And it seems to have left behind the "revolving door" experience of the state hospital.

It is reasonable to suppose that this innovative, helpful new mode of dealing with the young person during her first psychotic episode would be widely hailed and eagerly supported. Not so. To understand the reasons, we need to look at the politics of Diabasis, and the threat it constitutes to the traditional politics.

It is easy to see why orthodox psychiatrists and even Jungian colleagues look upon Diabasis with uneasiness and criticism. At Diabasis the best therapists often have proven to be relatively untrained paraprofessionals. This is disturbing to the ordinary professional. They are mostly volunteers, thus posing a vague economic threat. There is no strict medical control, in the ordinary sense. This offends physicians. The doctors do not even use their prerogative to prescribe medication. Dr. Perry thinks he has given two tranquilizers in the past ten months! The organization itself is not *directed* by physicians. They are simply facilitators of a process. This is a staggering departure from tradition.

Consequently there is grumbling and criticism about "low standards." Financial support is very difficult to come by. Like all person-centered therapy, it is revolutionary in its implica-

27

tions, and the professional establishment is fearful of it. To see psychiatrists relinquishing control of "patients" and staff, to see them serving only as successful facilitators of personal growth for deeply troubled "insane" persons rather than being in *charge* of these people is, I am sad to say, a very frightening scene to psychiatrists, psychologists, and other mental health professionals. Revolutionaries are seen as dangerous—and there is no doubt that they *are* dangerous to the established order.

A person-centered approach, when utilized to encourage the growth and development of the psychotic, the troubled, or the normal individual, revolutionizes the customary behaviors of members of the helping professions. It illustrates many things: (1) A sensitive person, trying to be of help, becomes more person-centered, no matter what orientation she starts from, because she finds that approach more effective. (2) When you are focused on the person, diagnostic labels become largely irrelevant. (3) The traditional medical model in psychotherapy is discovered to be largely in opposition to person-centeredness. (4) It is found that those who can create an effective person-centered relationship do not necessarily come from the professionally trained group. (5) The more this person-centered approach is implemented and put into practice, the more it is found to challenge hierarchical models of "treatment" and hierarchical methods of organization. (6) The very effectiveness of this unified person-centered approach constitutes a threat to professionals, administrators, and others, and steps are taken—consciously and unconsciously—to destroy it. It is too revolutionary.

Chapter 2 | The new family— and the old

An individual who is attempting to live his life in a person-centered way brings about a politics of family relationships, and marriage or partner relationships, which is drastically different from the traditional model. The child is treated as a unique person, worthy of respect, possessing the right to evaluate his experience in his own way, with wide powers of autonomous choice. The parent respects himself also, with rights which cannot be overridden by the child. In the relationship between partners, married or otherwise, issues are confronted with as much openness as the partners are capable of. In other realms there is much freedom for each partner to pursue a life direction, to make choices, to engage in work or other activities in his own way.

In these relationships the eventual choice lies in the person, as does the responsibility for that choice. The relationship is one of a changing expression of feelings and attitudes, with the other endeavoring to hear and to listen acceptantly, but with a right to his own feelings and attitudes as well, which also need to be acceptantly heard. It is a most difficult kind of relationship to achieve, which would certainly not be worth the investment were the results not so rewarding.

One facet of this complex scene is the manner of relating to

(I was going to say the rearing of) children. I am acquainted with a number of parents in their twenties, thirties, and forties who have been exposed to a person-centered approach—through student-centered classes, workshops, encounter groups, therapy or a combination of these experiences. These parents have a new way of dealing with the child, from infancy through late adolescence. His earliest tears and wails, his beginning smiles and his mouthing of sounds are efforts to communicate, and an earnest and respectful attention is given to those primitive communications. The effort is also made to allow the child the right to choose, in any situation in which he seems capable of bearing the consequences of his choice. This is an expanding process, in which increasing autonomy is given to the child and adolescent, autonomy bounded only by the feelings of those who are close to the youngster.

If this sounds like a completely child-centered family, it is not. The parent has feelings and attitudes too, and tries to communicate these to the child in a way this smaller person can understand. The results are fantastic. Because they are continually aware of many of their own feelings and those of their parents, and because these feelings have been expressed and accepted, the children develop as highly social creatures. They are responsive to other people, open in expressing their feelings, scornful of being talked down to, creative and independent in their activities. They are sensitive to the feelings of others about them, and though at times they may be confronting, it is only occasionally that they consciously attempt to hurt another. Thus there are two disciplines in their lives: the self-discipline that is always inherent in autonomy with responsibility, and the flexible boundaries—and hence discipline—set by the feelings of those who are close to them.

These children are not good material for a traditional school, which expects to mold them into conforming robots, but they are extremely eager learners when exposed to a climate that encourages learning. They are a great hope for the future. They are accustomed to living as independent beings, openly relating to others, and they expect to continue in that fashion—in their school life, their work life, and in their relationship to partners. These children are growing up with a minimum of repressed feelings—feelings denied to awareness out of guilt or fear—and with a minimum of inhibitions imposed by others through external controls. They come closer to being truly free creatures than any adults I know.

I don't wish to paint too rosy a picture. I have seen some of these parents forget, temporarily, that *they* have rights, with resultant spoiling of the child. I have seen parents and children revert temporarily to the old ways—the parent commanding, the child resisting. Both parents and children are sometimes exhausted, and react badly. There are always frictions and difficulties to be communicated and worked through. But all in all, in these families we find parent and child in a continuous *process* of relating, a developing series of changes whose final outcome is not known but is being shaped by an infinite number of daily choices and actions. The politics of control and obedience, with its pleasing static security, is gone. The politics of a process relationship between unique persons, a very different politics, takes its place.

How early can this relationship between unique persons begin? While I have been fascinated by the horizontal spread of the person-centered approach into so many areas of our life, others have been more interested in the vertical direction and are discovering the profound value of treating the *infant,* during the whole birth process, as a person who should be understood, whose communications should be treated with respect, who should be dealt with empathically. This is the new and stimulating contribution of Frederick Leboyer,[1] a French obstetrician who, after delivering thousands of babies, began to change his methods in very striking ways and who has assisted in the delivery of at least a thousand infants in what can only be called a person-centered way.

Leboyer has become indignant at our failure to understand, empathically, the struggles and cries, the fear and pain of the

31

newborn. He points out that the newly arriving infant is not blind, as is often supposed. He is instead ultrasensitive to light after nine months in the dark womb, and we blind him with floodlights in the delivery room. We assume that it makes no difference what he hears, and hence loud conversations and exhortations to the mother in labor to "Push! Push harder," are unimportant. Yet the baby is very sensitive to sound, and for some time after birth can be soothed and put to sleep by a tape recording of the sounds from inside the uterus—the movements of joints and muscles, the rumblings of stomach and intestines, and above all the steady rhythm of the mother's heartbeat. We assume that the baby's skin can stand the touch of dry cloth, when actually it is almost as raw as tissue that has suffered a burn. We assume that the first breaths are exhilarating, when the child's cries indicate that they are probably extremely painful.

Above all, the individuals involved are concerned with their *own* feelings, not those of the newly born. The doctor has completed his delivery—and is pleased with himself. The mother is smiling because the ordeal is over; she hears her baby crying and is proud of herself. The father is happy for having sired a son or daughter. So who pays attention to the infant's reactions? No one. He is too immature to have feelings or reactions, it is assumed. The infant is picked up by the feet, forcefully straightening a spine which has always been curved, slapped on the buttocks to force him to breathe, cut off from his alternate source of oxygen by snipping the umbilical cord, often placed on a cold metal scale for weighing, and then wrapped in dry cloth. The photographs of the screaming, terrified, blinded infants handled in this customary fashion are damning.

And what does Leboyer do about all this? He enters into the trauma of birth and new life and tries to understand this nascent person. In so doing he changes almost every step of handling an infant's birth.

First is the training of the mother for a natural childbirth. She is prepared for the steps the doctor will take. She will not be frightened by the fact that her baby will not loudly cry, but may simply utter one or two small cries or gasps as it starts to breathe. She is encouraged to feel "I am a *mother,*" not "This is *my child.*"

Then come the changes in the methods of delivery. As soon as the head appears, and it seems the birth will be normal, all the bright lights are extinguished, leaving only one soft light. During this time and afterward, the delivery room is *silent.* If there must be conversation, it is whispered.

As the child emerges, care is taken not to touch the head, which has borne the brunt of the pain of the birth canal. The child is then settled immediately on the mother's belly, now so hollow, where the warmth and the inner gurgles and the heartbeat can again be experienced. This placement makes it unnecessary to cut the umbilical cord, thus leaving the infant with two sources of oxygen, avoiding brain damage from anoxia. The baby, usually after a cry or two, begins to breathe. Sometimes, too, he stops breathing for a bit, and then starts again at his own pace. Since oxygen is still being received from the placenta, this is not dangerous. By the time the umbilical cord stops pulsating —usually after four or five minutes—the infant's breathing apparatus is working, he is cradled in the most comfortable place, second only to the womb, and is beginning to move and stretch. The baby has not been rushed. His natural pace has been respected. The umbilicus is now cut, having ceased to function. Leboyer adds, "We must behave with the utmost respect toward this instant of birth, this fragile moment."

As the child begins to use its limbs to explore the new space on the mother's abdomen, touch becomes the means of communication. Hands—preferably the mother's—are placed quietly and softly on the infant, or the back is stroked rhythmically as a reminder of the internal rhythms previously experienced. This touching assures the baby that "We are both still here; we are both alive."

When the infant seems ready, it is lifted from the mother's body and lowered slowly and gently into water that is heated to body temperature—98 or 99 degrees. Here it begins to move its limbs, to turn its head from side to side. Then the eyes are opened! Photographs of these newborn show them to look astonishingly older than we would expect. They are calm and exploratory, not in panic or fear, nor sobbing in pain. They begin clearly to enjoy themselves and their movements. Only when the child seems fully relaxed, and showing a welcoming attitude toward these tremendous new discoveries, is he removed from the water and placed in warmed cloth. The transfer from the womb to the world has been successfully begun.

Though it is too soon to know the long-term effects, this new way of handling the birth process is profoundly important. By respecting the infant, and endeavoring to deal with him understandingly, the psychological scars of the birth trauma have been enormously reduced. To come into the new life so gradually, with security and a caring, loving touch is much better for the child's psychological development than for him to be suddenly exposed to all sorts of terrifying stimuli and *forced* into a fearful new way of being. A French study of 120 of these infants up to the age of three shows them to be astonishingly free of feeding and sleeping problems, and to be more alert, coordinated, and playful than other children. They are also relaxed and agreeable.

What happens when parents regard their children as unique persons in an ever changing communicative relationship? The story of Ben and Claire illustrates the dynamics of this process.[2] Claire had raised her children along authoritarian lines until her divorce and remarriage to a man who was committed to the person-centered approach. Each partner brought to this marriage children by previous marriages, and there were many new relationships with varying degrees of trust and communication. Claire found herself changing.

In trying to resolve some of the new issues, Ben and Claire decided to have meetings in which every member of the family, no matter how young or old, was free to express his feelings—the complaints, satisfactions, or reactions—to the others. The father of Walter, Claire's oldest son, had disappeared from Walter's life with little warning. Otherwise Claire's statement is self-explanatory. I simply asked her how their family group meetings had started.

CLAIRE: We scheduled them. We picked a time. It turned out that it was every Tuesday. And nothing interfered with Tuesday—not a business meeting or a movie or entertaining, or if somebody came over we had to ask them to leave and come over another day. The children learned to count on that. There were a lot of adjustments to be made between me and Ben, between Ben and my children, and me and his children, and between the children. And Ben had been involved in group work before and wanted this kind of experience—the closeness and sharing and expression of feelings—to be a natural part of the family unit. He called a meeting following dinner. We all stayed at the table —the children wondering what was going to happen. He started it by trying to teach them how to express feelings and get away from accusations, you know—"You are a bully," or "You pick on me." I was picked to be the first one to start going around the circle. There were eight of us at the table and I had seven people to cover and to tell them how I felt about them, each one. And not only the positive but some of the negative things, some of my concerns and worries that were very different with each child. And it was really the first time I had talked about negative things in a constructive way in front of everybody else. That usually is a private thing. I could say to one of the boys how proud I felt of his scholastic accomplishments but at the same time how worried I was about what I perceived as selfishness—that I didn't really understand where it came from and I wanted to talk to him more about it so that we could resolve it or I could understand it better. It was the first time

I hadn't just shouted at him and said, "Share this with your sister, what's the matter with you?" And he could *hear* me. The children were restless and embarrassed at first. And then Ben, my husband, was next and he was a lot more skilled than I and topped off what I had said from his point of view. By that time the children had settled down and one of them was first and went around the circle—they really did a darned good job. I was surprised and very pleased. And they were proud and surprised and pleased with themselves.

And then an important thing happened. My oldest son, Walter, had had the hardest time with my divorce. He was the one who was chewing his fingernails and having nightmares. And not doing very well in school. He adored Ben. He was so happy to have Ben for his father—his stepfather. When he went around in the circle he said a lot of things about all of us, but when he got to Ben he just said, "And of course I love you," and passed right on. And we were all aware of something missing there. But as soon as Walter was finished, Ben was the first one to say, "Gee, Walter, I feel cheated. Everyone seemed to get so much more from you, and I love hearing that you love me but there must be more and I really want some of that." And Walter in kind of a cool way said, "Well, ah . . . I don't want to give you any more. I don't want to love you too much or get too close to you because I am afraid you are going to leave me." Wow! Tears started all around the table. We never would have heard that coming from Walter, would never even have known that was a part of him if we hadn't had this kind of structured scene to get in touch with this sort of thing. It gave Ben an opportunity to let Walter know he understood him, like, I know how you loved your father and trusted him to be with you always and he left you and then your mother has had two other men she was seriously interested in who claimed to love you and they left. And now here I am and I claim to love you and you don't have any guarantees about me. And then he said, "But I'll tell you something: I want you to know that I am going to love you just as long as I live and you can trust me to be available to you and never leave you for as long as you want me." And Walter looked at him and started to cry and got up and walked around the table and just threw himself in Ben's arms and they sobbed. And everybody did. And the children at the table . . . got up and touched Walter. It was just a natural thing for them to do. At any rate, you can imagine it was something.

This family meeting offers some astonishing contrasts with the usual family relationships: (1) The focus on relationships between the members of the family had higher priority than any other engagement of any kind. (2) The effort was made to focus on owned feelings, not accusations of judgments of another. (3) This shift was fully as hard for the parents as for the children. For Claire to change from "Share that with your sister!" to "I don't understand your (as it appears to me) selfishness" is an enormous change. (4) The new approach is not initially trusted. Everyone is uneasy, a bit suspicious, except possibly Ben. (5) The respect for the children is highly rewarded, because they turn out to be worthy of respect. (6) The openness which develops leads to a totally unexpected self-revelation, and a deep communication. (7) The relationship between all members of the family as separate but interdependent persons is much strengthened.

This is a family communicating as psychological equals. It is a far cry from both the traditional family, which is slowly dying today, but still prevalent, and the more modern family that is the norm in our culture. In the traditional family, the father is head of the household. He makes all the decisions. No one undertakes any significant action without his permission. Negative feelings or resentments, whether by spouse or children, are not permissible, and consequently almost everything important is kept secret from him. In the modern family, the father and mother jointly make all the important decisions. They attempt to control all the actions of their children, often unsuccessfully, especially with teenagers. Consequently the relationship often

37

resembles guerrilla warfare. Between these families and the family of Ben and Claire sitting around the table there lies a political revolution.

In the traditional family the politics of the situation is very clear. The father's authority is backed by religious and legal sanctions. The only way that family members can to any degree live independent lives is to do so secretly, deceiving him.

In the usual present-day family, control is theoretically unified in the hands of both parents, but in practice they often disagree. This opens the way for a power struggle between family members, with temporary or permanent factions forming. Subtle strategies are used by the children to set the parents against each other. The sanctions for parental authority are no longer so strong, further weakening the control structure. Consequently one of the most frequent characteristics is a continual wrangle over decisions involving control. "Why do I have to help with the dishes?" "Why can't I have the car tonight?" "I *want* to wear my blue jeans!" "Why do I have to come home at eleven, when my friend Suzy can stay out till midnight?" The children are struggling for more independence of parental authority. The parents are in the position of a weak government, alternatively being very firm and then giving in to demands. The politics of the family is very unstable.

Ben and Claire often fall into this same pattern. But at its best the politics of their family life sets a whole new pattern. This is not a family trying to make the traditional family structure work better. It is an entirely new and revolutionary way of being together in a family.

So much for the person-centered approach as it applies to the emotional interactions in a family. Is it capable of dealing with practical, everyday problems of behavior and discipline?

CLAIRE: Definitely. I can give you an example of one that I think is just marvelous. I would come home from work and walk in the door, anxious to be there, I really dig my family, and I like to be with them, but the first things I'd see would be coats and sweaters and books and baseball mitts and dirty glasses and cookie crumbs. The kids were glad to see me but I'd begin with "Good heavens, what's going on? Pick this up and put that away," and I'd be punishing and ugly and the kids didn't like me and I didn't like me and they felt guilty and ashamed. I began to think about it and I realized that they really didn't notice the things, because if I pointed to them they would pick them up and if I didn't point to the thing three feet away they didn't see it. It was strange. But they really didn't see it. And so I called a meeting. We had regular meetings, but you can also call one. And I called a meeting and for the first time really owned this as my own problem. *I* have a problem. I can't bear to have the house cluttered the way it is.

CARL: It wasn't a problem to them but it was very much of a problem for you.

CLAIRE: Exactly. They didn't care. They didn't care how messed up the house was. It wasn't their problem. It was mine. I'm a member of the family and have a right to some consideration here. They accept that. I said, "I need some help with this problem." We must have been at the table an hour and half. The children came up with the solution to my problem. It was ultimately called the "disappear box." We had a box, and any item found by anyone in the common rooms—the kitchen, living room, bathrooms, the hallway—was thrown in this marvelous old cardboard box and it would disappear. And they decided that it would stay there for a week. Whatever it was. I didn't have to enforce it. The kids made it, and there's no percentage in beating their own system. They were delighted with it and they policed each other. Beautifully, you know. A twelve-year-old knew just when a fourteen-year-old had lost something in the box, and if he took it out twenty-five minutes early it was . . . it just wasn't going to happen.

CARL: It had to be there the whole week . . .

CLAIRE: Right. Exactly. To the minute. At any rate things just disappeared like magic. The box was absolutely overflowing. And it was tested. There were a lot of times when we could have just blown the whole thing. For instance, one of the boys lost his school shoes the first day. He came home from school and took them off and they disappeared. And the next day he searched and couldn't find them and nobody told him, and he finally realized, oh, Good Lord, they were in the "disappear box." So he wears dirty old smelly tennis shoes and the next day he lost those. And you know, here's the test. What's mother going to do? He kind of looked to me. OK. I have to go to school and I don't have any shoes. And it was just not my problem. I turned and walked away from it. And the kids told him absolutely not. You don't get those shoes and you don't get the tennis shoes and what are you going to do? Anyway they came up with his house slippers. That's all he had left. He went to school in his slippers. And it was hard for me to do that. But I let him do it. . . . And it worked.

But another thing that happened as a result of this was something I didn't realize. When I walked in from work I took my shoes off and left them by the door. I didn't *see* my own shoes, but they did. I had three pair of shoes, green ones, blue ones, and black ones. I lost my blue and I lost my black and I wore green shoes to work for a week with every color of outfit. Ben lost two of his sports jackets, several ties, and a pair of shoes. Oh, they just gathered up all of our things that we left around. It really worked both ways and it was great. It was a lesson for me.

CARL: I think that what makes it really great is that it did work both ways and that it was their solution. I have often been impressed with the fact that kids faced with a problem are a good deal more ingenious than adults in thinking up ways of solving it.

CLAIRE: I never would have thought to leave things there a

week. They are harder on themselves, but it's fair. They're great.

The politics of the relationships here is clear. First is Claire's typical nagging parental control. Then comes her recognition that she is spoiling her relationship to her children, a result she doesn't wish. Then the realization that, incomprehensibly, it doesn't seem a problem to them, but it is to her, and *she* has rights. Next comes the risk—process is always a risk—of asking for help in solving *her* problem. Then the ingenious solution created by the whole family—the "disappear box."

This is a marvelous example of letting children (and adults) bear the responsibility for choices (even unconscious ones) where they can bear the consequences.

The final learning is that every problem is largely in the eye of the beholder. Her shoes had not been "a household mess," but the children's things obviously were. To learn that she too "makes a mess" is a painful lesson. But now the power is truly equalized and experienced as such.

A person-centered approach, wherever it exists in family life, changes markedly the politics of child-parent and parent-child relationships. It is a new pattern for family living.

Chapter 3 | The revolution in marriage and partnerships

So many deeply significant social factors have influenced the marriage relationship that it is virtually impossible to isolate the specific impact of a person-centered approach. Each of these factors has made a difference in the "politics" of marriage.

First of all there is the effect of greatly improved methods of contraception. The tremendous impact of contraception was brought home to me in reading *Thomas Jefferson: An Intimate Biography,* by Fawn Brodie.[1] Jefferson and his wife, Martha, were very much in love, and very close to each other. During their marriage, according to Jefferson, he lived "ten years in unchecquered happiness." But it is hardly an exaggeration to say that she was killed by their love. She was physically fragile, pregnant most of the time, had serious difficulties in childbearing, and died from the complications of childbirth a few months after the birth of their sixth child. Three of the six died before she did. Jefferson was thirty-nine, she was thirty-four at the time of her death. The story is not unusual. Martha's mother had died three weeks after Martha's birth. Her father then took another wife, who lived only a few years, and a third, who survived for only eleven months. After this her father turned to one of his female mulatto slaves, who, seemingly less vulnerable to infections than his white wives, bore him six children.

These are not isolated stories. With variations, they are repeated throughout Brodie's book, and involve the families of Jefferson's relatives and friends. Being a wife was certainly one of the most hazardous occupations of the time. Wives were expendable because there seemed no other alternative. Only celibate or infertile women had a reasonable life expectancy. Now all that is changed. The availability of effective contraception means that marriage can become more of a partnership, since the wife is no longer fully occupied with pregnancy, nursing, and child-rearing. It also means that physically she is as free as her husband to explore relationships outside of marriage. Premarital sex and sexual relations outside of marriage have increased markedly among women. She also has a chance to choose between family and career, or to balance the two. For the first time in history she is physically a free agent. Effective contraception has made possible the release of woman from her subjugated role. The impact on the politics of the family has been incalculable.

A second circumstance has also greatly affected marriage. This is the lengthened life span of both men and women and the consequent lengthening of the potential span of marriage. In less than a hundred years our life expectancy has doubled. In the United States a white woman may expect to live to age seventy-six, a white man to sixty-nine. Non-whites have a somewhat shorter life expectancy. The actuarial expectancy for the length of any marriage was over thirty-one years in 1971, the latest year for which figures are available. Compared to the historical past, this is an unheard-of span. A marriage of the past, with a possibility of lasting ten to fifteen years before being broken by death, is very different from a marriage of today, where it is possible that the two may live for fifty years before death takes either one. The flaws in a relationship which might be endured for ten years will not be endured for fifty. The number of elements that can change lives and make a relationship unstable is multiplied, unless the couple grows together and adjusts well to a continually changing relationship.

Another social factor that has entered in is the increasing social acceptance of divorce. No longer does either partner necessarily feel bound to the other "till death do us part." Neither partner any longer has lasting power or control over the other. Each individual always has the power of choice over whether to preserve the marriage.

Family mobility and transiency have had a profound effect on the interpersonal relationship of marriage. This puts the emphasis of the marriage on the quality of the relationship between two people. No longer is there an extended family to buffer the strains. Hence any deficiencies in the relationship become highlighted.

One little-recognized factor deserves mention. In 1940 17 percent of wives held jobs. In 1972 it was 42 percent, with 7 percent earning more than their husbands. The woman is more independent of her spouse, and she is much more likely to be in contact with other men at work. Again the possibilities of strain in the relationship are decidedly increased.

Increased sexual freedom has profoundly affected marriage. It is reported that 90 percent of the young people approaching their first marriage have engaged in intercourse, though only 37 percent of the population believe such behavior is permissible. Furthermore one study shows that where the partners in a first marriage are from twenty to twenty-five years of age, they engage in more extramarital sex during the first two years of marriage than during an entire married lifetime for older individuals.[2] The significance of these facts for the future of marriage patterns can hardly be exaggerated.

All these factors make a person-centered marriage or partnership more possible. But they also make marriage more risky, more open to tensions, less likely to endure. We face the dilemma that the more person-centered the sexual partnership becomes, the more it is open to disruption; on the other hand the more person-centered it becomes the more it is open to fulfillment and enrichment for each of the partners.

Each of these social circumstances gives the woman more

options, more chance for dignity, more possibility of discovering her own self-worth. They have all come together in one of the most rapid and effective "quiet revolutions" of our time—the women's liberation movement. Here we find an insistence on doing away with discrimination against women—in job opportunities, in property laws, in civil rights, in pay. Even in less obvious situations like our language—*man*kind, chair*man,* homage to *Him*—we are being made sensitive to the subtle way of holding down the self-esteem of women.

In its consciousness-raising efforts, as well as in its political and legal activities, the women's liberation movement is essentially person-centered. At its philosophical best it carries with it a deep trust in the capacity of the individual woman to live a life of her own choosing, to become an independent and creative person, if society will only create an acceptant climate for growth. The individual man may also become much more of a whole person—tender, loving, and emotional as well as intellectual and achieving—if the social climate can make room for this. Yet many men see "women's lib" as nothing but a threat—to their masculinity, to their position in the family, to their jobs. It is thus obvious that the women's liberation movement and its implications constitute an extraordinary force in altering the dynamics and the politics of marriage.

Here are some learnings I have gained from partners who have been involved in a person-centered climate—couples groups, encounter groups, individual therapy, or reading. These partners have found more of an acceptance of their own unique selves. The person-centered approach has had a variety of effects on these partnerships:

Difficulties already present in the partnership are brought into the open. A young couple had been living together and were planning to marry. They were together in an encounter group and asked the group's permission to explore their relationship

45

with the help of the participants. As they began to open up to each other, it was clear that they knew each other hardly at all. They had differing goals and sharply differing perceptions. For example, the young woman thought of herself as reasonably adequate, certainly not inferior. She was astonished and hurt to find that her lover saw her as much inferior to him in social status and intellect. As they explored their differences, they became much more open with each other, but their partnership seemed highly precarious. Yet a letter more than a year later told me of their marriage, their growing areas of mutual interest and work, and their current satisfaction with their relationship. Evidently the risk they took in exploring their profound differences had deepened the bonds of partnership rather than breaking them.

The areas of difference may occur in a variety of fields. In one couple the husband is hedonistic, works when he has to, regards himself as essentially "a lazy bum," while his wife is strongly imbued with a work ethic. Says she, "My heart skips a beat when I hear him say, 'I just want to be rich and have fun.' " She thinks he should be more serious about his work. It is an indication of the incredible complexity of human relationships that the work-oriented wife is, with her husband's consent, a topless go-go dancer, while the "lazy bum" is in business! But exploration of their differing goals is helping to bring them together.

The gulf that exists between partners may be due to old hurts. Hal and Jane have been married for fifteen years, have worked out many difficulties due to differing religious and cultural backgrounds, and their relationship now seems quite stable. Yet in an interview she reveals that she has held back much of her affection, and is not now freely giving toward him, because of an old resentment. During the early years of marriage Jane felt she did 90 percent of the giving, Hal 10 percent. She has never talked out her resentment, and has carried evidence of this old scar into her present relationship with him. Both of them are now sad that she didn't express her feelings much earlier—the partnership might have been much improved.

Another effect is that *communication becomes more open, more real, with more mutual listening.* One can sometimes see the exact moment in which this process is taking place. In a couples group a husband and wife were constantly attacking each other. The group tried to help them to listen more, to express their *own feelings,* not their judgments. The husband seemed to absorb something of this, and took the risk of stating, rather poignantly, the trap he felt he was in. The moment he ceased speaking, his wife took off in her attack on his motives and his behavior toward her. The facilitator interrupted, "Did you hear what your husband was trying to tell you?" "Of course I did." The facilitator said, "Would you just tell him the essence of what he said, so that he knows you heard him?" She fell silent, obviously searching her memory. She began to look very embarrassed. Finally she said to her husband, in the softest voice she had used since the group began, "What *did* you say?" It was the beginning of more listening.

In the climate of a person-centered approach *the partners come to recognize the value of separateness.* Carol and Bob had all the external trappings of a happy marriage. Both were educated, and things went well for them—they had a suburban house, a baby, and a new car. They did everything together. Everyone regarded theirs as a very successful marriage. Inwardly they both found the marriage dull and frustrating. They were disillusioned and angry—at each other, but especially at life.[3]

They attended a couples group, and began to realize that they had stopped growing when they married, and more important, that they were not communicating. Finally Bob risked revealing himself and told Carol of the affairs he had been having with other women. She was frightened and jealous. She had assumed that there was security in her world, and now that world had collapsed. Her marriage was out of her control, and she was very threatened. But even in her fright there was a dawning realization, "If he can be separate, perhaps I can too." She became much more open in the group, and hence was seen as more lovable. But to see that she was lovable in the eyes of the group members was scary to Bob. He in his turn felt threatened and hurt.

But his courage in being open about his affairs led her to be more courageous. Soon they were talking all night, each discovering new and interesting facets of the other. More and more each became aware of their separateness. They now can permit each other to date and pursue other relationships. Carol especially has dropped her "nice" image and become more of a real self, a self in which she feels much more confidence.

For Carol and Bob, a growth-promoting climate has meant a complete alteration in the politics of their marriage. No longer are they controlled by society's expectations—that they must do everything together, must follow a conventional pattern, must submerge their lives in each other. They are becoming unique and separate persons, pursuing differing paths, and bound together by communication and mutual love, not by some imagined conventional pattern from outside.

Another result of such a climate is that *the woman's growing independence is recognized as valuable in the relationship.* This is another example of the separateness we have just been noting, but it is such an important part of modern partnerships that it deserves special mention.

Jerry recently experienced what he called a "blockbuster" in his marriage. He has been preoccupied with his work. Jane has carried the difficult task of raising their son, not without buried resentment. As her time became more free with the passing years, she returned to the university for further education, being exposed to several person-centered influences. She decided that she wanted to take a professional position in the town where they had formerly lived. She told Jerry, but he simply could not take it seriously. When it did hit home that she *meant* it, and that he would either have to give her up or change jobs himself, it was, as he says, a "blockbuster." The family discussions were heated, and Jane fortunately talked out some of her resentments, becoming more willing to make accommodations. But the family is moving, Jerry is changing jobs, and the dynamics of their relationship has altered dramatically. Jerry has more respect for his wife; he sees more clearly the role he has played of being married to his job; and the ability of each of them to share their feelings has been markedly increased. Even in regard to their sexual relationships, which have never been ideal, there is more communication and hope. Part of the problem is that successful sexual intimacy has been difficult when Jane has been harboring a buried resentment toward her husband.

The problem of where to live, when both husband and wife are working and have attractive opportunities in different communities, is an increasing one. Solving it demands the utmost of shared feelings, exploration of all the options, and willingness to reach a solution that may not be ideal for either. Such problems are certain to occur more frequently as marriage is seen as an equalitarian partnership, with each spouse being respected as able to make important choices.

This new trend is often especially threatening to the husband of the developing professional woman. Her increased independence makes him feel unneeded as a provider, his old role. There is always the possibility that she may earn more than he. Where both are in the same or similar professions, competition becomes implicit in their relationship. As a consequence the *quality* of their sexual relationship, the degree to which each is growing, the extent to which they are developing mutual interests—all of these become far more important than in conventional marriages.

Inevitably, in a person-centered situation, *there is increasing recognition of the importance of feelings, as well as reason,* of emotions as well as intellect.

A feeling is "an emotionally tinged experience, together with its personal meaning. Thus it includes the emotion but also the cognitive content of the meaning of that emotion in its experiential context. [They are] experienced inseparably in the moment."⁴ Including as it does both emotion and meaning, feeling is the broader term. The stress that recent centuries have placed upon reason, thinking, and rationality is the attempt to divorce the two actually inseparable components of experience, to the detriment of our humanity.

This divorce of reason from feeling is one of the first myths to disappear in a person-centered approach. Individuals find themselves communicating with their whole beings, expressing their experiences, not some desiccated intellectual representation of them.

This is one of the major reasons why a person-centered approach has been so valuable to married couples and those living together in relationships. "Pure" reason and "objective" evaluation are *not* a basis on which two human beings can effectively live together. It means that they are attempting to exclude half of their experience (and perhaps the most important half) from their communication. Through intensive groups, student-centered classes, books, couples groups, and other sources more and more persons are learning the folly of such pseudo-communication. They are rediscovering what it means to communicate themselves as they are. I will not attempt to deal here with the ways in which such real communication can be thwarted by jargon or by an encounter-group ritual. "I want to know what you *really* feel," can be as much a pseudo-communication as any other, if it is not based on what the speaker is experiencing at the moment. Our American culture has been so corrupted by Madison Avenue that anything can be turned into a "gimmick." There is no doubt that this has often happened in the encounter groups and in the training of parents to be "real." These false notes do not, however, change the importance of true communication, which is also on the increase.

Exposure to a person-centered approach means that *there is a thrust toward the experiencing of greater mutual trust, personal growth, and shared interests.* The partners tend to develop more trust in each other as they are more real with each other. Being more real, they take more risks in being open, and thus enhance their growth as persons. As they communicate more deeply, they are likely to discover, and to wish to develop, more interests that they do or can share.

Experience in a person-centered psychological atmosphere has another result. *Roles, and role expectations, tend to drop away and are replaced by the person, choosing her own way of behaving.* Here are the expected roles of the male in the partnership. The man is head of the family. He is the sole provider. He is the stronger, the superior individual in the pair, though helped by "the little woman." His life is governed by intellect, not by emotion. He alone may occasionally have need of an outside "affair." He takes the lead in all sexual activity. He is the stern disciplinarian of his children. All these roles and expectations collapse in a person-centered experience. The focus becomes the man as an individual person—human, fluctuating, behaving in the light of his immediate feelings and his long-range goals.

The expectations for the woman are likewise open to challenge. The wife is submissive to her husband. She finds complete satisfaction in her home and children. She does all the tasks of making and keeping a home. She is the nest-builder. In comparison with her husband she is weak physically and inferior intellectually. She is capable of feelings, but not of organized thought. She subordinates her interests to those of her spouse. Her sexual urges are weaker than those of her husband. She is not to engage in extramarital sex.

Again, the behavior that is expected in playing these roles collapses in an encounter group or in person-centered therapy or in a women's consciousness-raising group. The individual woman emerges, with a sharply defined personality that is hers alone, behaving in the way that suits her needs and her choices. The sociological role loses its force in a person-centered experience.

The male and female roles are rarely put forward so bluntly

in today's culture. They have already been weakened by social forces. But we find them implicit in our social structure. Why are men paid more than women for the same job? Why are women permitted to weep when hurt, but not men? These roles are still very much alive and functioning, even though weakened. But they lose their force completely in a person-centered encounter group. Here we find a man weeping, and a woman with the strength to help him find his way out of sorrow. Here we find a man who feels secure only in his present nest, with an adventurous wife who takes steps toward a new life. We find all of the usual role expectations being contradicted in the experience of men and women struggling to *be* their own experiencing. This leads to behavior that is sometimes in line with role expectations, and sometimes not, but at no time is the behavior governed by the role the person is expected to play.

There is a more realistic appraisal of the needs each can meet in the other. When a man is thinking of his partner as a *person,* it becomes apparent that it is most unlikely that he can meet all of her needs—social, sexual, emotional, intellectual. With equal force it strikes the woman that she cannot be *everything* to this man. These statements become especially true when we are thinking not just of today but of years of being together.

So it becomes only realistic to recognize that each partner will need to grant the other more living space for outside interests, outside relationships, time alone—all of the elements that enrich life. This in no way contradicts the continuing search for a wider and deeper mutual life. It simply means that, as Bob and Carol learned, they do not have to do everything together. Experiencing that greater freedom leads them to a more rewarding life together.

So-called satellite relationships may be formed by either partner, and this often causes great pain as well as enriching growth. Satellite relationship means a close secondary relationship outside the marriage which may or may not involve sexual intercourse, but which is valued for itself. It seems much preferable to such terms as "extramarital sex" or "an affair" or "mistress" or "lover."[5]

When two persons in a partnership learn to look upon each other as separate persons, with separate as well as mutual interests and needs, they are likely to discover that outside relationships are one of those needs. And when that outside relationship involves the possibility of sexual intimacy, it poses problems for the primary partners. Nancy, for example, gives her partner, John, the freedom to date other women, and knows that the dating can lead to sex. Intellectually this has her full approval, but her emotions lag behind this logical stance. She is often jealous and hurt, yet also feels confirmed by the fact that John always prefers her, returns to her.

I often observe in encounter groups, or groups where couples are involved, the beginning development of such satellite relationships. An emotional, volatile wife who is resentful of her husband's compulsive dedication to his research forms a new relationship with another man in the group. He is playful, which her husband is not. He is feelingful and expressive of emotions, qualities lacking in her husband. The relationship becomes very close. The woman is very open with both her husband and her new-found love about her excitement and satisfaction in the new alliance, and also the confusion and conflict it generates in her. Her husband had a great many good qualities, and she feels disloyal to him, but—. As for her researcher-husband, who has described himself in the group as being without feelings, he discovers a depth of jealousy and anger in himself that frightens him. He is suffering intensely. He and his wife talk and talk, sometimes bitterly, sometimes caringly, at times really understanding one another, at other times experiencing nothing but anger.

Because all of this was so much in the open, the group and I were a part of the situation. We could not help but observe the sharp swings in mood between husband and wife, the alternating closeness and distancing in the satellite relationship. Different members of the group listened understandingly to all three members of the triangle, especially to the pain and anger and conflict experienced by the wife and her husband. As the group experience came to an end, I wondered whether a person-centered approach would be responsible for breaking up a marriage which, with all its flaws, had lasted for many years. It is a heavy question to ponder.

Months later a member of the group told me of a letter she had received from the wife. Their marriage, she said, had never been better. They were talking with each other in ways they had never done before, sharing feelings they would previously have hidden. The marriage had more value, to each of them, than in all its previous years. The dynamics of their marriage has drastically changed. Previously the hard-working, achieving husband cared for and looked after the woman he regarded as overemotional and needing restraint. Meanwhile his wife resented his dedication to his work, felt unfulfilled, regarded herself as definitely his inferior. Now it has come much closer to being a partnership of equals.

This is a pattern I have observed on numerous occasions. There is no doubt in my mind that when partnerships are exposed to a person-centered approach satellite relationships become more likely. Individuals—both men and women—discover that it is possible to feel love for more than one person at a time. One or both may experience a second love, outside of their primary relationship. This nearly always leads to jealousy, pain, and fear of loss. Yet that crisis can be lived through with a consequent enrichment of the partnership.

The core of the problem is jealousy, and the depth of its roots. For Rollo May, "Jealousy characterizes the relationship in which one seeks more power than love."[6] The O'Neills say, "We do not believe jealousy has any place in open marriage."[7] I have admitted much more uncertainty.[8] The frequency of jealousy has made me wonder whether it is simply the result of cultural conditioning, in which case it might disappear in a generation or two, or whether it has some basic biological foundation, like the territoriality that we find in animals, birds, and ourselves. There is evidence in the lives of many couples to indicate that feelings of jealousy can be modified and worked through, though not without feelings of hurt.

To the extent that jealousy is made up of a sense of possessiveness, any alteration in that feeling makes a profound difference in the politics of the marriage relationship. To the degree that each partner becomes truly a free agent, then the relationship only has permanence if the partners are committed to each other, are in good communication with each other, accept themselves as separate persons, and live together as persons, not roles.[9] This is a new and mature kind of relationship toward which many couples are striving.

One woman, speaking out of her own personal experience in her marriage and also as a counselor, expresses a point of view full of person-centered wisdom: "I think that there is one essential condition for living through the crises and enriching the relationship. It is the ability to believe that you have the right to experience what you are experiencing, and that you don't need the permission of your partner to do it. At the same time, you care enough for your partner to stay with him while he is having his feelings, and listen to them without feeling overresponsible and letting them control your behavior. What I see frequently happening is that the partner who is involved in another relationship feels controlled, guilty, and angry when he is not received unconditionally by his mate. That increases the feeling of threat and abandonment in the other, who becomes more clinging. Pretty soon they are involved in a terrible vicious cycle that is very hard to break. I think the ideal situation is when one can tell the partner: 'I need and I owe it to myself to experience this other relationship now. I'm hearing your hurt, your jealousy, your fear, your anger; I do not like to receive them, but they are a consequence of the choice I'm making, and I love you enough to want to be available to work through them with you. If I decide not to have this other experience it is because I choose to do so, and not because I let you stop me. In that way I won't feel resentful of you, and I won't punish you for my lack of courage in making my choices and being responsible for the consequences.' "

This is a mature kind of striving for both independence and richness.

Here is a marriage that was highly conventional in its orientation at first but changed markedly as the partners were exposed to a variety of person-centered influences. In response to my writings I receive a great number of letters, many of them highly personal. I have chosen the letter that follows because it is such a vivid account of the process of the partnership between Ruth and Jay over a number of years. It also reveals the changing politics of the relationship. In view of the purpose of this book, this is the aspect on which I wish to focus—the ways in which control is exercised, consciously or unconsciously; the locus of decision-making about oneself and one's partner or partners; the consequences of those choices on the dynamics of the whole system of which the marriage is one part. My comments on the changing politics of her experience are bracketed and in italics.

Dear Carl:

I feel as if I know you. Though I've never seen you, your mind has touched mine and I am changed. It is scary but it is great, and I feel a need to write to you and give you yet another story of human life and evolvment. [*Though she has been exposed to a person-centered approach through my writings, it is clear from her account that this is very recent. All of the first portion of her love life is quite untouched by any such concepts.*]

I will begin at the beginning of my marriage. While a junior in college I met and loved a fellow student. He was not my first love, nor will he be the last, but he is my only completing love. I became pregnant and we were forced to marry. I doubted that he loved me and felt he had married me only because I was pregnant. (However, he later convinced me this was not true.) [*Here the locus of decision-making is almost entirely external. One "must bear the child." One "must marry the father." She felt forced into these steps, and since the decisions were not really hers or Jay's, she did not feel sure of him.*] Jay, my husband, tried so hard that first year but I was miserable in my self-pity and was not ready for marriage or a baby. I made life very difficult for him and turned off my love for my own protection. [*Feeling martyred by the decisions that life has forced on her, she rebels. She is not ready for marriage or a child, so she withholds the love she feels for a loving husband. "Turning off" her love seems to be the only choice that gives her a feeling of being responsible for herself. It does preserve her as an autonomous person, sad though it is for their relationship.*]

After our child, Gordon, was born things were better. Jay went into the army and we moved near his army base. After a year and a half of marriage, he left for Vietnam. [*Here again the decision about separation is made by the government, and is not a choice either can feel responsible for.*]

That was a very difficult year. I finished my B.S. and started work on my M.A. I devoted all my energies to Gordon and later to my pupils when I began teaching that fall. I always feared Jay would not return, but he did. [*She is beginning to become a more independent and giving person.*]

But the Jay I thought I knew did not return. Jay had always been quiet and rather withdrawn, but he came back from a year at war and isolated himself completely. He gave to no one. For a year and a half things went on. I taught and enjoyed my world of students. Jay disliked his job and himself. I finished my M.A. and began teaching at a small university near our town the next year. [*The relationship appears to be dying. Jay is off in his own (probably tortured) world, and she is invested in her work. It would seem the end of the partnership is not far off.*]

Then we met Doug and Mary. They were so open, so honest, so loving. We learned to really talk to each other and to them.

57

I admitted to my fears of domination and my disgust with my body. Everything was beautiful. We loved and were loved. Then we went to bed with each other's spouses. [*The open communication with Doug and Mary is her first exposure to a person-centered approach, and as so often happens, Ruth began to blossom, particularly in the acceptance of herself and in the mutual communication with Jay and the other couple.*]

The first two or three times were beautiful. We all felt good, but Jay was impotent with Mary. This really bothered him. We talked some, but not enough. Suddenly one night I was watching Jay and Mary talking and being very loving. I became very frightened and cried. I could see Jay giving to Mary all the love and affection I had wanted from him but had not taken when he gave it (the first year) and now he didn't give it to me. Needless to say we stopped the physical part and almost broke up our relationship with Doug and Mary because I felt so threatened. [*As sometimes happens when two couples are mutually close, the closeness finds expression in physical and sexual ways. The sexual relations were evidently threatening to no one.*

[*The fact that Jay cares for and communicates with Mary proves terribly threatening to Ruth. She imposes control, evidently unconsciously. "Needless to say, we stopped the physical part." She appears to feel this doesn't even need discussion, though obviously she brought it about. She further distances Doug and Mary to quell her fears. She is not condemning of Jay, because she realizes that here is his loving self, the self she had rejected early in the marriage.*

[*It is fascinating that she does not even mention Jay's reaction to this breakup of a relationship that was becoming meaningful to him. She evidently does not see this as an issue and decision in which they both have a stake.*]

Then the next spring one of my students fell in love with me. I had always given much love and understanding to students, but I had never had college students. I was twenty-six and John was twenty. Before I knew it, we loved each other. Jay and I were talking then but evidently not saying all. My love for John only made my love for Jay stronger. But Jay was not able to accept John. He did really try. It was a great emotional strain on all of us. I loved Jay too much to see him so miserable. So I gave up John and went to teach at another college in the fall. John and I never went to bed together. [*Now Ruth finds that it is possible to love two persons at the same time in different ways. She also discovers that being giving and understanding and self-revealing to other persons can sometimes lead to love—as it did to her love for John. But now the jealousy comes from her husband, and though all three are trying hard to communicate, it doesn't seem possible to work it through. So again the same solution to jealousy is utilized—drop the "satellite" relationship. She seems to attach considerable importance to the fact that she and her lover never went "all the way."*]

The whole incident left a grave effect on me. I found myself afraid to give to my new students for fear of another such encounter and hurting Jay all over again. I began to narrow my world and refused to give as much of myself. [*What Ruth appears to have learned from this is that being open and giving is risky business. Don't give of yourself and all will be well!*]

Jay's dissatisfaction with his job led him to begin graduate school. My and Doug's interest in and talk of education probably influenced him in that direction. All of this time we had been reading and talking and growing some intellectually, but not much emotionally. [*Throughout this whole account it is evident that Ruth and Jay are continually trying to improve their communication—a good sign for the future.*]

Then the bomb dropped. Jay took an education class this fall and a group consisting of Jay, seven fellow students, and a faculty facilitator began an encounter group. They met once a week for six or seven weeks and then all day one Saturday.

How to explain how I felt? I wanted Jay to grow and learn to give to others and to be happy. Yet this threatened me because I saw a new Jay and feared he no longer needed me and would not stay with me when I needed him more than ever. I had narrowed my own world and his was widening. [*When Jay has a chance in a person-centered climate, he responds, but any change in a system of relationships is upsetting. Here is exactly what Ruth has been hoping for—that Jay would come out of his shell and be more expressive, but the realization of that goal terrifies her. The fear is that she will no longer be necessary to his life.*]

Communication broke down at home. We got angry and upset and hurt instead of talking and understanding. I feared I was losing him and in a way must have been driving him away.

Jay formed a close relationship with one of the girls in the group, Laura. Her own marriage was breaking up and she needed someone desperately. Jay went to her. He didn't tell me about Laura but I suspected the worst. Maybe even I subconsciously drove him to it. At least an affair was something I could understand or try to deal with. [*Interesting the way the learnings bounce back and forth in this relationship. Ruth had learned that being open, giving, and expressive could lead to love, and now Jay too rediscovers it, more deeply than with Mary.*]

Then I left Jay one weekend for a visit with my mother. I wanted him to decide what we were going to do about our marriage. He spent Saturday with Laura and they went to bed. He was impotent at first but then he overcame it. He came to me that night in my mother's house. I was happy because I thought he wanted to stay with me and make our marriage work, I wanted to make love but he didn't and I was confused.

The next week was good and bad. Jay still didn't tell me about Laura and I knew something was wrong. [*Though this is Ruth's account of her own pain, Jay's uncertainty, confusion, and agony show through as well.*] We hurt each other and took everything the other said in the wrong way. [*This is an example of the fact that when a couple has tried to communicate openly, a conscious holding back (in this case by Jay) leads almost certainly to miscommunication and hurt.*] Finally on Sunday Jay said he needed to get away for a week by himself. He was going to stay in a nearby town with Doug and Mary. I was scared and miserable but I wanted him to be happy and he wasn't. I let him go without a tear. But after he left, that day and the next two days were pure misery for me. I wallowed in fear and self-pity. I was afraid he was gone for good, and I was so lonely. But I did not call him or try to make him feel guilty. I didn't even tell him about how this was affecting our son so adversely. I really wanted to give him the freedom he needed. [*Clearly Ruth is trying so hard to be what she would intellectually like to be—willing to give her husband freedom—that her real feelings drive her to despair.*]

Jay came back on Tuesday night. We talked almost all night and each night after. He confessed on Saturday about Laura. She loves him and he loves her. It was all I had feared, but the knowing was somehow easier than all the fears and doubts. [*Somehow, because of the commitment each feels to the other, communication is reestablished. And when communication is open, the facts are never as devastating as imagination without the facts.*]

I began reading your book about encounter groups. [*Here is Ruth's second exposure to a person-centered approach.*] If I had only understood earlier it might never have gone so far. But it's not too late.

Jay is a changed person. He feels Laura needs him and he will go to her at times. He is able to give of himself in ways he never could. He is a loving person.

And what about me? Well, I love him more than ever. I want him to give to and love others. Oh, I still feel threatened and lonely at times. I still want a security that is never possible. But I am understanding more and more. I am giving more of myself both physically and emotionally to Jay now than at any other time in our marriage. I still have occasional relapses of fear and loneliness, but the biggest battle is over. [*The growth toward a mature and nonpossessive love, which is so briefly covered in this paragraph, is tremendous.*]

Your books have helped me to reach an understanding of myself and Jay and Laura. It is a little fearful, and change isn't ever easy, but I am changing. Instead of forcing Jay into a decision between me and Laura, I chose to let him have love for us both. At this moment I feel full of love and good will. Tonight, while Jay is with Laura, the old doubts may come back, but I am much better able to deal with them. I once more find myself more loving and giving with my students. And it is worthwhile. [*This is a daring, risky, growthful way that Ruth is choosing. Will it "work"? Who knows what that word means? But Ruth and Jay are in better communication, they are more giving, and life goes on. It is especially noteworthy that now she can again be her open, loving self with her students as well as with Jay. Life does not seem quite so frightening.*]

This is probably far from the last chapter in our lives. We are both young and will experience many more changes and emotions. But I am better able to deal with them now than ever. And Jay and I are talking and are giving to each other. Right now I'm doing most of the giving, but in time I feel he will give more and more to me. Thank you for helping.

Ruth_____

There have been astonishing shifts in the locus of power, of influence, of control in this relationship, and it is a dramatic example of the fact that a change in one facet of the relationship alters the dynamics of the whole system.

At different times circumstances were in control. The unwanted pregnancy made Ruth a self-doubting, suspicious, ungiving wife. The draft and Jay's year in Vietnam appear to have had devastating effects on him, but led to much greater independence and satisfaction on Ruth's part as she pursued her own life and built her own confidence.

Each time either of the partners has been involved in a relationship including caring, openness, and respect it has brought closeness, pain, and growth. The first was their experience with their friends, Doug and Mary. For Jay this led to a giving, communicating kind of love. For Ruth it led to fear and jealousy and withdrawal. But then came Ruth's openness with her students, which led to love both for John—the student—and Jay, her husband. But for Jay it meant threat, and they both withdrew. Next came Jay's exposure to the openness and caring of an encounter group. Here he found himself again as a giving, loving person, which changed the whole dynamics of the relationship because *he* had changed. Then his love for Laura confused him and upset Ruth. Through pain and hurt there gradually came more and more real communication. Jay became a loving person: Ruth is taking the risk of letting him love two women, and has become far more mature in the whole process. She is trying to understand and accept not only her own needs, but those of Jay and Laura. She is risking a difficult but person-centered relationship. She has come a long way, and, from her account, so has Jay.

As in every person-centered relationship, the exact course of the future cannot be predicted. All that we can safely say about the future is that it is being faced openly by two trusting, communicative partners, endeavoring to face life and its difficulties and rewards in relationships, without trying to control each other. And in that way it is probable that each of them, and Laura, and Ruth's students, will benefit.

I felt that I should try to discover the next chapters in the life of Ruth and Jay. Now, two years later, I was not optimistic about locating Ruth in view of the transiency of modern life, but my letter of inquiry was forwarded, and I received responses from *both* Ruth and Jay.

Ruth, in her letter, goes back over some of her experiences and amplifies the story a bit. She mentions that several months after meeting Jay they became lovers, and three months later "I discovered I was pregnant (pills were not so easy to get in our area in those days!). I really did not want to get married— I hadn't really planned to ever marry because I wanted a career —but Jay very much did want to get married. He was ready and he loved me, so with parental pressure from both sides we did marry."

During much of the time Jay was in the army, and while he was in Vietnam, Ruth lived with his parents, her in-laws—"they are really the most, best, everything I can say." During the year he was in Vietnam, "I started work on my M.A., and taught school. I was lonesome and wrote him every day. I don't think it ever really occurred to me to be unfaithful that year. At that point such extramarital activities just never really entered my mind. I know some people would find that difficult to believe, but it's true.

"Jay returned after a year. He was changed and it was almost like discovering each other for the first time. I finally relaxed enough to have orgasms when we made love and things got better and better. Jay got out of the army and took a job in his hometown. He was going through a lot then (he is a very peaceful, mild, considerate man for whom having to go to war was almost too much) but we were very contented with our lives."

She passes briefly over the three-year period which included their experience with Doug and Mary, and Jay's beginning his graduate work, knowing she has covered this before. Here let Jay pick up the story: "I will begin with my feelings that led to my involvement with Laura. After returning from Vietnam, I suppose outwardly I appeared to readjust. I went to work, made money, came home, watched TV, read some, spent money and did the things that are supposed to make you happy. Although I loved Ruth and Gordon very much I was not pleased with myself. I continued to torture myself about Vietnam and the nagging feelings it left in me. Attempting to break out of this, I decided to take a few graduate classes at night. The more involved in graduate school I became, the more new feelings of excitement over the learning process began to build. It is difficult for me to now realize the joy and excitement that can be found through learning. I discovered how many unnecessary limits we place on ourselves by saying I don't know.

So I committed myself to never again place limits on the things I was willing to learn about my world or the people in it.

"It was at this time that as part of one of my courses I decided to investigate encounter groups. Five other students and myself decided to actually experience an encounter group rather than read about them. We asked help from a professor in the psychology department to facilitate for us. Laura, also a student, became another member of this group. This was a very emotional encounter for all of the participants. Laura and I became very close and eventually became lovers. I rationalized that everything was fine with Laura and me and Ruth and me. Ruth realized something was wrong with me so we began to talk about Laura. Just going through the process of talking to Ruth about Laura diminished the intensity of the affair. After confessing the affair to Ruth, Laura and I did not go to bed again although we still saw a lot of each other at school. I suppose this was the hardest part for Ruth to understand. I told Ruth we were not going to bed anymore, but it was impossible for her to understand why we were still seeing each other. This I don't understand either; we just couldn't turn loose."

Ruth takes up the account at about this time. It was now summer, Jay was working full time on his master's degree, and she felt his relationship with Laura had cooled. She went to Europe for five weeks with a girl friend. "I was still wounded (in pride only) but my vacation was fantastic and the long absence made both of us see things differently. Ever since I returned that summer things have been better and better. We are closer and more in love than we've ever been. We are no longer just contented but truly happy. Our sex life is better than ever and I am actually aggressive many times."

Jay also gives his version of this period and brings us up to date on his love, his life, and his work. "That summer Ruth took her trip to Europe while I was still attending graduate school. Laura was still around although I did not see her while Ruth was away. I think Laura realized how much I loved Ruth and knew I would not want to see her while Ruth was away.

When Ruth returned I think we both decided to commit ourselves to our relationship which had always been very good. No verbal commitments were made, it was simply one of those nonverbal communications that people who love each other can make."

Laura's need for someone with whom she could communicate intimately at the time her marriage was breaking up was very great, "desperate." Ruth and Jay were not communicating well. As often happens, the sharing of feelings in the satellite relationship was almost certainly deeper, more honest, more feelingful than in the marriage. There is no doubt that Laura enriched Jay's life—and this led, after a stormy period, to an enrichment of his marriage. How did Laura feel? Was she full of conflict and guilt for her intimacy with Jay? Or did she regard their relationship as natural? Was she content with the distance Jay put between them when Ruth went to Europe, or resentful? Could she accept the gradual demise of the relationship, or did she suffer great pain? We tend to be so concerned with the marital partners that we forget that the outsider is a person also, with, in Laura's case, a real and genuine love. Jay recognizes the depth of their involvement when he says, "We just couldn't turn loose." It is clear that Laura, by talking with and loving Jay, brought Ruth and Jay much closer together and restored their marriage. But I wish we knew more of what the whole experience meant for Laura herself.

Jay continues his account by telling of his professional activity. "Now I'm teaching elementary school in a small rural school with a group of children I truly love. You know, if you love a bunch of kids and are willing to show them you do, they will learn from you in spite of all your clumsy efforts and failures. 'Freedom to Learn' has been and continues to be a big help in my teaching. Be good to yourself and those in your world and thanks for helping Ruth during a time when I could not."

Ruth is in agreement that Jay is "an *unbelievably excellent* elementary school teacher!" They have moved, but she is still teaching and working toward her doctor's degree. She makes two statements that give a very clear picture of their current relationship. "We have been married almost nine years and I wouldn't trade my life for any other life that I know! If I had *planned* to get pregnant back in college, I couldn't have picked a better father and husband and person.

"Neither one of us would dare say that we will not perhaps try an affair or swapping or something else someday. Who knows what we will do? But right now we just don't need it and aren't looking for anything else. Maybe in a few years we will want to try something else entirely, but I know now that we are closer and happier than ever. I don't think either one of us will ever be afraid of 'losing' the other. (I know you can't lose what you don't own but you know what I mean, anyway!) Everything that has occurred in our marriage has worked to strengthen it in the end. Maybe we're just lucky; maybe we had good parent models (both of us came from happy marriages); maybe we are just suited to each other. It doesn't really matter to me why; I'm just glad we have what we have."

As I have studied these current letters, it has become clear to me that I *had* to follow up on the later experiences of Ruth and Jay. I am often criticized for being too optimistic about human nature, about communicative relationships, about the growth process. I had ended my commentary about Ruth and Jay optimistically and I could hear critics saying, "Ridiculous! Here is an initially forced marriage, presently in a mess because the husband is in love with two women, and you have the *nerve* to picture the situation as constructive!" As I thought it over, while I believed what I had said, I realized that my critics could be right. The marriage might have broken up in bitterness. They each might be feeling terrible guilt. Their career hopes might have been destroyed. I *had* to find out! I could not leave the story there.

Once again, as so often before, the experience justifies a constructive view. Ruth and Jay show, as clearly as can be shown, that partners committed to a *process* relationship, partners who take the risk of open communication of feeling, who try to build relationships rather than guarantee the future, are going to find life enriching and rewarding, though certainly not always smooth. They can, as Ruth says, be "glad we have what we have."

So I have no apology for my earlier summary. I would suspect that Laura regards her experience with Jay as a growth experience in her life, and hope that John feels the same way about his closeness to Ruth. I am sure Ruth's students gain from the person-centeredness she has attained. The thing I did not foresee was that Jay's openness of being would be a great boon to his students as well. Like Ruth, I am quite content to leave the future as an unknown, but not a fearful unknown.

Here is a partnership in which initially a great deal of the control was from outside: the circumstance of pregnancy, parental pressures, social expectations, the draft—to mention a few. We have been privileged to watch it change over a period of nine years. In spite of periods when Ruth tried to control Jay, when Jay tried the strategy of deceit, we have seen each exposure to a person-centered approach lead to a weakening of the power of external controls and a relinquishing of attempts to control each other. As they have each grown, through periods of stress and pain as well as satisfaction, they have had less and less need to control. As a consequence they each have increasingly supplied a growth-promoting climate for the other. Where at first they were pawns, now they are persons. They have a great and loving *influence* on each other, but each is a respected person in his own right. The politics of their relationship is now thoroughly equalitarian, with each partner clearly in control of his and her own life and behavior. They have developed a person-centered politics in their marriage.

Chapter 4

Power or persons: two trends in education

The educational system is probably the most influential of all institutions—outranking the family, the church, the police, and the government—in shaping the interpersonal politics of the growing person. We will take a look at the politics of education as it is and has been in this country and compare it with the politics of an educational enterprise when it has become infused with a person-centered approach.

Here is how the politics of the traditional school is experienced:

The teacher is the possessor of knowledge, the student the recipient. There is a great difference in status between instructor and student.

The lecture, as the means of pouring knowledge into the recipient, and the examination as the measure of the extent to which he has received it, are the central elements of this education.

The teacher is the possessor of power, the student the one who obeys. The administrator is also the possessor of power, and both the teacher and the student are the ones who obey. Control is always exercised downward.

Authoritarian rule is the accepted policy in the classroom. New teachers are often advised, "Make sure you get control of your students the very first day."

Trust is at a minimum. Most notable is the teacher's distrust of the student. The student cannot be expected to work satisfactorily without the teacher constantly supervising and checking on him. The student's distrust of the teacher is more diffuse—a lack of trust in teacher's motives, honesty, fairness, competence. There may be a real rapport between an entertaining lecturer and those who are being entertained. There may be admiration for the instructor, but mutual trust is not a noticeable ingredient.

The subjects (the students) are best governed by being kept in an intermittent or constant state of fear. There is today not much physical punishment, but public criticism and ridicule, and a constant fear of failure, are even more potent. This state of fear appears to increase as we go up the educational scheme, because the student has more to lose. In elementary school the individual may be an object of scorn, or scolded as stupid or bad. In high school there is added to this the fear of failure to graduate, with its vocational, economic and educational disadvantages. In college all these consequences are magnified and intensified. In graduate school, sponsorship by one professor offers even greater opportunities for extreme punishment due to some autocratic whim. Many graduate students have failed to receive their degrees because they have refused to obey every wish of their major professor. They are like slaves, subject to the life and death power of an Oriental despot. It is the recognition of this abjectness which caused Farber to title his biting criticism of education *The Student as Nigger.*[1]

Democracy and its values are ignored and scorned in practice. The student does not participate in choosing his goals, his curriculum, his manner of working. They are chosen for him. He has no part in the choice of teaching personnel or in educational policy. Likewise the teachers have no choice in choosing their principal or other administrative officers. Often they, too, have no participation in forming educational policy. The political practices of the school are in striking contrast to what is taught *about* the virtues of democracy and the importance of freedom and responsibility. *There is no place for the whole person in the educational system, only for the intellect.* In elementary school the bursting curiosity of the normal child and his excess of physical energy are curbed and, if possible, stifled. In secondary school the one overriding interest of all the students—sex and the relationships between the sexes—is almost totally ignored and certainly not regarded as a major area for learning. In college the situation is the same—it is only the *mind* that is welcomed.

If you think that such views have vanished, or that I am exaggerating, we have only to turn to the Los Angeles *Times* of December 13, 1974. Here we find that the University of California (embracing all of the state universities—Berkeley, UCLA, and others) is lobbying to keep John Vasconcellos, a state legislator, off of any committees having to do with university policy. Vasconcellos for the past three years headed, with distinction, a legislative study of higher education. And why is the university trying to keep him from having anything to do with university policy? Because of two changes he favors. First, he favors setting aside a percentage of the budget for innovative educational programs. This is strongly opposed. But the most important reason for opposing him is that he favors the inclusion of *both* "affective and cognitive" learning, according to Dr. Jay Michael, a vice-president of the university. Says Michael, "We believe . . . there is knowledge that exists separate and apart from how a person feels . . . and that accumulated knowledge of mankind is cognitive. It can be transmitted, it can be taught and learned, and the pursuit of that kind of knowledge is academic research." He continues, "It appears to us that he [Vasconcellos] would like to abandon cognitive learning, or at least reduce its importance to a level unacceptable to scholars. . . ."

In reply Vasconcellos says he values cognitive skills, "but I also believe that the affective, the emotional component . . . is terribly important." He believes cognitive skills should be combined with better knowledge of self and of interpersonal behavior.

The politics of this difference is quite fascinating. The vice-president clearly holds to the "mug and jug" theory of education, where the faculty possesses the knowledge and transfers it to the passive recipient. So threatened is he by the possibility of change that he opposes any innovation in educational procedure. But most threatening of all is the idea that faculty and students alike are human in their experiencing of a feeling component in all knowledge. If this were even partially admitted, students and faculty would be on a more equal level, and the politics of domination would be weakened. This was the position of one of the "great" university systems in 1975.

Although this traditional picture of education is exceedingly common, it is no longer the one and only way by which education may proceed. A decade ago, only a few lonely, quiet pioneers offered an alternative to the traditional picture. Today, in every major city in the United States, there are dozens of "alternative schools," "free schools," "universities without walls" in which humanistic, person-centered, process-oriented learning is taking place.

Here are the fundamental conditions that may be observed when person-centered learning develops in a school, college, or graduate school.

Precondition. A leader or a person who is perceived as an authority figure in the situation is sufficiently secure within himself and in his relationship to others that he experiences an essential trust in the capacity of others to think for themselves, to learn for themselves. If this precondition exists, then the following aspects become possible.

The facilitative person shares with the others—students and possibly also parents or community members—the responsibility for the learning process. Curricular planning, the mode of administration and operation, the funding, and the policy making are all the responsibility of the particular group involved. Thus a class may be responsible for its own curriculum, but the total group may be responsible for overall policy.

The facilitator provides learning resources—from within himself and his own experience, from books or materials or community experiences. He encourages the learners to add resources of which they have knowledge, or in which they have experience. He opens doors to resources outside the experience of the group.

The student develops his own program of learning, alone or in cooperation with others. Exploring his own interests, facing the wealth of resources, he makes the choices as to his own learning direction and carries the responsibility for the consequences of those choices.

A facilitative learning climate is provided. In meetings of the class or of the school as a whole, an atmosphere of realness, of caring, and of understanding listening is evident. This climate may spring initially from the person who is the perceived leader. As the learning process continues, it is more and more often provided by the learners for one another. Learning from one another becomes as important as learning from books or films or community experiences, or from the facilitator.

It can be seen that *the focus is primarily on fostering the continuing process of learning.* The content of the learning, while significant, falls into a secondary place. Thus a course is successfully ended not when the student has "learned all he needs to know," but when he has made significant progress in learning *how to learn* what he wants to know.

The discipline necessary to reach the student's goals is a self-discipline and is recognized and accepted by the learner as being his own responsibility.

The evaluation of the extent and significance of the student's learning is made primarily by the learner himself, though his self-evaluation may be influenced and enriched by caring feedback from other members of the group and from the facilitator. *In this growth-promoting climate, the learning is deeper, proceeds at a more rapid rate, and is more pervasive in the life and behavior of the student than learning acquired in the traditional classroom.* This comes about because the direction is self-chosen, the learning is self-initiated, and the whole person, with feelings and passions as well as intellect, is invested in the process.

The political implications of person-centered education are clear: the student retains his own power and the control over himself; he shares in the responsible choices and decisions; the facilitator provides the climate for these aims. The growing, seeking person is the politically powerful force. This process of learning represents a revolutionary about-face from the politics of traditional education.

What is it that causes a teacher to reverse the politics of the classroom? The reasons are multiple.

First I cite my own experience. As my point of view in therapy became more and more trusting of the capacity of the individual, I could not help but question my teaching approach. If I saw clients as trustworthy and basically capable of discovering themselves and guiding their lives in an ambience I was able to create, why could I not create the same kind of climate with graduate students and foster a *self-*guided process of learning? So, at the University of Chicago, I began to try. I ran into far more resistance and hostility than I did with my clients. I believe this had the result of making me more defensively rigid, putting *all* the responsibility on the class rather than recognizing myself as a part of the learning group. I made many mistakes, and sometimes doubted the wisdom of the whole approach. Yet with all my initial clumsiness the results were astonishing. Students worked harder, learned more, did more creative thinking than in any of my previous classes. So I persevered, and improved, I believe, in my ability as a facilitator. Although I began to talk and write about my experience, and some of my students worked in similar ways with classes they were conducting, there was always the nagging doubt that perhaps this procedure worked simply because of something in me, or some peculiar attitudes we had developed in the Counseling Center at Chicago. Consequently it was enormously supportive to find that others had gone through similar struggles, were adopting the principles we had outlined, and were having parallel—indeed almost identical—experiences.

An English teacher named Jacqueline Carr, with whom I had had no contact, recorded her own account of the ambivalent way in which she "took the plunge."[2] Here is how the political climate in her classroom shifted, and why.

"Recently, while reading some material written by Carl Rogers, I became increasingly excited, frustrated, and obsessed with some of the 'idealistic' concepts he presents. I asked myself, 'Just how much freedom can be given to high school students? How much responsibility can they accept for their own education?'

"I wanted to believe that if given freedom, high school students could accept some responsibility for their own education. But I kept thinking, 'It just won't work . . . impossible to put into practice . . . the kids will go wild . . . the administration won't allow it . . . etc.' I was disturbed by the hypocrisy of believing what I read, yet refusing to act upon these beliefs."

Clearly the basis for change lies in a questioning, doubting, gestation period in the person of the teacher. Little by little the groundwork is laid for taking the risk, for changing from teacher to facilitator.

"Then one Friday I announced that Monday we were going to begin reading *Romeo and Juliet*. One boy complained, 'How come we never get to read anything good . . . anything different . . . just Shakespeare, Dickens, Hugo . .' I justified class reading on the basis of district requirements, curriculum guides, college expectations, cultural demands, and personal satisfactions.

"As soon as I had finished my explanation, one of the girls said, 'How come we never get to do what *we* want?' Questions similar to these two have been asked of teachers for generations. I stopped talking, took a deep breath, sat down on the top of my desk, and looked around. Every student was watching for my reactions. I said 'OK! Monday, each of you can bring to class an individual plan of study for the next six weeks. You can study any area that interests you, providing it involves reading and writing.' "

In one statement she has turned upside down the politics of the interpersonal relationships in her class.

"There was a dead silence. Then one youngster said, 'But then how are you going to test us?' I answered, 'No tests for six weeks.' Another student asked, 'Then, how will you grade us?' I said, 'We'll work out something by mutual agreement based on what you've accomplished, how much you think you've learned in comparison to the last six weeks, and how much you've done in relation to other students in your class.'

"Several of the students were worried, confused, and upset. One boy asked, 'Could we just follow the work you had already planned to do for the next six weeks?' Some of the students were obviously afraid they couldn't handle the freedom, the responsibility."

The reactions to this political upset are those that I, and many others in Ms. Carr's position, have met. The students who have been clamoring for freedom are definitely frightened when they realize that it also means responsibility. There is also a healthy skepticism as to the reality of the change. Won't the teacher still dominate through grades and exams? Isn't this a pseudo-freedom? As they become convinced that it is real, a new spirit is released.

"I suggested we talk about things they might like to do. One boy said, 'I'd like to spend the whole six weeks reading about writing short stories and then trying to write one.' Another student said, 'I'd like to spend six weeks just reading all the books I've wanted to read but haven't had time for.' Several students wanted to spend their six weeks reading books by one author. One girl wanted to read material on semantics, another on psychology, another on Communism. One boy was interested in investigating the concepts of 'free will' and 'determinism.'

"This same kind of excited discussion went on. . . . The 'average' students seemed far more excited than the college-prep group. I imagined I could hear their comments when they left the classroom. 'Mrs. Carr is going to let us do anything we want, and what's more we get to grade ourselves.' So I went directly to the head of the English Department and also to the principal. Their cooperative and interested responses convinced me that we teachers often use the 'administration won't let us' excuse for our own supposed lack of freedom."

Ms. Carr's students did much more creative work than they had done before. "Students came to class before school, at lunch time, and after school. During classtime, they worked industriously all period long." But, as she says, "the subject matter of the student products seemed less important than their personal reactions to the projects."

Here are four quotations from the statements of her students. The first two indicate how placing the power of choice in the hands of the student brings a totally different sense of responsibility, and much greater effort. The third indicates the increase in self-insight, the fourth the growing sense of maturity. All of these are typical outcomes when there is a person-centered approach to the classroom.

"Because I disliked school, I was surprised to find out how well I can study and learn when I'm not forced to do it."

"I've never read so much in my life."

"Various 'free' discussions have helped me a lot to understand myself."

"It was like I was an adult—not supervised and guided all the time."

Not everyone has been so fortunate in attempting a person-centered approach. Joann Lipshires[3] took over the teaching of three high school seminars in Human Relationships. She had great difficulty working through the problem of negative feelings—her own and those of the students. She thought one of the seminars was "a disaster." But her department chairman encouraged her to continue, and gradually she could say that "I believe that my efforts finally have been successful in providing young people with something they desperately need."

When she restricted her seminars to fifteen students, provided a more relaxed and comfortable environment, and made a rule that put-downs or killer comments would not be tolerated, her seminars began to follow the patterns that have become familiar. Students were almost unanimously favorable.

Her report adds two other aspects that are not always so well documented. She shows how the changes in the school atmosphere, including a greater self-respect, and an improved ability to listen to others affects the politics of the family. Here is one student's report: "By listening to my mother at home I learned to care about her as well as the things she has to say. I no longer classify her 'mother' or 'parent' (which to me is a sign of authority which I would defy under any circumstances) but as another human being who deserves just as much love and attention as I or anyone else does. We don't try to change each other's thoughts on life anymore but we try to understand them first."

A parent of a sophomore who had taken Human Relations had this comment to make: "As a parent of a child who has taken the course Human Relations I would like to recommend it for other students. This course gave my child a chance to think about herself in many ways. It made her realize why she said things and how she felt about others. Her sense of values seems to have taken on a more positive form. The honesty in dealing with one's feelings makes for a better person. I believe this is the type of course that could be taught in grade school." In addition Ms. Lipshires has the report of two observers— student teachers assigned by the Education Department of a nearby college—on the discipline in her seminars. The reports have a similar tone:

"Not only do they enjoy the class, but the trust the teacher places in them is returned by the students' efforts to keep the class going and orderly."

"Discipline is a problem for most teachers. It is always viewed as the students walking all over the teacher's authority —'these kids have no respect!' In Human Relations there never seem to be any serious discipline problems or even any smaller troubles, like getting everyone's attention in class. The teacher is the key: she always expresses herself in terms of honest and real *feelings* and has enormous respect for the *feelings* of her students."

There could scarcely be a clearer statement of the way discipline by external authority is changed to self-discipline.

Change is never easy. To pioneer is anxiety-arousing for the teacher and threatening to colleagues. It seems it would be much simpler to go back to being the authority. It is hard being a person to one's students. And then there are, at the elementary and secondary level, the attitudes of skeptical or antagonistic parents to deal with. Many teachers have found that the only way to handle parental doubts is to find ways of including parents in the learning process. Some have invited parents to volunteer in different ways in the classroom. One imaginative secondary school teacher invited parents of her students for "An Evening of Learning" where they were exposed to, and discussed, the facilitative approach she was using with their children.

A new approach to education demands new ways of being and new methods of handling problems. Individuals are also finding that if they are to carry out a quiet revolution in the schools, they definitely need a support group. This can be small, perhaps only two or three people, but a resource of persons where one does not need to defend one's point of view, and can freely discuss the successes and failures, the problems faced, the difficulties unresolved.

I have spoken mostly of the risks the teacher takes in the teacher-student relationship when the politics of the classroom changes. But a facilitator is also taking the risk of threatening the administration. How is this dealt with?

In many states and communities, instructors are being held more and more accountable. They are expected to write down "behavioral objectives" for each student or for each course, and later to give evidence that these objectives have been achieved. The anxiety that underlies these demands—sometimes encased in law—is understandable. The public hopes that young people are learning, and this has been the only way they can see of determining whether learning is taking place.

From the viewpoint of any good teacher, conventional or innovative, this becomes a new strait jacket which prevents any deviance from the expected, any ventures into exciting bypaths of learning. Dr. David Malcolm, a university professor, tells how he met this request for behavioral objectives.[4]

"My university is on an 'accountability' kick right now, and writing 'behavioral objectives' for students is the big thing. Both do total violence to all my personal beliefs about learning and what people are for. My protest has been to refuse to write objectives for 'my' (what arrogance!) classes. Instead I wrote down some tentative ideas trying to express objectives for my own behavior. They fell into place pretty well, and I'd like to share them with you."

Here they are, in shortened form.

A SET OF BEHAVIORAL OBJECTIVES WRITTEN BY AND FOR DAVE MALCOLM

(The following is written on the assumption that behavioral objectives begin at home.)

QUESTION: Okay, just what *does* the faculty member (specifically, *me*) do in my idealized "learning place;" i.e., one *not* contaminated by gate-keeping?

ANSWER: Well . . . *first,* I have to give the learners accessibility to me as a person, to my experience, to my expertise . . . *second,* I have to be as ready as I can to suggest experiences (materials to read, things to do, people to touch, processes to observe, ideas to ponder, practices to try, whatever) that they might not otherwise have thought of, thereby increasing the options open to them; *third,* I have to respect each learner's autonomy and freedom, including the freedom to fail; and *finally,* I have to be willing to (perhaps, better, I should say *have the courage to*) give each learner honest feedback, as straight as possible, to the very best of my ability, on as many of the following as I can:

(He describes nine areas, including ability to conceptualize; demonstrated skill in practice; effectiveness in oral and written communication; degree of self-understanding, insight and skill in interpersonal relationships; innovativeness; my best judgment as to his progress or growth. He is *willing* to give feedback in these areas if the student desires.)

Here is a conscientious and inspiring statement of the true "objectives" of one person-centered facilitator of learning. Malcolm is up against the impossible task of defining his aims for students, being expected to follow the old conventional authoritarian framework. His own politics of education simply does not permit this. So he bravely sets forth, thoughtfully and precisely, the objectives he has for *himself,* not the student. His statement can be a guideline for teachers. Most of all, however, it shows the complete incompatibility of the old politics and the new, and thus fits a definition that has been given of revolution.

"What is a revolution? A redefinition of the facts of life, such that the new definition and the old definition of the same facts cannot coexist."[5] Clearly, to advance a revolution threatens the power of a conventional administration, and a consequent risk to the facilitator, who is a radical in the true sense of going to the root of the problem. This risk cannot be ignored.

Too little attention has been paid to the problems of the student in meeting the challenge of a person-centered way of education. Initially students feel suspicion, frustration, and anger, and then excitement and creativity replace those feelings. No one has caught these changing reactions better than Dr. Samuel Tenenbaum, who was a member of a seminar I offered at Brandeis University in 1958. His account indicates the impact upon the learner of a sharp change in the power relationship in a class.[6]

I have often pondered the reasons why, in this seminar, the reactions were more strongly negative, and eventually more strongly positive, than in any other class I have led. I believe it is due in part to the fact that they were so eager to learn from the "master," the "guru," that they were loath to accept any shift in authority. Perhaps another reason is that they were all graduate students, most of them already employed professionally, or, like Dr. Tenenbaum, taking the course as a postdoctoral seminar. Such students are, I believe, even more dependent upon authority than are elementary school children.

I took up most of the first meeting of the seminar (about twenty-five students) by introducing myself and my purpose and asking if others wished to do the same. After some awkward silences, the students told what brought them to the seminar. I told the group about the many resources I had brought with me—reprints, mimeographed material, books, a list of recommended reading (no requirements), tapes of therapeutic interviews, and films. I asked for volunteers to organize and lend out these materials, to run the tapes, and find a movie projector. All of this was easily handled, and the session ended. As Dr. Tenenbaum takes up the story:

Thereafter followed four hard, frustrating sessions. During this period, the class didn't seem to get anywhere. Students spoke at random, saying whatever came into their heads. It all seemed chaotic, aimless, a waste of time. A student would bring up some aspect of Rogers' philosophy; and the next student, completely disregarding the first, would take the group away in another direction; and a third, completely disregarding the first two, would start fresh on something else altogether. At times there were some faint efforts at a cohesive discussion, but for the most part the classroom proceedings seemed to lack continuity and direction. The instructor received every contribution with attention and regard. He did not find any student's contribution in order or out of order.

The class was not prepared for such a totally unstructured approach. They did not know how to proceed. In their perplexity and frustration, they demanded that the teacher play the role assigned to him by custom and tradition; that he set forth for us in authoritative language what was right and wrong, what was good and bad. Had they not come from far distances to learn from the oracle himself? Were they not fortunate? Were they not about to be initiated in the right rituals and practices by the great man himself, the founder of the movement that bears his name? The notebooks were poised for the climactic moment when the oracle would give forth, but mostly they remained untouched.

Queerly enough, from the outset, even in their anger, the members of the group felt joined together, and outside the classroom, there was an excitement and a ferment, for even in their frustration, they had communicated as never before in any classroom, and probably never before in quite the way they had. . . . In the Rogers class, they had spoken their minds; the words did not come from a book, nor were they the reflection of the instructor's thinking, nor that of any other authority. The ideas, emotions, and feelings came from themselves; and this was the releasing and the exciting process.

In this atmosphere of freedom, something for which they had

not bargained and for which they were not prepared, the students spoke up as students seldom do. During this period, the instructor took many blows; and it seemed to me that many times he appeared to be shaken; and although he was the source of our irritation, we had, strange as it may seem, a great affection for him, for it did not seem right to be angry with a man who was so sympathetic, so sensitive to the feelings and ideas of others. We all felt that what was involved was some slight misunderstanding which once understood and remedied would make everything right again. But our instructor, gentle enough on the surface, had a "whim of steel." He didn't seem to understand; and if he did, he was obstinate and obdurate; he refused to come around. Thus did this tug-of-war continue. We all looked to Rogers and Rogers looked to us. One student, amid general approbation, observed: "We are Rogers-centered, not student-centered. We have come to learn from Rogers."

After more of this, individual students attempted to take leadership and organize the seminar around certain topics or ways of planning, but these attempts at structure were largely disregarded. Gradually the group became insistent that I lecture. I told them that I was just completing a paper, and would be willing to give that as a lecture, but I also informed them that I was quite willing to have it duplicated so that each could read it. They insisted that I give it as a talk, and I agreed. It was a topic I was much involved in, and I believe I delivered it as well as I was able, taking somewhat more than an hour. Tenenbaum reports the results.

After the vivid and acrimonious exchanges to which we had been accustomed, this was certainly a letdown, dull and soporific to the extreme. This experience squelched all further demands for lecturing.

By the fifth session, something definite had happened; there was no mistaking that. Students spoke to one another; they by-passed Rogers. Students asked to be heard and wanted to be heard, and what before was a halting, stammering, self-conscious group became an interacting group, a brand-new cohesive unit, carrying on in a unique way; and from them came discussion and thinking such as no other group but this could repeat or duplicate. The instructor also joined in, but his role, more important than any in the group, somehow became merged with the group; the group was important, the center, the base of operation, not the instructor.

What caused it? I can only conjecture as to the reason. I believe that what happened was this: For four sessions students refused to believe that the instructor would refuse to play the traditional role. They still believed that he would set the tasks; that he would be the center of whatever happened and that he would manipulate the group. It took the class four sessions to realize that they were wrong; that he came to them with nothing outside of himself, outside of his own person; that if they really wanted something to happen, it was they who had to provide the content—an uncomfortable, challenging situation indeed. It was they who had to speak up, with all the risks that that entailed. As part of the process, they shared, they took exception, they agreed, they disagreed. At any rate, their persons, their deepest selves were involved; and from this situation, this special, unique group, this new creation was born. . . .

After the fourth session, and progressively thereafter, this group, haphazardly thrown together, became close to one another and their true selves appeared. As they interacted, there were moments of insight and revelation and understanding that were almost awesome in nature; they were what, I believe, Rogers would describe as "moments of therapy," those pregnant moments when you see a human soul revealed before you, in all its breathless wonder; and then a silence, almost like reverence, would overtake the class. And each member of the class became enveloped with a warmth and a loveliness that border on the mystic. I for one, and I am quite sure the others also, never had an experience quite like this. It was learning and therapy; and by therapy I do not mean illness, but what might be characterized by a healthy change in the person, an increase in his flexibility, his openness, his willingness to listen. In the process, we all felt elevated, freer, more accepting of ourselves and others, more open to new ideas, trying hard to understand and accept.

This is not a perfect world, and there was evidence of hostility as members differed. Somehow in this setting every blow was softened, as if the sharp edges had been removed; if undeserved, students would go off to something else; and the blow was somehow lost. In my own case, even those students who originally irritated me, with further acquaintance I began to accept and respect; and the thought occurred to me as I tried to understand what was happening: Once you come close to a person, perceive his thoughts, his emotions, his feelings, he becomes not only understandable but good and desirable. . . .

In the course of this process, I saw hard, inflexible, dogmatic persons, in the brief period of several weeks, change in front of my eyes and become sympathetic, understanding and to a marked degree nonjudgmental. I saw neurotic, compulsive persons ease up and become more accepting of themselves and others. In one instance, a student who particularly impressed me by his change, told me when I mentioned this: "It is true. I feel less rigid, more open to the world. And I like myself better for it. I don't believe I ever learned so much anywhere." I saw shy persons become less shy and aggressive persons more sensitive and moderate.

One might say that this appears to be essentially an emotional process. But that, I believe, would be altogether inaccurate in describing it. There was a great deal of intellectual content, but the intellectual content was meaningful and crucial to the person. In fact, one student brought up this very question. "Should we be concerned," he asked, "only with the emotions? Has the intellect no play?" It was my turn to ask, "Is there any student who has read as much or thought as much for any other course?"

The answer was obvious. We had spent hours and hours reading; the room reserved for us had occupants until ten o'-clock at night, and then many left only because the university guards wanted to close the building. Students listened to recordings; they saw motion pictures; but best of all, they talked and talked and talked. . . .

The Rogers method was free and flowing and open and permissive. A student would start an interesting discussion; it would be taken up by a second; but a third student might take us away in another direction, bringing up a personal matter of no interest to the class; and we would all feel frustrated. But this was like life, flowing on like a river, seemingly futile, with never the same water there, flowing on, with no one knowing what would happen the next moment. But in this there was an expectancy, an alertness, an aliveness; it seemed to me as near a smear of life as one could get in a classroom. For the authoritarian person, who puts his faith in neatly piled up facts, this method I believe can be threatening, for here he gets no reassurance, only an openness, a flowing, no closure.

I have nowhere found such a vivid account of the initially chaotic, gradually more fluid way in which the group, as it fearfully takes responsibility for itself, becomes a constructive organism, listening and responding sensitively to its own needs. It is the outwardly confused, inwardly organized, politics of an ever-changing group purpose, as the class moves to meet its intellectual, personal, and emotional needs.

Does a person-centered education bring results? We have a definitive answer from research. For ten years Dr. David Aspy has led research studies aimed at finding out whether human, person-centered attitudes in the classroom have any measurable effects and if so what these effects are.[7] He collected 3,700 recorded classroom hours from 550 elementary and high school teachers and used rigorous scientific methods to analyze the results. He and his colleague, Dr. Flora Roebuck, have found that students of more person-centered teachers contrast sharply with students of teachers who are less person-centered. They showed greater gains in learning conventional subjects. They were more adept at using their higher cognitive processes such as problem solving. They had a more positive self-concept than was found in the other groups. They initiated more behavior in the classroom. They exhibited fewer discipline problems. They had a lower rate of absence from school. They even showed an increase in I.Q. among their students.

Teachers can improve their facilitative, person-centered attitudes with as little as fifteen hours of intensive training. Of significance for all of education is the finding that teachers improve in these attitudes *only* when their *trainers* exhibit a high level of these facilitative conditions. In ordinary terms this means that such attitudes are "caught," experientially, from another. They are not simply intellectual learnings. These teachers have a more positive self-concept than less person-centered teachers. They are more self-disclosing to their students. They respond more to students' feelings. They give more praise. They are more responsive to student ideas. They lecture less often.

Geographical location of the classes, racial composition, or race of the teacher have not altered these feelings. Whether we are speaking of black or white or Chicano teachers, black, white, or Chicano students, classes in the North, the South, the Virgin Islands, England, Canada, or Israel, the findings are essentially the same.

Aspy's findings are confirmed in practical experience in medical education. The Medical School of McMaster University has taken a person-centered facilitative approach to the training of physicians. Though these young men and women have never had the conventional medical courses, they have learned intensively for three years the medical knowledge they need to deal with patients. They show up very well on the tough Canadian licensing exam, and in addition are more creative and humane. As another example, nine hundred top-ranking medical educators in the United States, concerned about the dehumanizing effects of medical training, have enlisted in the program, Human Dimensions in Medical Education. In intensive four-day and ten-day conferences they have learned to listen, to be more person-centered in their teaching, to be more communicative in their personal relationships. The changes in some of the medical schools are already striking.

In short, whether at the elementary, high school, college or graduate level, *person-centered attitudes pay off,* changing the politics of education in the process.

Chapter 5
The politics of administration

Organizations—whether governmental, industrial, educational, or medical—have traditionally been administered through a hierarchical distribution of power. At the top is one person, as in a corporation or in the Catholic Church, or a small group, as in the Communist party. Though in various ways power flows to the top from those who are governed, the organization is usually *experienced* as a process of control flowing down from the top. This may be through the medium of orders and regulations, or through selectively given rewards such as promotions and salary increases.

In recent years many large American corporations have been modifying this extreme hierarchical control. They have endeavored to diffuse authority, responsibility, and initiative throughout the organization, especially in all levels of management. In other countries—notably Sweden—experimentation is being carried further to the worker level. In all these efforts, those in control have tried to increase open communication in all directions: from below upward; from top management downward; horizontally from department to department, and from skilled specialist to skilled specialist. Constructive effects have been felt in certain industries. Much has depended upon the genuineness of the desire of top management to create opportunities for individuals in the organization to maximize their personal development.

Such constructive trends, however, are often neutralized or contradicted by two elements. One is the fact that almost without exception management retains the "right" to hire and fire. The second is the fact that increasing profits, rather than the growing of persons, is seen as the primary goal.

A few years ago I had the opportunity to present to the heads of large corporations the possibility of a person-centered approach to administration. I distributed to the group in advance of our meeting some notes to provoke discussion. These notes represent my personal view of the meaning of a person-centered administration.

Some Notes on Leadership:
TWO EXTREMES

Influence and Impact	*Power and Control*
Giving autonomy to persons and groups	Making decisions
Freeing people to "do their thing"	Giving orders
Expressing own ideas and feelings as one aspect of the group data	Directing subordinates' behavior
Facilitating learning	Keeping own ideas and feelings "close to the vest"
Stimulating independence, in thought and action	Exercising authority over people and organization
Accepting the "unacceptable" innovative creations that emerge	Dominating when necessary
Delegating, giving full responsibility	Coercing when necessary

91

Offering feedback, and receiving it	Teaching, instructing, advising
Encouraging and relying on self-evaluation	Evaluating others
Finding rewards in the development and achievements of others	Giving rewards Being rewarded by own achievements

*Here are my personal preferences, convictions
and experiences, which focus on the left end
of the leadership continuum.*

I want very much to have influence and impact—by influence and impact I mean behavior on my part which makes a *difference* in the behavior of others, but not through imposing my views on them, or exercising control over them—but I have rarely desired to, or known how to, exercise control or power.

My *influence* has always been *increased* when I have shared my *power* or *authority*.

By refusing to coerce or direct, I think I have stimulated learning, creativity, and self-direction. These are some of the products in which I am most interested.

I have found my greatest reward in being able to say "I made it possible for this person to be and achieve something he could not have been or achieved before." In short I gain a great deal of satisfaction in being a facilitator of becoming.

By encouraging people's ability to evaluate themselves, I have stimulated autonomy, self-responsibility, and maturity.

By freeing people to "do their thing," I have enriched their life and learning, and my own as well.

The element in myself I prize most is the degree of ability I have to create a climate of real personal freedom and communication around me.

I love to be in contact with younger people, with their capacity for fresh thought and creative action, or with the fresh and growing portion of a person of any age.

These were not simply theoretical ideas. They had grown out of a revolution in my own way of being as an administrator, a way of being which changed markedly about 1945, when I founded the Counseling Center of the University of Chicago. It was a person-centered approach to *therapy* which changed my view of administration. In a talk in 1948 I said, "For nearly twenty years I have had administrative responsibility for staff groups of one sort or another. I had developed ways of handling administrative problems—ways which had become fairly well fixed. Certainly as I became more and more deeply interested in a client-centered type of counseling, it was furthest from my mind that it would ever affect the way in which I dealt with organizational problems. It is only in the last two or three years that I have been really aware of the revolution in administrative procedure which it might bring about. I would mention again a point I made at the outset, that the effectiveness of a client-centered approach in counseling means that these concepts continually force themselves into other areas where one had not thought of using them.

"For myself, I have found it both difficult and rewarding to attempt to apply these concepts in administration."[1]

I did indeed find it both puzzling and difficult to *practice* a person-centered administration at the Counseling Center. We followed many directions in our attempts, and even some of those which seemed blind alleys at the time later proved to have value. In a staff group which grew to approximately fifty, there was always excitement and change and personal growth. I have never seen such dedicated group loyalty, such productive and creative effort, as I saw during those twelve years. Working hours meant nothing, and at all hours of the day, far into the night, and on weekends and holidays, staff members were working because they wanted to.

I learned many strange things from the experience at the Counseling Center. It was quite dismaying to me at first that we never seemed to be able to find the *right* way of operating the Center. First all decisions were made by consensus. That was too burdensome. We delegated decision-making to a small group. That proved slow. We chose a coordinator, and agreed to abide by her decisions, though like a prime minister she could be given a vote of no confidence. Only gradually did I realize that there is no right way. The life and vitality and growing capacity of the Center was closely bound up with its lack of rigidity, with its continually surprising capacity to change its collective mind, and to utilize a new mode of operation.

I found that when power was distributed, it was no big thing to be the coordinator or chairman of the budget committee or whatever. Consequently administrative tasks were very often sought by the newest members of the staff, because it was an avenue of becoming acquainted with the workings of the operation. An intern might chair a group making up next year's budget. The newest staff member might head a planning group, or a group to pass on membership or promotions. We never did do away entirely with distinctions between secretarial staff, graduate students in training, interns, and staff members. Senior members of the group were freed to spend more time on research and therapy, knowing that if the various administrative task groups failed accurately to represent the sentiment of the members, their decisions would be rejected by the staff as a whole.

I found the enormous importance of personal feelings in administrative matters. Often the staff would spend *hours* (or so it seemed) in arguing some trivial issue, until a perceptive member would see and state the feelings underlying the issue —a personal animosity, a feeling of insecurity, a competition between two would-be leaders, or just the resentment of someone who had never really been heard. Once the *feelings* were out in the open, the issue which had seemed so important became a nothing. On the other hand when the staff was in open communication with one another, heavy issues such as the allocation of the budget for the following year, the election of a coordinator, the adoption of an important policy might take only minutes to decide. In a working group with close and often intimate communication, it is very difficult to terminate a member of the group. Only once in the twelve years was a person fired, and that after many attempts to help him, and after several warnings that his questionable work and practices simply could not be tolerated by the group. On the other hand many of our appointments were to one-year internships, and we could not take all of these people onto our permanent staff. Consequently in this area it might be a problem of selecting two people, and terminating four or five. This too was a very painful experience for the staff, and many were the compromises in the way of nominal and unpaid appointments, or part-time assignments, in order to find a human solution to a potentially hurtful termination.

We developed quite effective ways of dealing with crises. When the threat or crisis arose from outside the group—a drastic budget cut or an attack by the department of psychiatry, for example—the group tended to coalesce immediately and to delegate full authority to a member or members to deal with the crisis on the basis of their best judgment. When the crisis was internal—a smoldering feud between two staff members, or a question about the ethics of a staff member's actions—then the tendency was always to call special meetings of the whole staff to air the personal feelings involved and to facilitate some sort of acceptable interpersonal solution.

It is very rare for the impact of a person-centered approach to move upward in the organization. Our way of working in the Counseling Center did *not* change the administrative practices of the dean under whose supervision we operated. Certainly we had no effect on the total administration of the university, which was decidedly hierarchical. I believe this learning is simply one of the facts of life. An individual with a person-centered philosophy can often carve out an area of freedom of action, as

I did in my relationship with the dean, and then implement this philosophy to the full with those who are, in the organization chart, "under" him. But it is not likely that this approach will seep upward in the organization unless there is a high degree of receptiveness to innovation among those in the top posts. There is one other learning which comes partially from my experience at the Counseling Center, but even more from experience with other groups. If I am somewhat insecure, not quite willing to share power and authority with the group, feeling some need to control, then I *must* be *open* about it. It is perfectly possible for an organization or a group to function with some freedom and some control if it *knows,* clearly and unequivocally, those behaviors which will be controlled by the one in power and those areas in which the individual or the group is free to choose. This may not be an ideal situation, but it is a perfectly viable one. I have found, however, from bitter experience, that to grant to the group pseudo-control, which I may take from them in a crisis, is a devastating experience for all concerned. I have learned that my wish to vest authority in the group must, above all else, be *genuine.*

Is there any evidence that an organization which focuses on persons and their potential can function as effectively as a conventional hierarchical outfit? There is indeed.

A team of investigators under Rensis Likert made a study of supervision in an insurance company.[2] First they measured productivity and morale in the supervised groups and divided them into those that were high and low on these measures. They found significant differences in the behavior, methods, and personalities of supervisors of the high-productivity, high-morale groups and the qualities of the supervisors of the low groups. In the working units with high records, supervisors and group leaders were interested primarily in the workers as people, and interest in production was secondary. Supervisors encouraged group participation and discussion, and decision-making about work problems and policies was a shared process. Interestingly, supervisors in these "high" units did not supervise closely the work being done, but trusted the worker to carry the responsibility for doing good work. The supervisors of units where productivity and morale were low showed the opposite behaviors. They were concerned primarily with production, they made the decisions without consultation, and they supervised the work very closely. One could hardly find clearer evidence of the results of a person-centered approach.

Later this initial study was extended by Likert to some five *thousand* assorted organizations.[3] Again, he had gone into these companies and identified the high-producing managers and the low-producers, ignoring, for purposes of his study, all those in between. Harold Lyon,[4] who endeavored not very successfully to introduce a person-centered approach into the administration of a government bureaucracy in a federal department, gives an excellent summary of Likert's findings.

The high-producers were very "people-oriented." People were unique individuals to them. The low-producers, on the other hand, were "production-oriented." People were tools to get the job done.

The high-producers were good delegators; the low-producers were not.

The high-producers allowed their subordinates to participate in decisions. The low-producers were very autocratic.

The high-producers were relatively nonpunitive. The low-producers were quite punitive.

The high-producers had good, open, two-way personal communication flow. The low-producers were closed and relatively inaccessible.

The high-producers had few formal meetings at which only one or two people spoke. They didn't have to meet often, since they had such open communication flow. This is interesting, judging by the frequency of meetings in the bureaucracy. The low-producers had frequent formal meetings at which only the chiefs spoke, usually giving explicit instructions.

The high-producers had a lot of pride in their work groups. The low-producers were plagued by low morale.

The high-producers planned ahead effectively. They weren't just soft or goody-goody human-relations types. The low-producers didn't plan well.

In times of crisis, the high-producers maintained their supervisory roles, whereas the low-producers rolled up their sleeves and pitched in with the work. If there was a hole in the dike, the low-producer would go down and put his finger in it. Then, when another hole developed, there was no supervisor to send to the crisis area.[5]

A quite different type of study was completed by G.W. Cherry in 1975.[6] He utilized highly sophisticated research methods and appropriate statistical techniques to study the following questions and their interrelationships:

What kind of person is the "fully functioning person" (Rogers) or the "self-actualized person" (Maslow)? Can behavioral scientists objectively define this person?

What kind of person does the large organization—private or public—wish to have as a high-level manager? Can this person be objectively defined?

How does the desired manager of question 2 compare with the fully functioning person of question 1?

How do the characteristics of the fully functioning person relate to the real productivity, creativity, interpersonal cooperation, and job satisfaction of actual managers?

Without going into his methods I will try to state his findings in a simplified fashion. He found in the first place that experienced behavioral scientists were in very substantial agreement in giving an objective description of the fully functioning person.

He found that thirty-seven senior level managers, in significant executive posts, were able to give an objective picture of the kind of manager desired by the organizations they worked for.

Not too surprisingly, there was a considerable difference between the two pictures. The sharpest differences:

The self-actualizing person has significantly *more* of these characteristics than the desirable manager.

> Engages in personal fantasy, daydreams, and fictional speculations.
>
> Expresses hostile feelings directly.
>
> Enjoys sensuous experiences (including touch, taste, smell, physical contact).
>
> Thinks and associates to ideas in unusual ways; has unconventional thought processes.
>
> Is concerned with philosophical problems; e.g., religion, values, the meaning of life, etc.
>
> Enjoys esthetic impressions, is esthetically reactive.
>
> Has insight into own motives and behavior.
>
> Is skilled in social techniques of imaginative play, pretending, and humor.
>
> Values own independence and autonomy.

Clearly, from these examples one gets a picture of the self-actualizing person as a warmer, more original, more open, expressive individual, with broad philosophical and artistic interests, with more appreciation of his psychological and physical self. The "ideal" manager, for instance, holds back negative and positive feelings. The fully functioning person expresses both warm and hostile feelings openly. The "ideal" manager is much closer to the public stereotype of a "leader"—dependable, productive, serious, candid, someone you can lean on, but not a dreamer or a philosopher, nor an entirely autonomous person.

One may well react, "So what? These are simply two different ideals. The self-actualizing person probably wouldn't be a good manager."

Here Cherry's answer to his fourth question is of interest. Would a self-actualizing person be a good manager? By an ingenious method he was able to answer this question. He discovered that the cluster of traits having to do with warmth, capacity for close interpersonal relationships, compassion, and considerateness correlated very significantly with the qualities of productivity, creativity, cooperativeness and job satisfaction. A person-centered manager, it would seem, would be of more value to the organization than a stereotypical leader.

Another finding was that the person who recognizes and shares negative feelings and information (as well as positive), who is feelingful but not overprotective, is more likely to be productive—and less likely to be satisfied with his job!

Finally, a cluster of characteristics often associated with management—power-oriented, aggressive, exploitative, achieving goals by manipulation and/or deceit—is not correlated with productivity, and has a negative correlation with creativity, cooperativeness, and job satisfaction.

All of this seems to point to the somewhat surprising conclusion that the person who is able to develop close interpersonal relationships, who is primarily person-centered, who does not place a high value on power, who is a growing person with understanding of himself, is, all in all, likely to be the most effective and productive manager of an enterprise.

The skeptic—and there are many of these in administrative posts—may still have many questions. "These research studies are all very well, but would such ideas really work in a typical industrial situation? And above all, would such an organization be able to maintain itself financially? Would it be profitable?" For such individuals the following story may be of interest. I vouch for its accuracy.

I know a man who has, for many years, been a consultant for a very large industrial firm. The business of this firm is diversified, but for the most part its units of manufacture are small and widely used.

This man has, by his way of being, by his training approach, and through cognitive methods, brought into being in this organization a person-centered way of management—not with the whole organization, of course, but with a sizable number of middle and upper management personnel.

So highly has he been regarded, and so effective the managers who had trained with him, that a number of years ago he was permitted to set up an "experiment." Certain factories were set aside as experimental manufacturing plants, where the consultant had trained, and continued to work with, management and nonmanagement personnel. Other plants were designated as control units. It should be stressed that this is a very modern industrial giant, with generally good labor relations, a high level of efficiency compared with other firms manufacturing the same types of items, and of course a rigorous cost-accounting system. Hence both the control and experimental plants started the experiment as "well run" systems.

During the past seven years the people in the experimental plants have become more and more deeply involved with a person-centered philosophy. Employees tend to be trusted by those in charge, rather than having their work closely supervised, inspected, and scrutinized. Likewise, employees tend to trust each other. The degree of mutual regard among the employees is unusually high, as is their respect for each other's capabilities. The emphasis of the consultant and of the plant personnel has been upon building up good interpersonal relations, vertical and horizontal two-way communication, and a dispersion of responsibility, choice, and decision-making.

Now the results are clearly apparent. In the experimental plants the average cost of a particular unit is about 22¢. In the control plants the average cost of the same item is 70¢! In the experimental plants there are now three to five managers. In the control units of comparable size there are seventeen to twenty-three managers! In the experimental units workers and supervisors come sauntering in from the parking lots in earnest conversation, generally about their work. In the control plants they come in quickly, mostly singly, to punch the time clock.

What is the name of the company? Who is the consultant? When I told my acquaintance that these findings *must* be published, he said he was not permitted to publish them. The profit gain to the company is so great that this is regarded as a trade secret which must *not* be leaked to other firms in their highly competitive industry! When I exclaimed over the irony of this —that treating people as persons was a trade secret!—he explained that top management has little understanding of his work. They see only the balance sheet. "Once a year I get dressed up for lunch with the president. He tells me he is greatly impressed by the work I have done in the plants and wants to know what budget I need for the coming year. That is about the limit of his understanding."

Since I cannot give the documentation for this story, I can readily understand the skepticism of any reader. Yet the story is true, and I have checked it. The fact that it cannot openly be told is a reflection on the confused purposes of a modern capitalistic enterprise—truly interested in persons, so long as that interest turns a profit.

As I have collected the foregoing evidence, theoretical, practical, field-tested, I find I am asking myself, why do I want to present it? That question starts an inner dialogue. Is it because I want to convince you, intellectually, that a person-centered approach is best? No, because even if intellectually convinced, you would not have the basis for the attitudes that are essential, the gut-level learnings that make such an approach possible. Is it because I believe that reading such evidence would cause your behavior to become person-centered? No. I believe it rare indeed that behavior changes to a significant degree just from reading something. Why then?

As I mull it over, I have come to believe that the presentation of factual evidence—whether from empirical studies, action research, case examples, or subjective report—may have one effect that makes it worthwhile: it may intrigue you into opening your mind to new possibilities. And this may increase the chance that you will try out, in your *own experience,* in a small way, some of the hypotheses of a person-centered approach. You may try them out to prove they are wrong. But if you try them at all, you open yourself to visceral learnings that may change your behavior and change you.

You may begin to be more open, empathic, and trusting of an adolescent son or daughter. You may, if you are an executive, see what happens if you give more responsible autonomy to one or two of your subordinates. Or you may try understanding your wife (or husband) purely from his or her point of view, not trying to change or control those perceptions. You may, if you are a teacher, give your students freedom of choice in some small part of their learning where you feel comfortable in doing so. In every case you would be altering the politics of the relationship in some small way, and then carefully observing the attitudinal and behavioral consequences. It is this slight opening of the door to possible sharing of power and control, to more communicative and human ways of being, which, for me, justifies the presentation of evidence.

I hope I have made clear that it is entirely possible to have a person-centered organization in which the basis of power and control is *experienced* by each individual as residing within himself. Solid evidence indicates that in such an organization these individuals can and do work responsibly together to set goals, to determine policy, to deal with administrative details, to utilize a variety of organizational modes, and to handle the crises that inevitably arise. The group is more capable of wise decisions than one person, because it is calling on the leadership potentialities of all.

I believe the problems of a person-centered organization are fully as complex and difficult as those of a hierarchical organization. They are, however, quite different in kind, and with far more personal growth involved in their resolution. I believe a person-centered organization never *looks* particularly efficient. Routine procedures are frequently disrupted for human reasons. The organization never *looks* very good to the outsider, because he can't readily find who's "in charge." Its efficiency is human, its leadership is multi-faceted, and one of its most important "products" is the development of persons toward their full capacity.

I have not often used the term "politics" in this description, but it should be clear that the politics of a person-centered organization is 180 degrees removed from that of a traditional organization. It is based on different values, works on different principles, achieves effectiveness through different operations. A person-centered organization is not a modification of a traditional one. It is a collective organism, totally unlike present-day organizations. It is a revolution in the achievement of human purposes.

Chapter 6

The person-centered approach and the oppressed

Frequently, the issue of the oppressed comes up when I speak to large audiences, and even more bluntly in workshops. The point is made that a person-centered approach is a luxury which may be appropriate for an affluent middle class, but that it can have no meaning in dealing with an oppressed minority. Whether with blacks, Chicanos, Puerto Ricans, women, students, or other alienated and relatively powerless groups, it is said that such a "soft" approach has no relevance. What these groups need are jobs or equal pay or civil rights or educational opportunities—things that must be *wrested* from the oppressor, that he will not give up willingly. Therefore a person-centered approach is too "weak" to deal with these situations.

I could respond that though my opportunity for work with racial and ethnic minorities has been limited, my experience runs directly counter to these assertions. But I believe the best answer comes from the thinking of Paulo Freire, who has worked with illiterate Brazilian peasants whose state was only slightly better than the medieval serf's. Freire's book, *The Pedagogy of the Oppressed,*[1] was first published in Portuguese in 1968 and translated into English in 1970. My book, *Freedom to Learn,*[2] was published in 1969. There is no indication that he had ever heard of my work, and I had never heard of his. I was addressing students in educational institutions. He is telling about work with frightened, downtrodden peasants. I tried to use a style that would reach students and their teachers. He writes to communicate with Marxists. I like to give concrete examples. He is almost completely abstract. Yet the principles he has come to build his work on are so completely similar to the principles of *Freedom to Learn* that I found myself openmouthed with astonishment.

Here is how he worked and the effects that he had on the peasants. He had only five years to work in Brazil before he was jailed; the old order and the military junta that took over in 1964 feared him. He was "encouraged" to leave the country and went to Chile, and has since worked with various international organizations. I have often said that if a dictatorship took over in this country, one of their first acts—if they were at all intelligent—would be to jail me and others who hold a person-centered point of view.

Freire bitterly opposes the "banking" type of education in which the teacher knows everything and teaches, and the students know nothing and are taught. He moves on to a new concept which, developed in practice, means that an interdisciplinary team goes into a geographical area of, say, a high degree of illiteracy and apathetic dependence. In informal meetings the team states its aims, endeavors to begin building trust, and enlists volunteer assistants. The team members act "as sympathetic observers with an attitude of *understanding* toward what they see."[3] They do not attempt to impose any values, but to see the people from the inside—how they talk, the way they think and construct their thought, the nature of their interpersonal relationships. This is discussed with the volunteer assistants, who participate in all the activities of the team. Particularly, they look for the contradictions, problems, and issues that exist in the minds and lives of the poor. These issues they try to place before groups of the local people, often in pictorial form.

For example, working with a group of tenement residents,

the investigator—with the intent of focusing on the problem of alcoholism—showed a scene in which a drunken man was walking on the street and three young men were standing on the corner talking together. The group participants were in agreement that "the only one there who is productive and useful to his country is the souse who is returning home after working all day for low wages and who is worried about his family because he can't take care of their needs. He is the only worker. He is a decent worker and a souse like us."[4] Wisely the investigator (I would call him a facilitator) dropped his initial aim, and drew from the group more of their real feelings—about low wages, about being exploited, about drinking as an escape from reality and the frustration of powerlessness.

In the process of discussion, the facilitator runs into the same problems any student-centered teacher encounters. After a bit of lively discussion, a group may suddenly stop and say to the leader, "Excuse us, we ought to keep quiet and let you talk. You are the one who knows, we don't know anything." In another group a peasant says, "Why don't you explain the pictures to us? That way it'll take less time and won't give us a headache."[5] But Freire has developed the realization that only by letting the people face these problem situations in their own way will true self-initiated learning take place. Gradually they become fully aware of their world and its problems. Then they begin to seek answers. The issues "which have come from the people return to them—not as contents to be deposited, but as problems to be solved."[6]

Though Freire tells little of the general outcomes, the changes in attitudes are clear. At first, "The peasant feels inferior to the boss because the boss seems to be the only one who knows things and is able to run things."[7] They regard themselves as lazy, unfit, worthless, less free than an animal. Because of this they feel attracted to the oppressor and his way of life, and their highest dream is to be like him, and oppress others. But gradually the self-concept and the goal change. Peasants make such statements as these: "I now realize I am a man, an

107

educated man." "We were blind, now our eyes have been opened." "Now we will no longer be a dead weight on the cooperative farm." "I work, and working I transform the world."[8]

Freire's approach follows this process. First the curriculum for learning is drawn from the problems as the peasant sees them, the staff facilitating that process. Then resource materials are prepared to point up the issues and contradictions, and free discussions gradually emerge in groups that have never before articulated their thoughts or feelings. Now the excitement of self-initiated learning occurs. The members, as they reveal themselves to one another, begin to trust themselves as persons, and other members of the group as well. They change their goals. Instead of simply aspiring to become oppressors themselves, they envision a new type of social system, more human. Finally, they begin to take considered steps to change the terrible conditions under which they live.

You may say that Freire failed, since he was expelled from the country as a dangerous revolutionary. Perhaps. But my experience with a person-centered approach is that for every person who is fired or expelled, a dozen agents of change, independent in thought and action, have been created.

The experience I've had with oppressed groups—students, first of all, but including blacks, Chicanos, and women—causes me to agree with Freire that this approach is a basically revolutionary process, subversive of any authoritarian structure. Here are four of his major points. First is a statement about the change in power relationships. Speaking of breaking the vertical authority patterns characteristic of "banking" education, he says, "Through dialogue, the teacher-of-the-students and the students-of-the-teacher cease to exist and a new term emerges: teacher-student with students-teachers. The teacher is no longer merely the-one-who-teaches, but one who is himself taught in dialogue with the students, who in turn while being taught also teach. They become jointly responsible for a process in which all grow."[9]

His belief in the importance of this shift in power is very deep. "The important thing, from the point of view of libertarian education, is for men to come to feel like masters of their thinking and views of the world explicitly or implicitly manifest in their own suggestions and those of their comrades. Because this view of education starts with the conviction that it cannot present its own program but must search for this program dialogically with the people, it serves to introduce the pedagogy of the oppressed, in the elaboration of which the oppressed must participate."[10]

In a third statement, he refutes the notion that a revolutionary movement can succeed only by insisting *first* on a propagandistic, dogmatic leadership. "Problem-posing education does not and cannot serve the interests of the oppressor. No oppressive order could permit the oppressed to begin to question: Why? While only a revolutionary society can carry out this education in systematic terms, the revolutionary leaders need not take full power before they can employ the method. In the revolutionary process, the leaders cannot utilize the banking method as an interim measure, justified on grounds of expediency, with the intention of *later* behaving in a genuinely revolutionary fashion. They must be revolutionary—that is to say, dialogical—from the outset."[11]

Finally, in the foreword is a glimpse of the far-reaching implications of this work. "A distinguished Brazilian student of national development recently affirmed that this type of educational work among the people represents a new factor in social change and development, 'a new instrument of conduct for the Third World, by which it can overcome traditional structures and enter the modern world.' "[12]

I concur with Freire's basic views. I have already indicated, in speaking of education, that I would extend the basic principles, on which we both seem to agree, to all learning situations.

The National Health Council is an organization made up of representatives of the American Medical Association, the American Dental Association, nurses' organizations, health insurance companies, health-oriented agencies, and many other similar groups. A few years ago these "health providers," as they termed themselves, decided to include in their annual conference a group of "health consumers" from the urban ghettos and the rural underprivileged. They should receive full credit for this humane and courageous decision, which clearly involved risk to themselves. The health consumers were elected or selected by local groups in their own areas. They were all poor, many black, some Mexican-American. As the time of the conference approached, the planners became uneasy and invited the staff of the Center for Studies of the Person to act as facilitators of groups at the conference. The invitation was accepted.

When the conference opened, the hostility of the "consumers" was so thick it was palpable. After the usual bland opening events, the conference threatened to split wide open. The "consumers" were going to withdraw. The conference was seen as just another attempt by the establishment group to give a meaningless token representation to the poor. They would have none of it. Only the statements of the facilitators that they had come all the way across the country, for no fee, simply to make certain that *everyone* in the conference would be *heard,* that everyone would have a truly representative voice, held the conference together temporarily.

Twenty groups of twenty to twenty-five each were formed, with "providers" and "consumers" in each group. I remember the group I facilitated. The bitterness of the poor erupted in full force. Their anger at white professionals, at the lack of health services, at the lack of any voice in their own health care was so strong that some of the professionals were frightened, while others were self-righteously angry in response. The value of a facilitator, who could truly understand and clarify the feelings expressed, was most clearly demonstrated. Without the facilitators there is no doubt the conference would have blown apart. Voicing his hatred of oppression, one black man said that the Marines had trained him to kill, and if need be he would use that training against the people and institutions that were holding him down. A black woman with little formal education was undoubtedly the most influential person in the group. Highly skeptical of everyone's motives, including mine, she spoke out of a long and terrible personal struggle against poverty, prejudice, and oppression. Whenever she spoke, everyone listened— and learned.

As the group sessions continued, there was a small but significant growth in understanding. The white professionals began really to see their functioning as it appeared to the recipient. A ghetto member who hated health insurance companies realized that the insurance company executive in our group was not all bad, and that they could communicate. A white social worker finally gained the courage to tell how she had constructed a "cover story" for herself as an unemployed worker needing health care, and how, playing this role, she had approached various health-oriented "helping" agencies. The appalling treatment she had received had disillusioned her about her own profession, but now she could begin to see some hope. Some blacks began to differ with others of their color, to their great embarrassment, because they felt they should keep a united front against whites. A Mexican-American woman finally told tearfully of how she felt totally scorned and uncared for by *both* blacks and whites.

To put the process in more general terms, the existing conflicts, such as those between haves and have-nots, between blacks and whites, between professionals and recipients, between establishment and radicals, burst into the open. But these violent outpourings occurred in a climate in which each person was respected and permitted to state his feelings without interruption; a climate in which the facilitators showed that their caring concern was for the dignity of each person, and their primary purpose was to foster open communication. In this atmosphere the issues became greatly clarified, and, what is perhaps equally important, persons emerged as separate, unique individuals, each with his own perception of those issues. Little by little real interpersonal communication began.

At this point, some radicals will say, "See, what you are accomplishing is better, less angry communication! You are destroying the possibility of revolutionary change! You are defusing the hatred and bitterness which alone can spark any real change for the oppressed!" I would only ask such readers to hear the rest of the story.

Although the "health consumers" had never known one another before, they quickly coalesced and began to formulate resolutions which were circulated to the various groups, where they were discussed, revised, amended. Then we were all told that it was "the established policy" of the National Health Council to be a forum only, and that it did not take stands on health issues, so no resolutions could be adopted. Undaunted, the "consumers" waited until the long final meeting of the whole conference, which was scheduled to be a series of talks "summarizing" the conference, though some of the speakers had not even attended. A "consumer" spokesman immediately moved that the whole program be dropped and that the time be spent considering and voting on the resolutions that had been circulating. Excitement was high, and the pros and cons emotional. The motion carried by a large majority, and the would-be speakers were thanked and dismissed. The conference then, after heated discussions, passed a long series of resolutions, with no mention of "established policy." The conference ended with highly affirmative feelings, not only on the part of the "consumers" but on the part of most of the establishment members as well. The surprising result was that in the ensuing year a very large number of these resolutions were carried out.

Here are my own conclusions from Freire's work, as well as from my experience with the "consumers," summarized in an "if-then" form.

In a situation involving minority groups, the oppressed, or anyone who feels powerless, I conclude that:

If a person with facilitative attitudes can gain entry into the group;

If this facilitator is genuinely free of a desire to control the outcome, respects the capacity of the group to deal with its own problems, and has skills in releasing individual expression;

If a respectful hearing is given to *all* attitudes and feelings, no matter how "extreme" or "unrealistic";

If the problems experienced by the group are accepted and clearly defined as issues;

If the group and its members are permitted to choose, collectively and individually, their own next steps;

Then a process is set in motion that has these characteristics:

From some members long-suppressed feelings will pour out —mostly negative, hostile, bitter feelings.

Finding these attitudes accepted and understood, more and more members of the group feel free to express the whole range of experienced feelings.

With more complete expression individual persons are recognized for their uniqueness and strengths, and mutual trust begins to develop.

The most irrational of the feelings are somewhat defused by being fully expressed, and by the feedback from group members.

The feelings based on experiences common to the group are clarified and strengthened.

Confidence grows—self-confidence in the individual, and general confidence in the group.

There is a more realistic collective consideration of the issues, with less overload of irrationality.

Trusting each other more, there are fewer "ego trips," with members competing for leadership, or trying to take credit for, or defend, a proposed solution.

The group moves toward innovative, responsible, and often revolutionary steps, steps which can be taken now, in an atmosphere of realism. Leadership in the group multiplies. Each individual tends to respect himself and the leadership qualities he has. Constructive action is taken, both by the group and by the individual members, to change the situation they are in. Individuals feel enough support by the group to take actions they know will be regarded as radical, even when high risk to themselves is involved.

Chapter 7

Resolving intercultural tensions: a beginning

Am I fiddling while Rome burns? What possible difference can a new approach to family life or to psychotherapy make when our very planet is threatened with dissolution? If our schools become more person-centered, will that be important if a nuclear war wipes out *all* schools, *all* students, *all* teachers, *all* advocates of any educational philosophy—of whatever brand? We cannot dodge the fact that our world—the planet Earth—is in mortal danger. In 1969 U Thant, Secretary General of the United Nations, said, "I do not wish to seem overdramatic, but I can only conclude from the information available to me . . . that members of the United Nations have perhaps ten years left in which to subordinate their ancient quarrels and launch a global partnership." Somewhat more optimistic, the authors of a powerful recent volume on international relations title their book *7304* to indicate that there are only 7,304 *days* in the twenty-year period in which they believe the fate of the planet will be decided.[1]

Topping the list of world problems which will decide whether we *have* a future are the ancient as well as the modern feuds that divide cultures, ideologies, religions, and nations. No one knows whether the hatred between Arab and Israeli will spark a new—and possibly catastrophic—

115

war. The centuries-old feud between Protestants and Catholics in Northern Ireland may at any moment become an unrestrained deadly explosion. The situation in South Africa is a lethal time bomb. The tensions between the Soviet Union and the People's Republic of China constitute a smoldering threat of unknown proportions. The discrepancy in wealth and income between the "haves" and "have-nots" of the world is laying a basis for present as well as future hatreds. Here at home, whites have been warring with blacks over busing and other issues around integration. On a broader scale, terrorist groups roam the world, wreaking violence on totally innocent people. There seems no end to the list of undying feuds between races, cultures and nations.

Our shrinking world and our burgeoning technology make each of these feuds a life-and-death issue for every citizen of the globe.

Does a person-centered approach have anything useful to offer in solving these immense and dangerous global issues? There are already significant models on a small scale for handling these tensions; there is every reason to believe these could be imaginatively expanded and utilized. The cost would be infinitesimal compared to the 280 *billion* dollars that the world as a whole spent on arms in 1975.[2]

Political scientists are themselves beginning to point in the direction of the person-centered approach. Finlay and Hovet say that "to deal constructively with world problems a global strategy is necessary. Such a strategy must attempt the seemingly impossible: *to establish a sense of common cause among the vastly disparate and competing nations of the world.* It requires that nations move beyond self-interest defined in terms of power and concentrate on common interests defined in terms of realizing man's fullest potentialities."[3] While the authors italicize the second sentence of the paragraph, I would strongly underscore the final sentence. A desire for their citizens to develop their potentialities is one of the few items on which most of the nations of the world might agree. And it is precisely at this point that experience with a person-centered approach may have something to offer.

In a time of major social change, there is a long quiet period of gestation, experimentation, and model building before anything happens. Information is gathered, solutions are discovered, and often unsuccessful attempts are made to promulgate these solutions. Meanwhile the average citizen is becoming acutely aware of the problem and frustrated by the superficial attempts at correction. Then, sometimes suddenly, the public as a whole sees the problem clearly, looks more deeply for solutions, and discovers that the answers, on a small scale, are already at hand. There develops a clear public *will* to deal with the problem, and enormous forces are set in motion. This does not mean that a miraculous solution is quickly reached, because most social problems—and technological problems too—are highly complex, and many unforeseen difficulties arise. But once the corner has been turned, once that amorphous creature "the public" has made a decision to attack the problem, there is a great deal of forward movement.

The telephone, the radio, the automobile all went through a slow gestation period before the public realized the value of each, and demanded their rapid development.

Margaret Sanger established the first birth-control clinic in 1916. The public displayed negative interest in its bitter opposition. Nevertheless, due to a dedicated group working on a small scale, many of the problems of contraception were faced and resolved, and an enormous amount of data gathered on the exploding population rate and its effects. It was not until the 1960s and overpopulation was a serious problem that the public woke up. Now nations are taking positive action to promote family planning and control reproduction.

We have known of pollution by factories, mines, and automobiles for years. Masses of data were accumulated. But suddenly —dramatized most strongly, perhaps, by smog in Los Angeles and the death of Lake Erie—pollution became a *national* concern. The public had decided to deal with pollution.

For generations blacks were denied the right to vote and could not hope to receive equal justice before the law. In the 1950s and 60s the public decided to do something about it. Changes began to occur, sometimes with surprising speed, sometimes with tragic slowness. But they *are* being made. Just when it seems too late, the great social collective mind grasps the seriousness of a problem and begins to move dramatically ahead. Because the collective decision is so late, the outcome is always in doubt—the world may still be drowned by overpopulation, we may still die of pollution, we may still see violent racial strife—but at least we are making massive efforts to deal with those issues. It is this knowledge of the past that gives me courage to propose methods for dealing with intercultural, interracial, and international tensions. I believe that if the public becomes truly aware that present-day policies are targeted directly toward the destruction of all of us, then they may decide to look for alternatives. And the person-centered approach offers just such an alternative.

In presenting this alternative, I begin with the most minute examples of resolution and conflict, first within the individual, then between individuals, then between small groups, and finally with the bitter feuds and tensions between large groups. We already have available small-scale solutions, minute solutions, to some of the most baffling of international feuds. I am well aware that these small-scale models will run into enormous difficulties if translated into global terms, but these will be *technological* difficulties, which our culture is most adept at solving. Some of the basic *principles* have a coherence, a consistency, and a demonstrated effectiveness that deserve scrutiny. Many of these underlying principles involve the person-centered approach to the problem of power, control, and decision-making.

Conflict within the individual is the most basic of all feuds and tensions. One of the commonest problems I faced as a psychotherapist was the individual who feels at war within herself: "Outwardly I'm a reasonably acceptable person; I'm able to make a living [or a home]; I have some degree of recognition from people in my world. But inwardly I feel I'm a fraud. I'm worthless, incompetent, full of bad impulses and evil intentions. There is an irreconcilable discrepancy between what I *seem* to be and what I really *am*. If people knew me as I am, they would reject me."

Here is a power struggle within the person. In order to "get by" she *must* keep up her façade, yet this fraudulent front is continually undermined by "the real me." She is sure that, whichever might win out, life will be dissatisfying or frightening, or both.

As a therapist, I learned to accept each of these flatly contradictory feelings. There was one young man who just "went blank" at crucial points—his mind failed to function, he became confused and almost disoriented, he flubbed important examinations, was unable to carry out important duties. For a time I was unable to see why this seemed to him such conclusive evidence of a bad and evil aspect of his nature, though I accepted his very contradictory feelings. Then he revealed more about his relationship to his father and others in authority. Finally I ventured, "I wonder if what you are telling me is that you have, through this blankness, found a sure-fire way of defeating all of those who want to control you and mold you into the image they have fashioned for you?" After a moment of silence in which he seemed to be digesting this, he broke into wildly uncontrollable laughter, which was very embarrassing to him—and puzzling to me. Then haltingly, and with some feeling of shame, he recognized that not only was my statement accurate but that the wild laughter was a full experiencing, for the first time in his life, of the glee he had felt in defeating his father and everyone else through these distressing periods of "blankness."

In subsequent interviews came the slower and more difficult recognition that these two parts of himself could each be accepted, that they could live comfortably in one person, that they were not fundamentally incompatible. He began to see that it

119

was not true that one part of him was bad, another part good; one part right and one wrong. More specifically he came to realize that he could work openly for approval of others and could strive for recognition, but that he could also resist control by others. He recognized that he could do what *he* wished, and not simply what others expected or demanded of him. The two elements of his emotional life, formerly so incompatible they were not even in touch with each other, could perhaps live comfortably within one person.

How can the chasm between individuals be bridged? Some of the forces that create rifts between people are marital conflict, sibling rivalry, athletic or academic cutthroat competition, and racial and educational differences. Look for a moment at the enormous gap in life experience between a member of a black ghetto in one of our inner cities and the educated white professional person who has never known a day of real hunger, who has never lived a street life, never been the victim of unreasoning prejudice. How could these individuals possibly feel any commonality? Recently I received very touching evidence that such a gap can be bridged. An instructor in an adult education class sent me a paper turned in by Michael, an uneducated and inarticulate black man who was a student in one of his classes. Michael had read and been moved by the chapter entitled "This Is Me" from my book *On Becoming a Person*.[4] "This Is Me" describes the struggles and learnings that have had meaning for me, my internal, personal life. There is *nothing* that would seem to connect it with ghetto experience or the black man's struggle for personhood. And yet, here is Michael's illiterate but powerful report:

I backed up and returned to the first chapter I read for this course. This chapter was a well written piece of literiture which had come so close with defining myself as I am existing today.

I have been on that same frequency this author is unfolding in this piece of his work. I have delt with these same ideas, concepts, and experinces the author is talking about. I am also puzzled by the story that I have claimed to understand up to now [by this chapter that I am claiming to understand] for the simple reason, I feel that the author is a well educated white person that is so far from being a poor black man according to society today. So if society places us upon two different levels of being, then I should not be thinking on the same level as this fine writer. The capability [possibility] of me thinking on the same level as this man isn't [cannot be], so a question have been put inside me from reading this chapter, and that is why can I understand what this author has written that fits me like my skin?

I also got some positive feelings from reading this mans work and those were a feeling that me and this man was no different from each other realy because I have found out that the only thing in a persons life that makes him different from some body else are the thoughts in your mind that you know of an no one else do. Now I got the feeling that this author knows this also from the way he came on with his willingness to let you inside of hiself, so that you would be able to know the real him that he had discovered in hisself.

I understood what he was saying about hisself because I understood myself to that point which he was talking about in hisself. It was like reading something formiua [a formula?] that i hadn't read before, but I had lived the exact experinces of this mans trip inside hisself. Now if by chance this wonderful man did not write [had not written] about his trip inside hisself then the chances of me figuring out that what had been drilled into [me] earlier by society was wrong [would have been almost nil] and that's why there had seemed at the time something wasn't right with what society was saying about all men being alike within. If this [chapter] had not crossed my path when it did then I would still be searching for that clearification. I thank this person for the understanding he has shared with me.

Though I have never met him, I feel close to Michael, just as he feels close to me. Why? Because it is in our humanness —the shared conflicts, and feelings, learnings, perplexities, "experinces"—that we can come together, in spite of lives that in their externals probably have *nothing* in common, except that we were both born and have both lived. Yet he feels that what I wrote fits him "like my skin," even though he *cannot* understand why an educated white man can possibly have anything in common with a ghetto-taught black man.

I have seen this demonstrated before. As human beings trying to cope with life, to understand it and learn from it, we have vast pools of commonality to draw on. It makes no difference that I am an older white middle-class American male, and you may be yellow or black or communist or Israeli or Arab or Russian or young or female. If we are openly willing to share, then there is a large area in which understanding is possible. It is in the "thoughts in your mind that you know of and no one else do" that we can begin open and intimate communication.

One learning stands out clearly from Michael's statement. To the degree that I, in my writing, was able to open myself to him —with no desire to lead, direct, or persuade—he was able to open himself and to empower himself as a separate and worthy person.

If by some tragic chance, Michael and I found ourselves on opposite sides of the barricades in a race riot, could we still communicate, could we discover a pathway to constructive resolution of the crisis? If we could get into physical communication—yes. We have, between us, the human basis for resolving issues of economics, ideology, civil justice, and revolutionary violence.

In tension situations, the pattern is simple. *Each* of the parties involved holds, with equal conviction, an identical view: "I am right and you are wrong; I am good and you are bad." This holds for tension between individuals and between groups, where it becomes *"We* are right and you are wrong; *we* are good and you are bad."* One of our greatest difficulties in any dispute is to recognize or, even more difficult, to accept that the certitude we feel about our own rightness and goodness is equaled by the certitude of the opposing individual or group about their rightness and goodness. If tension is to be reduced, it is this pattern that must somehow be dissolved. Here is where a person-centered approach is at its most powerful.

A number of years ago, a "helping" community called Changes was formed in a neighborhood on the South Side of Chicago by Eugene Gendlin and other individuals who had been associated with the Counseling Center. It reached out to the inhabitants of the neighborhood, many of them alienated or members of the counter-culture. It trained its members in "absolute listening," putting out a "Rap Manual" and conducting sessions on the same topic. How can a concept like empathy be explained to the average person? Here is a paragraph from the "Manual" about listening:

"This is not laying trips on people. You only listen and say back the other person's thing, step by step, just as that person seems to have it at that moment. You never mix into it any of your own things or ideas, never lay on the other person anything that person didn't express. . . . To show that you understand exactly, make a sentence or two which gets exactly at the personal meaning this person wanted to put across. This might be in your own words, usually, but use that person's own words for the touchy main things."

Another aspect of their training, "focusing," helps a person attain "conscious moment-to-moment touch with what goes on in you, how you feel, what affects that and how, what's really important, all the complex parts of it."[5] So the members of Changes are helped to become skillful in *listening*—to the other —and *focusing*—on what is going on within themselves. A member tells how these attitudes affect intergroup tension:

These techniques can radically improve group interactions. It happened when the women in our South Side Chicago Gay Liberation group were negotiating a monthly Gay Women's Coffee House with a local church that supported a number of radical community groups. A problem was the deeply rooted desire of the women to ban men, and the church commune's policy of keeping an open door to everyone at their coffee houses, regardless of who was sponsoring it that week. Most of the negotiation took place between a hypersensitive lesbian, who felt overrun by men in both gay and straight worlds, and a male member of the church commune staff, who wanted to protect the trusting, transcendent view of the open-door policy, and did not understand the history and necessity behind the defensive, strictly all-female approach to a lesbian coffee house.

There were personality clashes and strain in trying to work out a policy suitable to both sides; a number of events caused tension to escalate mostly through misunderstanding, until the existence of the coffee house was threatened, and a general meeting was called. Without advance planning, it just happened that members of both groups present were involved in the radical therapy community Changes and they had learned and incorporated these techniques in their behavior. Because of this, the two pivotal figures who had the history of difficulty negotiating were able, not only to state their positions, but to go into their hurt, misunderstood, distrustful feeling with the help of the rest of the group. That stopped the polarization, shifted the defensive energy inward for each, and cleared the air for a new negotiation, based on a clear, open, thorough sense of the underlying needs and fears of each group, from which developed a specific procedure for the Coffee House which compromised neither group's ideals. The incident, in fact, opened up possibilities of communication between the two groups at a level deeper than would have been likely given their original social alienation from each other. The Gay Women's Coffee House became and remained a flourishing community institution for the rest of this past year. All of this stuff does work.[6]

This small event demonstrates that initially the pattern is as usual: "The decision must be made my way, because I am standing on the good principle that oppressed gay women have a right to a closed meeting." "No, the decision must be made my way because I am standing on the good principle that meetings in this church are open to anyone." It is a head-on conflict between irreconcilable principles. The fact that some members of each of the conflicting groups had been trained by Changes in a person-centered approach gives the little struggle all the significance of a pure laboratory experiment. Through listening to the two main antagonists, through helping them focus on their own feelings of hurt and distrust, the conflict over "principles" becomes completely redefined. It is now a question of the feelings, the needs, the fears of each group and of the two primary figures. Redefined, each group now finds that it can meet its needs without violating the needs of the other group. New channels of realistic communication are opened up. The politics of a head-on collision over decision-making changes completely when each person is empowered to be all of himself —feelings, fears, ideas, hopes, distrusts. A decision is then reached on a human basis, not as a result of a political clash.

Judy Henderson, who told me the coffee-house incident, is a self-styled member of the radical Left. She believes the person-centered approach is useful in revolutionary activity but often she has seen radical groups destroy themselves through inter-personal tensions. She says that "these groups, in the name of radicalism, practiced on me both explicit and tacit kinds of authoritarianism. I'm talking about the tyranny of unspoken norms and roles subtly controlling what kind of thing gets said and what doesn't, who speaks most and who listens, who ends up supporting someone else's need or ideas, but not his or her own."

She realizes that concern for a person's feelings is considered counterrevolutionary. "Most of us have heard slogans such as: 'This is politics, not therapy! There is no solution but the collective one; individual solutions are cooptation.' I have been

125

around a number of groups where the idea of dealing with personal experience and interaction was looked down on as worse than useless, as a drain on energy, a digression from 'the real issues,' even as 'elitist, pampered, self-indulgent.' " But Henderson has come to see these ways of "listening" and "focusing" as new instruments for change. "They provide germinal tools for a radical self-experience, interaction, and group process. To me these techniques are the material basis for discovering a new politics and a new approach to politicizing others, coming from a rich, as yet untapped, understanding of and access to the locus of power in the individual. . . . But it doesn't happen without back-sliding and exhaustion. I say this after struggling for a year now, together with a number of people, to integrate these attitudes and processes into our personal, collective, political lives. It goes slowly; it requires large belief and perseverance. The beginning seems to last a long time; there is need to relearn what it means to be myself, then to be with another, and then to form a group. I have to keep sight of long-range goals when I feel mired down in personal hang-ups. I have to keep hold of the processes I have learned to trust, even when I am fearing and doubting everyone around me and what we are doing. I have to keep remembering, with some relief, what a new thing we are trying to find and how much we are up against, when I start envying the efficiency of established institutions and the easy action of groups that organize their power in the showy, familiar ways. . . . But it seems to me, after a year, to be very much worth it, because I see in myself, and in the real challenges we have begun to face as a community, *real* change and possibilities of a new social system that gets at the roots of our disease. . . . I feel good and right doing this particular struggle in a way that I never have before. There is something about clarity in myself, and about human beauty available to me in anyone I might work with, that I have a grip on now, that is strongly infusing my political vision and action, and bringing me great joy, in the oddest, unexpected ways, even when I 'love.' "[7]

Here is someone who has learned that revolutionary changes in social groups are best and most lastingly brought about by the subtle, difficult, seemingly "inefficient" attitudes embodied in a person-centered approach.

Community tensions, racial and otherwise, can be eased by using the person-centered approach to empower the people on both sides of the conflict.

A young minister in a Wyoming town of about nine thousand was disturbed by the sharp division between the Chicanos and Anglos and decided to try to do something about it. The town was divided by a railroad and the Chicanos (about a quarter of the population) lived on the south side and the Anglos on the other. The white Americans thought that everything was fine in the town, because there was no very overt discrimination. The Mexican-Americans, on the other hand, felt that they *were* discriminated against. They felt oppressed, believed that the community was not responsive to their needs, and harbored feelings ranging from passive resignation to burning resentment.

Lloyd Henderson, the minister, was able to get a modest grant to finance a program for the improvement of communication. First he chose nine leaders from the community, representing a cross-section—Anglo; Chicano; upper, middle, and lower class; men and women. He invited a facilitator from the Center for Studies of the Person to give an intensive weekend of training to the leaders. It helped them to discover that they were not expected to be leaders in the conventional sense, but facilitators of expression and communication. The groups were to be focused on communication, not on taking action. Then the nine groups were set up, with an attendance of eight to fifteen in each group. They met once a week for twelve weeks and they had an optional weekend together, which some of them chose to utilize and others did not. The groups, too, were cross-sectional; the local judge, in fact, was in with some Chicano youths who had always regarded him as their worst enemy.

First the groups turned to the leaders, expecting them to take responsibility, but gradually they realized that if the groups were to function, they had to take responsibility for themselves and for their own expression. The conversation was personal but focused on community issues. There was talk about unemployment. There was an airing of frustration with the railroad, which was a very central feature in the community. They discussed educational problems that their children were having. Thus, the major topics were community issues but set in a personal framework. The Chicanos were disheartened to be reconfronted with the lack of solidarity in their own group. Although the Anglos often thought of the Chicanos as a united group, the Chicanos themselves were aware of their disunity as a barrier to improving their situation.

One of the most characteristic discoveries in these meetings was that the attitudes of the participants, no matter what their backgrounds or ages, were more similar than they had supposed. When they discussed their children or the need for jobs, feelings were the same on both sides of the track. A look of wonder and awe came over the faces of two mothers, one Anglo and one Chicano, when they discovered how very much alike they were in their hopes for, and their problems with, their children.

Members of the groups were invited to participate on a local television show, telling of what they were doing and the progress they were making. This helped to keep the community in touch with the project and to give it some investment in better communication.

Gradually changes began to occur. Individuals who in the normal course of events would never have met built friendships across cultural and age barriers. The judge came to have a better understanding of the young people he was dealing with in his court. Toward the end, some groups did take action—for example, talking to employers about their hiring practices.

After the sessions had ended, the Chicanos banded together into a group, wrote a proposal and got a grant from the federal government, which had as its aims reducing school dropouts, providing job training, and taking Mexican-American parents to see the state university, to raise their educational goals. These are samples of the group's activities. They hired a director to manage this program. It was a decided morale booster for the south side of the tracks.

All this was accomplished through a person-centered approach on a budget of less than five thousand dollars. The minister had believed in placing responsibility on the local leadership. Then he had provided these leaders, and himself, with a very brief but intensive training period in listening skills and facilitative skills. He was able to start *enough* groups to create a "critical mass." One group might have been helpful to the individuals involved, but almost certainly would not have affected the community. But nine groups, involving only a little over one hundred persons out of nine thousand, proved to be a sufficient mass to initiate creative social action. The results speak for themselves, indicative of what can be accomplished when tensions are not too great and bitterness not too deep. Individuals on both sides of the track experienced and used their power because they were able to realize their strengths through open expression and personal communication.

I experienced a deep feud when I worked with a group from Belfast, Northern Ireland. It was possible to observe what happens in a group where the bitterness involves generations of economic, religious, and cultural hatred. There were five Protestants—including one Englishman—and four Catholics in the group. The nine were chosen to include extremists and moderates on both sides, men and women, older and younger. The Englishman was a retired army colonel. We wanted to facilitate straightforward communication and to film this interaction.[8]

In the early sessions the bitterness, horror, and despair of everyday life in Belfast was abundantly clear. Tom's sister was blown to bits by a bomb which might have been thrown by terrorists of either side. Dennis and his family have hidden behind mattresses as bullets struck their home during a wild burst of shooting on their street. Dennis has on several occasions had to help carry away the torn bodies, living and dead, from bomb explosions. Becky spoke repeatedly of the brutality of the British army patrols to her teenaged sons. After one episode where the boy was made to believe he would be shot, "that child came in and I never saw fear like it on anybody's face in my whole life."

Gilda, young and attractive, spoke of the hopelessness. "I just get so full of despair. I just give up, you know." Becky said, "I really feel hopeless. . . . If something is not done the bitterness is just going to keep eating away at those kids and eventually they could become IRA men."

The bitterness was on both sides. Pretty Protestant Gilda said, "If I seen an IRA man lying on the ground—this is the wrong thing I suppose in your eyes—I would *step* on him, because to me he has just went out and taken the lives of innocent people."

All the violent feelings leave their mark. Sean, a sensitive young Catholic teacher, told how he had been forced to pull down a "steel shutter" between his functioning self and the seething feelings within. Otherwise he would go berserk. In a very quiet, soft voice he spoke of this inner wild beast: "Yeah, I know myself. I'm quite aware of this kind of thing, and it scares me to know that it is there. 'Cause it is violent and emotional and daft. . . . I take long walks and let this thing inside of me talk. It isn't quite the same as human feelings—it isn't quite the same as having a beast inside you—some sort of animal feelings, you know—"

The whole mixed stream of hatred and violence, of fear and despair, seems so powerful that to think one weekend could possibly make *any* difference seems incredibly quixotic. Yet changes did occur. One small example composed of two inter-changes between Dennis, a Protestant, and Becky, Catholic:

DENNIS (*speaking about Becky*): The general impression back in Belfast is, if she is a Catholic she is a Catholic and you just put her in a wee box and that is the end of it. But you just can't do that. She has communicated to me that she is in a worse position than what I am. . . . I would hate to be sitting in Becky's chair . . . because I feel that she feels the absolute despair that I would feel. I don't know how I would react if I were one of her lads. I would probably go out and get a gun and finish up doing something radical and end up dead.

BECKY *(later):* Words couldn't describe what I feel towards Dennis from the discussion we had at dinner time. We spoke quietly for about ten minutes and I felt that here I have got a friend and that was it.

DENNIS: We sat here at dinner time and had a wee bit of a yarn quietly when you were all away for your dinner—

BECKY: I think he fully understands me as a person.

DENNIS: I do, there is no question about that—

BECKY: And for that reason I am very grateful and I think I have found a friend.

During our sessions the hatreds, the suspicions, the mistrusts of the two feuding groups were very evident, sometimes in covert form, gradually becoming more open in their expression. The individuals were speaking not only for themselves but for generations of resentment and prejudice. There were only six-teen hours of group interaction, yet during that incredibly short period these centuries-old hatreds were not only softened but in some instances deeply changed. It is evidence that facilitative attitudes can create an atmosphere in which open expression can occur. Open expression, in this kind of a climate, leads to communication. Better communication very often leads to understanding, and understanding washes away many of the ancient barriers. So rapid was the progress, so significant the changes, that some of the statements I have quoted here had to be deleted from the film. To show such understanding of the opposition would have endangered the lives of the speakers when it was shown in Belfast.

When the group returned to Belfast, almost all of them continued to meet at the home of the British colonel, whose neighborhood was the safest. After the film was completed they formed teams—one Protestant, one Catholic—and showed the film to many church groups of both sects, and led discussions. None of this had been planned. There were no funds to help out. It was done on their own spontaneous initiative.

For one group to make progress toward reconciliation hasn't ended the killings in Belfast. True, but suppose there had been a thousand or two thousand groups. The expense would be a fraction of what private Catholic armies, the British occupation army, and private Protestant armies have cost. As for facilitators, there are hundreds already sufficiently trained, and with three months' notice, they could be on the job.

This whole view is thoroughly confirmed in a recent interview with two Belfast men, very knowledgeable in the community, who have been acquainted with the project and who have seen the impact of the film on small audiences. They are all for training large numbers of Irish as facilitators. "We've got to get thousands of people involved. Once we do, it gets harder for the two percent of paramilitary gunmen [to control the public mind]. The whole idea of encounter groups—this is it! Encounter groups need to be done at a street-by-street level."

When will this come about? It will happen when the concerned public makes up its mind that the problem is so serious that something *must* be done. It is not experience or personnel or solid evidence that is lacking. It is the public will. The public is not yet convinced that there are any possible solutions, and even if there were, it is not willing—yet—to take the risk. When it is, a humanistic, person-centered approach has something to offer, even in situations of deadly antagonism.

I have had some experience working with black/white groups, groups composed of Chicanos and whites, and mixed groups with whites mingled with blacks, Chicanos, Filipinos, and others. Minority group members feel tremendous rage and bitterness toward the whites. With facilitative leadership, the group becomes a place for violent verbal expression of these feelings. Whites feel vilified as the abuse is heaped on them. The rage is overwhelming. There are several natural reactions on the part of white Americans which are of no help whatsoever: "I can understand your bitterness because I've been oppressed too"; "Yes, yes, I can understand how you feel, but I have never personally been a part of your oppression. It is the white society which has oppressed you." Whites who are effective seem to learn two attitudes—one toward self and one toward the minority members. The first is the realization and ownership of the fact that "I think white." For men trying to deal with women's rage, it may be helpful for the man to recognize "I think male." In spite of all our efforts to seem unprejudiced, we actually carry within us many prejudiced attitudes.

Rage needs to be *heard.* This does not mean that it simply needs to be listened to. It needs to be accepted, taken within, and understood empathically. While the diatribes and accusations appear to be deliberate attempts to hurt the whites—an act of catharsis to dissolve centuries of abuse, oppression, and injustice—the truth about rage is that it only dissolves when it is really heard and understood, without reservations. Afterward, the blacks or other minority members change in what seems a miraculous way, as though a weight has been lifted from their shoulders.

To achieve this kind of empathic listening the white needs to listen to his own feelings too, his feelings of anger and resentment at "unjust" accusations. At some point he too will need to express these, but the primary task is to enter empathically the minority world of hate and bitterness and resentment and to know that world as an understandable, acceptable part of reality.

In working with international groups it is fascinating to watch the development of appreciation for the customs and beliefs of very diverse nationalities, races, and cultures. The reactions of the participants and facilitators to the person-centered approach has been overwhelmingly positive. They speak of loss of fear in trying to communicate, a feeling of being heard, and an awareness of the beauty and richness of cultural differences.

I want to give the reader some feeling of what it is like to participate in a group that cuts across cultural, religious, racial, and national lines. Here is the report of a Swedish woman, Binnie Kristal-Andersson,[9] who speaks very personally of her experience in a ten-day group.

KRISTAL-ANDERSSON: I had had one previous experience with a three-day intercultural communication workshop in Stockholm, 1974. It was there I met Charles Devonshire when he came for this first pilot workshop in Sweden, and I felt those three days were for me one of the most meaningful experiences of my life—meeting and getting to know a group of totally different people from several different nations and talking about everything from fear of death to fear of living, and everything in between. We shared tears, laughter, anger, thoughts, fears, and insecurities, learned an openness to one another's values and customs, even if they were completely different from our own, learned to express feelings to people we normally would not open ourselves to, to listen, to express our inner needs without ambiguous or confusing signals. We experienced each other with a growing awareness, that we are more alike than different.

Could this ten-day encounter in Furudal be as rich an experience again? I had just finished a two-year psycho-dynamic oriented group (one and a half hours once a week). Within myself I felt that I had learned more about myself and other people in the client-centered three-day workshop than I had learned in the two-year group experience. I wanted to see again if I would feel this way.

The group gathered in front of a fire the first evening—sixteen very, very different people: organizational executives, psychologists, a black-American teacher working in Germany, a German woman working with mentally retarded children in Hamburg, a nineteen-year-old American university student, journalists from Swedish radio, two academically educated American housewives, a social worker and a Dutch psychologist. We ranged in age from nineteen to fifty-two. We ranged in different interests from tennis playing to writing poetry. We were different races, different nationalities—Dutch, German, American, black and white, Swedish, Malaysian. We had totally different religious beliefs—from the deeply religious American housewife, to the cool Swedish Protestants, to radical atheists. Different political colors, different political interests, and as many life-styles as there were participants. As one of the participants put it: "When I heard the different backgrounds of the group, then I thought this must go to hell, it couldn't work." And we all seemed to have very different motives for coming. . . .

Hard feelings came out in the beginning, the first days, aggression, clichés, false impressions about the person or his race or nationality. But these slowly disappear, explained away or become unimportant, as the person behind the nationality, the accent, the race or color is discovered. . . . When a woman described herself as an extension of her husband, another woman got angry and asked her if she was listening to the words she said and what they meant. The first woman got sad and then started talking about her anger toward her husband and sometimes her children, because of having sacrificed her life to them.

The girl of Chinese background has meekly asked for permission every time she wanted to say something in the group. "May I . . ." "Could I . . ." Another girl asks her why she has to excuse herself every time she has to say something—to ask for permission to say something. She gets very flustered at the comment, is silent for a while, and then angry and crying. The other girl says that she didn't mean to hurt her, but she did remind her of all the meek little well brought up girls who have to excuse themselves, feel guilty for having something to say, for being anything else than a picture someone painted for them. The Malaysian girl then started talking of her upbringing—in a bourgeois Chinese home—taught from early childhood to be silent, polite, to dedicate life to an eventual man, to learn, to go to school, even university—waiting for marriage. At the end of the group session these two women hug each other, walk away hand in hand. . . .

Charles Devonshire,[10] the facilitator of the group, is attacked from time to time by several members in the group for not leading, for not helping or mediating an argument, for not explaining, or calming anger, but he calmly repeats again and again that he cannot take responsibility for the group, but they must themselves—that he doesn't want to be made into their leader, their god—no, they could find answers themselves. Some thought it was a trick or he was just pretending or that he was waiting for the right moment to take over the lead. Even when he said that he felt very afraid and insecure one day, one member laughed at him and didn't believe it, wouldn't believe it. . . .

The large group often broke up into smaller groups, where the conversations continued from the larger group, often with a deeper, more intense contact, sometimes into the early morning hours. There was very little sleeping those ten days. The straightness and honesty of what we said constantly to each other gave an intensity to every situation—even the wordless

ones, running, swimming, boating, dancing, listening to fiddle
music in an ancient "fábod" high in the mountains—we could
no longer avoid confrontation, tension, closeness—both positive and negative—wherever we went. . . .
Difficult to describe in words—the giving of ourselves, the
dropping of masks, and all feelings of having to be nice, of
having to do anything. The fullness of being able to say from
morning to night what one is thinking and feeling. . . .
The last days, I interviewed the participants. All left with
some insight into themselves, their lives, the culture they live
in, their different roles in society, how other people see them as
people, and as a part of a culture. . . .
When I came to the group I was afraid of not being accepted.
I was looking for a space I felt I could not find within the group
(or in the world). I was afraid of not being accepted, and then
I found acceptance and a space and I realized that I *did not*
want to be accepted, didn't need to be accepted by everyone in
the group. I learned to accept rejection as well as acceptance,
and not be afraid of my strength, as a woman and as a person.
I could show so many different sides of myself, test them out,
and see that some were accepted and some were rejected. When
I was rejected one day by someone I was very fond of, I could,
after running away, come back, and I never came back before.

One of the most striking things about international groups is
that they are so similar to every other encounter group. As
Binnie says, the national and racial and cultural differences
come to seem unimportant as the *person* is discovered. In spite
of all the differences, there is a great potential for understanding
and closeness in the human issues we are all trying to cope with.
The participants in this workshop do not speak much of the
cultural issues. Instead they speak of things like "I've found my
family again"; "I was not being honest with myself"; "I can
cry, show feeling, instead of constantly joking"; "If I am going
to change, can change, or dare to change, I don't know yet, but
I am surer of myself"; "I am more self-confident"; "I have

learned to better trust my feelings." Think of these statements. Which was made by a black, by a German, by a man, by a Swede? It is impossible even to guess. These are *human* statements, and that seems to be the outcome typical of such person-centered groups. It is being human which dissolves the barriers and brings closeness.

This appears to be the result when persons of highly divergent cultures are empowered by being heard and accepted and permitted to be self-directed. This is the interpersonal politics of a cross-cultural application of the person-centered approach.

I hope I have been successful in demonstrating that models do exist for the constructive handling of almost every variety of intergroup tension. Whether we are speaking of religious differences or of bitterness based in poverty versus wealth or mistrust rooted in differing cultural customs or the seething rage growing out of racial discrimination or deadly centuries-old feuds involving a number of these elements, we are not without knowledge of, and experience in, utilizing interpersonal skills which help to resolve these tensions. We need to improve our skills. We need to recognize the problems that will emerge if these efforts are multiplied 100- or 1,000-fold. But experience with a person-centered approach indicates that there is no basic reason for despair. We have made progress in setting up test-tube solutions. When the world is ready, we can say tentatively and with humility that we are ready to begin.

Throughout every example there runs a consistent thread of interpersonal politics. The individual is not manipulated by powerful leadership; is not converted by some charismatic figure; is enabled to become more of self, more expressive, more open to feelings, good and bad. And it is out of that more complete and powerful humanness that person touches person, communication becomes real, tensions are reduced, and relationships become expressive and understanding, with an acceptance of the negative as well as the positive. This is the end result of a person-centered politics in intergroup frictions.

My purpose in this whole first section of the book has been to show that a new politics of relationships is possible. From the intimacies of marriage to disputes between countries, there are living, effective examples of what a person-centered approach means in practice.

In this new politics it has been discovered that the most powerful stance one can take in any relationship is, paradoxically, to leave responsible power in the hands of each person or each group. Then this self-empowered relationship can become constructively changing and growthful if one party or the other is able to take steps in the direction of providing facilitative conditions. Where power is relatively equal, either party can provide the conditions for change. Where power is unequal, or where one is *perceived* as more powerful—the teacher or administrator are examples—the first steps must be taken by the perceived leader, the perceived power.

The attitudes that make for change and growth and improved relationships are not mysterious, even though they may be difficult to attain. One is the willingness to "indwell" in the perceived reality of the other; a willingness to step into his or her private world and perceive it as if it were one's own. The more such profound understanding occurs, the more tensions relax, fresh insights occur, and communication becomes possible. Another facilitative attitude is the valuing and respecting and caring for the other person. The more this exists, the more the individual gains in self-esteem, and hence in a more responsible and responsive stance toward others. Finally, realness and absence of façade in one party draws out realness in the other, and genuine meeting (to use Buber's term) becomes possible.

I have not used a theoretical mode to present this new interpersonal politics. I have drawn on my own experience and that of others to show that functioning examples, living models, exist at every level and in every major area of our lives— whether we consider ourselves to be parents, spouses, therapists, teachers, administrators, social activists, or international mediators.

Perhaps most important of all, I have tried to indicate the revolutionary nature of this seemingly simple, straightforward approach. It threatens family life as it has existed in the past. It turns education topsy-turvy. It changes the whole pattern of the helping professions. It threatens the number, the power, and the importance of supervisors and administrators in industry or any other organization. It is threatening to both militants and conservatives alike in social issues, interracial tensions, international disputes. It is a genuinely new approach, though not necessarily in its ideas, which can be shown to have old roots. What is new and highly threatening to the establishment is that it presents evidence to show that it *works*. It is not a pie-in-the-sky ideology that can be ignored as unrealistic. In every area I have mentioned, it has been shown to be practical, constructive, and effective. It is the realization that it is a *viable alternative* to our present ways of seizing and using power that makes it most threatening of all. It is, not only in principle but in cold *fact,* a quiet revolution.

Part II

The person-centered approach in action

Chapter 8 | A person-centered workshop: its planning and fruition

During the past ten days I have become accustomed to the cavernous hall with its dark-paneled wood walls and the intricate beams supporting the high gabled ceiling. And I have met many of the 135 people who crowd together in an irregular mass, occupying the middle portion of the great room. Their faces are illuminated by the soft ceiling lights. They are restlessly settling themselves for a community meeting, the majority sitting close together on the floor so that they can hear each other, but ringed by a roughly circular fringe of chairs and couches which hold those who are too old or stiff to enjoy the carpeted floor. I see Clancy is here, he of the bright, merry spirit and the tiny, wasted body. He unstraps his artificial leg, lays down his crutch, and sits on the floor. And Rachel from Brazil, aristocratic and gentle; wild-bearded Frank from Argentina; smiling Betsy from Vermont; Jane, the clear-eyed horse lover from the Bay Area; Don, the dedicated music teacher from Kansas; Julia of the Netherlands, with placid face; and Clifton, whose chocolate skin only emphasizes her large, soulful eyes.

There is no one in charge. No one called the meeting. We just came together. Two or three people make announcements about meetings, about plans. Then Vicente stands up and speaks, making an emotional statement about the desperately poor people he works with in the Mexican ghettos. His English is not good, but his message is that we must be more socially conscious. It will not do just to understand ourselves while enjoying an affluent life. He questions whether a person-centered approach has any meaning in his oppressed and poverty-stricken barrios. He is struggling to convey the pain and the urgency of his situation.

He makes the mistake of pausing for a moment, and someone speaks up to rebut him. "There are oppressors and oppressed here, too. If we can make progress in ourselves, if we can get beyond the petty things here, we will be better able to deal with the petty things and the large things in the world outside." Someone else clinches the rebuttal. "By changing ourselves we are working to change the whole issue of wealth versus poverty in the world." Vicente has been effectively silenced. He sits down, but there is a sad, wry look on his face.

The issue is not dead, however. Another speaker stands and is soon silenced. The pros and cons of this issue tangle up in themselves.

Another theme comes up. "When the oppressors are overthrown, the revolutionaries just take over the old oppressive roles. But we have an opportunity here to alter the *nature* of the revolution. This group *is* the revolution. We will be carrying on a continuous dialogue with all kinds of institutions. Educators are learning to revolutionize schools. Some of us are learning how to infiltrate hospitals. Others are changing the churches. . . ." The speaker goes on, carried away by his thoughts.

Then Gary—bushy-haired, open-faced Gary—speaks up so quietly it is difficult to hear him. He works in a nearby clinic of strictly orthodox psychoanalytic ideology, very authoritarian in its structure. He had asked permission to come to this workshop under a policy of brief leaves for educational credit. Permission denied: "Rogers' ideas are speculative and of no value." Gary decided to act on his own. He made plans to take care of all his therapy cases in hours he could get away from the workshop. He brought all his reports, statistics, and paperwork up to date. He made arrangements to do any current reports immediately after the workshop. Then he came, without asking further permission. Today he was called on the carpet by the director. "I see you did not put in a full forty hours last week." Gary explained that he was being a fully responsible, professional person. He had taken care of, or had arranged to take care of, all his professional responsibilities. He was attending the workshop because he thought his learnings here about the process of growthful relationships would contribute to his work with his patients, to the clinical service, and to the larger hospital community, as well as benefiting himself.

This set off much discussion between the director and Gary. Finally the director indicated that Gary could be asked to leave for not following the rules and time schedule of the clinic. Gary replied passionately (though in this clinic feelings are always considered indications of immaturity, dependence, transference, narcissism or rebellion against father figures): "I've dealt responsibly with my work; I will make up the time I've lost; I am having experiences which will improve my work with my patients, help the clinic, and be full of learning for me. The only aspect I haven't dealt with is your power and authority over me. I *am* acting on my own responsibility, and I know you have the power to punish me." The director looked at him, seemed about to fire him, then dropped his gaze. His chin dropped to his chest and he was silent.

"I guess there's nothing more to say." Gary got up, left, and came to this community meeting where he is now telling us of the confrontation. He has no idea if he will be fired.

Individuals respond in a variety of supportive ways, but soon fragmented conversations start up again. People offer positive evaluations of their experience thus far. "I'm increasing my listening skills." "I have a greater tolerance for ambiguity." "I'm getting in touch with me."

But then Denny—tense, dramatic, very politically oriented

—takes the floor. "Self-actualization is not enough! We have only three or four years to control the spread of incredibly dangerous nuclear power plants! It's not *enough* to be feeling and thinking! We *must* be active! I need your *bodies* to block the roads where they are constructing these plants! I need your *energy* to fight this battle! The time is terribly short!"

Protests are immediate. This is not a group of followers, and Denny is made keenly aware of this fact. One person says, "This is the first time in this workshop that anyone has tried to tell me what I must do. I resent it." Denny sits down, squelched.

And then Anne speaks up. I have talked with her several times. She is in her late sixties, but in the last three or four years has remade her life. She is astonishingly adventurous and spontaneous in her way of being. She has become independent in her thinking and her interests. Sexually too she is more free, and she tells me that her marriage with her husband of thirty-five years is richer and more exciting than ever, with more freedom for growth for both of them, and an increasing ability to deal with the negative aspects of their relationship. She somehow learned to live her own life—a refreshing example of what the older years can be. She speaks softly, but with an unmistakable firmness. "I've been feeling distressed, because we never *heard* Vicente. We paid no attention to the fact that when he sat down he said, 'I wasn't finished.' He has been hurting ever since. I want to *hear* him."

The whole character of the meeting changes at this point. We pay attention to Vicente and hear his passionate despair. Then we listen to each of those who had been so summarily cut off —to Denny, who had antagonized so many with her crusade. We *understand* her urgency, without putting her down. What has been, up to this point, a disconnected cluster of 136 people gradually becomes a unified social organism. We are willing to receive, and learn from, and be nourished by the highly diverse individuals who are here. There is a very different spirit in the air. And it has happened intuitively, without anyone charting the course or leading the way. It seems to have happened because collectively an inner sense, operating in the group, wants it this way.

I feel very moved—and also very tired. I leave the meeting and go to my room to rest and sleep. But sleep will not come. So I get up and write these notes.

August 11, 1975

11:30 P.M.

I left the community meeting simply because I already had much more than I could digest; and I wanted to try to clarify some of my own feelings, which were getting jumbled by the fullness of the events. And I left comfortably because I knew that the community had the capacity for handling anything that might come up, and handling it far more wisely than I—or any *one* person here—could handle it.

And the first of my feelings that became clear to me was *pride*. I was proud to be a member of a community where there was so much caring concern for others, a caring that was broader and more sensitive than I, or any one person here, was capable of. I thought of Vicente, and the fact that someone finally realized—which I had not—that he had not been fully heard or accepted. I heard a community which insisted, through a number of its members, that Denny, her anger and her passion, be *heard*, even though she had expressed it in ways many resented. The resentment too was heard and accepted. I watched people really listening to one another. There was anguish and pain and anger and frustration—and a mixture of pride, joy, and sorrow around Gary's courageous confrontation. There were ideas and causes and solutions to problems—and we *listened*, whether we agreed or violently disagreed.

I don't mean we *all* listened, all heard. There were interruptions, misinterpretation, distortions, an inability to understand and sometimes no *desire* to understand. I was part of all that, too, in me. But finally, in almost every case, it seemed to me, someone *heard*. And I felt proud of us and of the stretching of myself into new areas, having to face new and sometimes over-

147

whelming issues, but moving, in process, getting better at whatever the hell we're doing.

I thought of one thing in my own experience that relates to all this: I had a part in initiating the attitude, the philosophy, the approach, which seems to me to be prevalent here. I didn't have the foggiest notion that it would spread beyond individual therapy. But there was one conviction I held that I now realize was very significant. It was this: I believed that if we could discover even one significant truth about the relationships between *two* people, it might turn out to be much more widely applicable. And of course I didn't mean truth with a capital T, but just an approximation to one truth about what goes on between a person with problems and a person who is trying to help. If we could discover that truth, that orderliness, that lawfulness, it might have many implications. And in my judgment that has proven to be true. What we discovered has had widespread application.

I like to remember that when the early astronomers began to discover that the earth was not the center of the universe but revolved around the sun, their discoveries were full of errors, but they had profound effects nonetheless. Their findings were absolutely revolutionary in their impact on all aspects of life—on religion, philosophy, art and culture. And just possibly we may be making discoveries like that.

As I participate in the struggling, difficult, trying, painful process of our beginning to become a community, I have two reactions. One is that at times I am so frustrated that I wonder if it's worth it. But the other reaction is much stronger. I watch with awe the birth pangs of something new in the world. And my earlier conviction returns. If we can find even one partial truth about the process by which 136 people can live together without destroying one another, can live together with a caring concern for the full development of each person, can live together in the richness of diversity instead of the sterility of conformity, then we may have found a truth with many, many implications.

I don't know how to solve the problems of the exploitation of the poor by the rich, nor the horror of the nuclear shadow, nor the incredible social injustices of the world. I devoutly wish I did. But if we can discover one truth about the process of building community, I'm not going to despair. The discovery of *anything* that is approximately *true* has an earthshaking revolutionary power. And I believe we are making some such discovery, though I can't define it, and can only observe some of its characteristics. So I have hope that some of the over-whelming world issues may be touched, in ways I can't even dream of now, by what we are doing.

The foregoing is a slice out of the middle of a sixteen-day intensive workshop in the person-centered approach. It is *my* perception of the meeting that night. I have come to believe that there were 136 different workshops going on, and that each of us saw the events somewhat differently, and found different meanings in them. This chapter is largely the planning and the process of the workshop as I perceived and experienced it in myself. I have, however, where possible, used material given to me by other participants to show some of the varying individual perceptions.

What led up to this project? In what ways is such a workshop different from any other conference, workshop, or seminar? I believe there are profound differences, and these will emerge as I describe the distinctive steps that led to the building of a vital, if temporary, community. The methods were the complete op-posite of procedures used in conventional enterprises.

First was the matter of choosing to hold a workshop. There were three of us who had been together as staff members in two workshops the previous summer, John, Natalie, and myself. We decided we would aim for one larger workshop in the summer-time, with approximately a hundred participants, lasting for sixteen days. For such a large number we wanted a staff of nine

—if small intensive groups were part of the experience, each staff member could facilitate a group of eleven.

We met to choose six more staff members and were surprised when we each made lists of people we would like to work with and discovered there was a good deal of consensus on four names. These were agreed upon, but there were difficulties over two of them. We talked out these differences until we had reached a solution genuinely satisfying to all. We also agreed that Joann, who had been the coordinator for administrative matters the previous summer, should be invited again, and if she accepted, would be made a full-fledged staff member, participating in all decisions. We were unhappy at the thought of having someone who was simply "hired to do a job."

All this may seem quite unremarkable, but I would like to point to the power aspects. The three of us functioned as equals. No one was in charge. No single person's ideas prevailed. I was the senior member of the group in age and professional status, but my ideas and feelings carried weight only when they made sense to the others.

Joann and the six others—Maria, Jared, Maureen, David, Marion, and Dick—were immediately invited, all but two by long-distance phone, and to our delight we had, within a day, seven acceptances.

Those in the vicinity of La Jolla met for the next planning steps. People offered to take on different responsibilities, and these offers, with modifications, were accepted. I offered to draft the brochure. The responsibilities could not possibly be evenly divided, so it was decided that each person keep track of the number of hours expended in pre-workshop activity and receive compensation on that basis, all with the same hourly rate.

At this point active work began. No important decisions were made without getting staff approval by mail or phone. Since our staff was geographically much divided—four in the La Jolla area, three in the San Francisco area, and one each in Ohio, Texas and Maine—obtaining group approval was not always easy, but we felt it important.

I drafted a brief brochure, sent it to the staff and was astonished to be bombarded with demands for major changes. There is such a thing as pride of authorship, and mine was a bit bruised. After a short cooling-off period, I realized how these changes would improve the brochure, and what a challenge it was to try to meld together the sometimes contradictory views. So a second draft, which elicited a smaller number of suggested changes. By this time the title of the workshop, our purpose, the description of the form it might take, and the qualifications of the participants had all been drastically changed. The third draft was accepted by all.

This may seem a very wasteful way of putting together a brochure. But again let me point to its politics. Ten people, only a few of whom have ever worked together, where no one of us is well acquainted with all of the other nine, have now come together by mail, as equals. Furthermore, the workshop is now *owned* by every one of the ten, because all have contributed to its preliminary description. No one feels "I have been hired to be on the staff of the workshop"; everyone feels "I am sharing the responsibility for *our* workshop."

Because the brochure played an important part in the way the group developed, here are the salient paragraphs.

A PERSON-CENTERED APPROACH: THE PROCESS OF INDIVIDUAL GROWTH AND ITS SOCIAL IMPLICATIONS
A Summer Workshop, August 1–16, 1975

PURPOSE

The aim will be to build a workshop around an approach to human relationships and human growth which recognizes that the potential to learn and the power to act lie *within* the person —rather than in an expert dealing with him or her, or in a system controlling him or her.

The workshop will provide a place where people who believe in the worth and dignity of the individual and in each person's capacity for self-direction can come together to create a community. The workshop values what each participant has to offer. We welcome every way of releasing the inner strength of the person. The community will, we hope, provide for a sharing of our professional worlds, our personal questions, problems, and satisfactions, our creativity and our innovations. We trust the workshop will demonstrate the psychological climate which we know can evoke self-understanding and self-directed behavior. It is hoped that the experience will not only lead to inner personal growth but to an increased understanding of one's responsibility in the world, and how one can act on that sense of responsibility.

It is anticipated that in pursuing its purpose the community may consider such topics as: the politics of the person-centered approach; the facilitation of problem-solving change in society and its institutions; the new roles of women and men; ways of living, working and relating with people who are different; ways of living in one's aloneness and in one's intimacy with others; the problems of life transitions; changes in life-styles; psychotherapy and healing; the "other worlds" of psychic phenomena; the development of a broader person-centered theory and philosophy; the problems of humanistic research.

Finally it is our belief that all of us—participants and facilitators—will gain support, and develop support, systems which will give us vitality, energy, and renewal as we take our learnings into the "back-home" situation.

THE FORMAT

The aim will be to combine experiential and cognitive learning—the personal and the intellectual approach. Consequently community meetings, interest groups, encounter groups, seminars, books, tapes, films, opportunities to practice and develop one's interpersonal skills, designed experiences for eliciting alternative ways of behaving—all will be available as elements upon which the group can draw as we work together in the construction of a program. The initial steps will be planned by the staff, but the total design and format will be a mutual product, created to meet the needs of the participants, including the facilitators.

In order to have the workshop open to individuals of different ages, races, occupations and socioeconomic statuses it was made clear that selection would *not* be on the basis of paper credentials. The major criterion would be "the degree of impact the individual is having, or potentially has, on persons involved in the crucial issues of the day." To further enrich the workshop, spouses/partners were encouraged to apply. As for tuition, we said, "We are attempting something new but something which is definitely in accord with the philosophy underpinning a person-centered approach. The tuition fee will be based on the participant's personal decision, based on his/her situation. Some persons will pay up to three or four times the average fee, some will pay much less."

The diversity of the staff experience was described, and the fact that they were not narrowly committed to any fixed approach and that each brought specialized knowledge and experience to the workshop.

This is not only an announcement of a workshop. It is a significant political statement, and was intended as such. There is no group of experts who are to instruct the participants. It is made clear that the control of plans and program will rest with the whole group. There will be no first-class and second-class persons—paper credentials are disregarded. It is political in the social as well as the interpersonal sense. It points to the social implications of this kind of an approach, to the individual's "responsibility in the world," and the problem of how to "act on that sense of responsibility." It aimed to make very clear the fact that power will be shared among all of us—staff and participants—and that we feel an obligation to use that personal power in the social milieu.

Even more unconventional in its politics was the manner of setting the tuition fee. It was a grave risk, but we decided to let people set their own fees. In this "rip-off" society that's indeed a gamble. Could people be trusted to be honest about their incomes? Especially in a recession year? We simply could not be sure, but we chose to find out. We agreed on a carefully worded "Financial Statement" to be considered by each applicant.

We explained our desire to break the pattern of having workshops and other learning experiences available only to the affluent. We wanted a broader socioeconomic and educational mix.

But we also made clear our need for an *average* tuition of $325 per person. Then a number of questions were raised, the most important being, "What is my total usable yearly income?" Applicants were encouraged to consider whether they had a financial backlog, and how great were the needs of their dependents. A table suggested fees based on *income* considerations: for example, incomes under $5,000, $50 to $150 tuition; $20,000 to $30,000, tuition of $600 to $900.

Finally the applicant was asked to sign a statement which concluded, "Having given careful thought to all of the above, I believe I am paying my appropriate share by paying a total tuition fee of $_____."

Our enterprise was ready for launching. The brochures were sent out to a modest mailing list in the United States. We had decided we would not try for foreign enrollments. We also placed notices in several journals and newsletters, including the newsletter of the La Jolla Program. This is a program for training group facilitators, sponsored by the Center for Studies of the Person, which during its nine-year history has attracted many foreign participants. Then we sat back and waited.

Soon the applications started arriving in a steady stream. Over a hundred and seventy applications came in from the United States and, to our astonishment, from twelve foreign countries. The selection committee was impressed by the diversity: penniless graduate students, the director of a conservatory of music, people with little education but working in very significant jobs, psychiatrists, educators; all ages from twenty-two to seventy-two; men and women about evenly divided. We had achieved our hope for a wide range of interests, occupations and ages, and had found an unexpected range of nationalities as well.

The financial statements were kept from the selection committee so that they would not be influenced by that factor. As the weeks went by, my feelings about finances went up and down with each new batch of applications. By early May, it was clear we were at a crisis point. The average fee was only slightly over $200. The staff met, determined we would not cancel the workshop, decided to increase the size of the workshop from 100 to 126, and to write the accepted applicants of our plight. They were asked to increase their tuition by 20 percent if possible. The response was most heartening. Some raised their fees by more than 20 percent, most by 20 percent, and those who could not called or wrote to explain the reasons.

Thus, to a degree beyond our expectations, the politics of the self-determined fee was important. It treated the applicant as a trustworthy person, responsible for his or her actions. An unexpected result was that because of the crisis it gave a sense of ownership of the program.

The thinking of the applicants about the policy was evident in their reactions, which we requested on the financial statement:

"I think this system is a very good one. At the same time, however, I have a strong need of wanting to explain why I have chosen such a small amount to pay. It looks so stingy and poor and this does not correspond to the worth that coming to your workshop has for me. The reason is that . . ."

"I believe this is the only way to handle a situation like this, and though I am not used to it and it hurts to pay more than the minimum that would be established in the conventional manner of charging, I feel good about it. I sure hope that it works and that it allows you to continue operating in this fashion. When writing these lines I had not decided on the exact quantity I wished to pay, and the more I write the higher my thoughts go, so I decided to stop now."

"My first reaction was 'That's great.' Then when I began to figure out, I considered a little dishonesty, then decided on $—— which was the lowest I could pay and stay honest. After two days of thinking (and some squirming) I decided on $——, a larger amount. It was an interesting experience. I feel good about the idea and (now that the decision-making is over) good about the whole deal."

A few women raised the question of the fee for a wife whose husband makes a fairly high income but who wants this to be *her* workshop, not something that *he* is financing. Some counter-culture persons had difficulty because they knew they could earn more money (and hence pay more) if they were willing to work at some conventional occupation, but "I only work until I have a little money ahead, then I live on that while I write or play . . . so I earn less than I'm capable of earning."

To our amazement, the fee structure never came up as a topic for discussion in the whole sixteen days of the workshop. To our surprise and pleasure, we broke even financially—barely so— and the staff did not have to take a salary cut.

Because a number of the staff were not at all acquainted with one another, we got together for four days of relaxation and planning. We met on the Mills College campus, which had been chosen as the most suitable location for the workshop.

Here again is an instance of the seeming wastefulness of a person-centered approach. If we had been providing a cluster of courses, one day or less of advance planning would have been sufficient, because each of us would have known what he could teach. And by such a process we would have cut ourselves off from learning—from each other and from the participants.

As we met and worked and played together, the purposes of the four days emerged:

We wanted to be ourselves with each other, with our problems, our pain, our competency, and our creativity, so
we could be ourselves with the whole group.

We considered how we could create a climate in the workshop that would encourage a diversity of being and a
self-responsible attitude. We planned carefully for the
initial moments and hours of the workshop because they
are important in setting the tone for what follows.

We took steps to make resources available for all kinds of
learnings.

We chose to set aside two "free days" during the sixteen to
allow all of us to relax.

We chose to set a simple schedule for the first three and a half
days which structured the blocks of time but did nothing
to structure the content.

We brainstormed about experiences and ideas we each
wanted to contribute, but left the scheduling to the future so that we could feel our way, rather than plan our
way into the workshop.

Here is the simple schedule we adopted and had duplicated
for the opening meeting.

	Friday	Saturday	Sunday	Monday	Tuesday
Morning 9–12		Small Groups	Community meeting	Small Groups	Community meeting
Afternoon 1–5:30	Registration	Rest & recreation. Resources: library, films, etc., available	Rest & recreation. Resources available	Small Groups	
Evening 7–10	Community meeting	Small Groups	Small Groups	Party	

We had decided to set aside time for small intensive groups because we believed that when people know each other in depth, they can better work together, learn, and contribute. We thought it unlikely that the small groups would continue for more than a few days, and we provided a staff member to meet with those who wanted no part of small groups. Likewise, even this simple schedule was to be adopted only if the whole group so elected. In other words, choices were to be honored.

John K. Wood was on the staff and here is his account of the experience: "We began . . . by convening the staff—ten talented and unique persons. We spoke with each other of our personal lives, our desires, our fears, our fantasies of the workshop. We talked of what we wanted to offer as resources and teachers and what we wanted to gain from the experience. We shared our commonalities and our differences. We laughed and cried and got drunk together." And finally we could "breathe together," experience together. "We certainly did not all have similar feelings, thoughts, beliefs, or expectations about being together or doing the workshop," but we could be together as living, breathing persons. We had reached some sensing of a unity, an unspoken agreement as to our intent, which was deeper than any of our disagreements.

"When we met together, the ten of us, something happened." We "decided" on a "design"—an attitude, a philosophy that reflected our different personalities and attitudes, and our "unity," our oneness in experiencing. "Later, in the community of 136, our individual personalities and moods were reflected. In a way each of the staff, by being who they were at the moment, sanctioned that way of being, and thus made it possible for persons in the community to be that way also. For example, if one of the staff was indifferent, then indifference became an attitude permitted by the staff and therefore available for anyone to express who had such feelings." When one of the staff was angry, this clearly permitted anger to be expressed. "The community reflected all the splits and polarities and indulgences of the staff, all the creative and facilitative and loving attributes as well, and since the staff breathed together, the community also reflected this unity."

I believe this catches the extremely subtle influence the staff had in making it possible for each person to be his feelings, his experiences, his thoughts of the moment. In this sense each person was empowered to be himself. I believe this influence would not have been nearly so strong if the staff had not explored their own very human aspects, and the issues which strongly divided them—for we were certainly not of one mind —before the workshop began.

Some of the most detailed advance planning had to do with the afternoon of registration. We wanted the person-centered atmosphere to be immediately felt. Joann, the coordinator, is likable and outgoing, and we felt good about having her handle the actual registration and fees. Some people arrived early and we asked them to take over various tasks, which they gladly did, such as meeting later arrivals at the bus and taking them to our complex of dormitory rooms. We permitted each person to select his own room. I thought this a bit silly, as the dormitory rooms were quite alike, but it proved very worthwhile. All the room doors were opened. Each new arrival was given a tour of the complex, chose a room, closed the door, and came back to complete registration. Early arrivals were asked to serve as guides for those who came later.

Then, to aid recognition and getting acquainted, a mammoth chart had been made (by an early arrival) with each participant's name, a place for a photo, and a space for the room number. The staff took turns taking a Polaroid picture of each person on arrival. This was pasted over the name. As soon as a room was chosen, the room number was listed too. Staff photos and rooms were listed also—at the bottom of the chart.

Why all this attention to detail? It had very important effects. Being put to work meant that you were a part of the enterprise, not a passive recipient. Choosing a room meant that you were in control, not being ordered. Having all the pictures up demonstrated strongly that interaction between participants was seen

159

as just as important as interaction with staff. It was a politics of equalitarian, self-responsible, self-directed activity from the very outset.

One of the sharpest differences in the staff had to do with the question of how to open the first meeting. There was no lack of opinions. It should be agendaless. It should be opened with a chart listing the issues to be faced by the workshop. Carl should open it. Carl didn't want to open it—it would look as though it was *his* workshop. The staff should sit in a circle in the middle, discussing the possibilities for the workshop. We could not agree, and no one wanted the responsibility. Finally, after a whispered consultation, Jared and Maureen, the two youngest staff members, said that if they could do it together, they would open the meeting. We agreed with relief, not knowing how they would handle it.

It may seem surprising that we gave so much thought to the initial steps. But experience had shown that a mind-set is developed in the first hours—often in the first few minutes—of any conference, which tends to set the personal and political form of the whole conference.

When opening night came, and 126 nervous participants and 10 uneasy staff members had gathered informally in the auditorium, Maureen and Jared spoke up. I don't remember what they said, but it was so transparently honest, so unassuming, so expressive of their own hopes and uncertainties, that the atmosphere became at once easy and welcoming. They had hardly finished before members were eagerly speaking up to tell of their own hopes and expectations, the reasons for their coming, all sorts of personal expressions. The evening flowed smoothly. At an appropriate moment the tentative schedule for the next three days was brought up and accepted by the group. A method of selecting the small groups so as to have a diversity of age, geographical location and sex was described, and was accepted with relief, participants saying they had been uneasy as to how the groups would be formed. The meeting ended with a number of necessary announcements, and the answering of questions about meal tickets and all the minutiae of living together. The participants had already accepted a large share of responsibility and decision-making for themselves. The staff had played a relatively small facilitative role, and certainly no controlling role.

Every encounter group is different, and I have only a vague impression of what went on in the other eight small groups, so I'll limit myself to the one I attended. I can only tell of a few small incidents without breaking confidences, but these minute episodes show how the small groups contributed to the workshop as a whole.

I met with our group the second morning—fifteen of us, including four foreigners. I opened the group, simply saying that the tentative schedule gave us fifteen hours together and that I hoped we could come to know each other well. Things seemed to me to start very slowly. This was one of the times I seemed to feel responsible for the group. Gradually my stomach began to churn with impatience and frustration, as I wished things would move *faster*. I said almost nothing, but I was inwardly pushing. Among the early speakers in the group was Ben, an elderly psychiatrist, whose contributions were of two sorts. On the one hand he wanted to quiz me, the authority, about therapy. This kind of dependence always annoys me. I told him I wasn't in the mood to answer his questions now, but if there was sufficient concern with such questions we might set up an interest group later. But he still raised the questions. Along with this he wanted to expound his philosophy of therapy and living, which was that feelings interfered with reasonable living, and he was proud that he had, for many years, been able to hold his feelings in check. Members of the group were at first incredulous, then probing and critical of his stance. Ben met these attacks with calm, Buddhalike responses. He was not, he said, touched by any of this. This lack of responsiveness infuriated some of the women, and the attacks were sharper. I felt a need to let Ben know that I understood his point of view, though I could not agree with it. The more he revealed how he had handled his close relationships, especially with his former wife, the more skeptical and angry the group became, until he admitted he did have some feelings about the attacks, but that he was successfully suppressing these emotions.

There were many other expressions by group members during that first session, but I still felt it had all gone too *slowly.*

During the afternoon (of rest, recreation, and resources) I came to terms with my own feelings of responsibility for the group. When the evening session started I led off by telling them how responsible I had felt, and that I didn't like the fact that my viscera had been trying to bring more rapid movement into our process. I had come to realize this was ridiculous. I am *not* responsible for the group. It is *our* group, and I want to participate, but not push, even internally. Someone said, "Welcome to the group," and that was that. From that point on, individuals were much more expressive. Probably my unspoken overconcern had been felt and experienced as a burden. I don't know.

Michele, an attractive woman in her late thirties, gradually and painfully disclosed her conflict. She is lonely since her divorce two years ago and both wants and fears closeness with a man. She has been hurt too much. She finds this conflict unbearably present here at the workshop. This afternoon she went with a man to join the group at the swimming pool. After a time she felt she had to escape. Without a word to him, and without his knowledge, she left and went to a movie the workshop was showing. But she was so much in turmoil that she left that too. A member of the workshop—a man—who saw her leave thought she looked disturbed and followed her. She was angry that she had not been able to shake him off, but it sounded as if she had gained something from talking with him. She said the workshop experience was stirring up all her conflict over being *alone.* She had finally chosen that route—to be *alone* with her children and her job and to isolate herself from hurtful relationships. But now her desire for closeness, which had brought her nothing but pain, was reasserting itself. "I'm always doing this pull-push thing. It's awful. I can't bear this stress."

I, and the group, tried to be understanding of her and to be with her in her feeling of being torn in two directions. I wasn't sure we were helpful.

Then Ben asked to be heard. He said he had spent a most difficult afternoon. He had come to realize that perhaps he was mistaken, that holding down his feelings might not be constructive. He saw what this stance had done to his relationship with members of the group—that he had seemed to them cold and unfeeling. He remembered that his wife had bitterly complained in just these terms. He thought he was not achieving what he wanted, and he was changing his policy of many years. He was going to try to be aware of and express his feelings instead of suppressing them.

I listened to his statements with interest, but with a good deal of skepticism. The about-face seemed too sudden, and a bit unbelievable. The group welcomed his new attitude. Then others spoke up, one after another occupying the focus of the group for a time.

Toward the end of the evening I found myself thinking about Michele and the painful tug of war within her. I felt a very strong impulse to hug her. This set off a dialogue within me, my mind being full of reasons why I should do no such thing. "Isn't sexual attraction one reason you want to embrace her? What makes you think she would accept it when her greatest fear is of closeness? This is only the second meeting of the group and it would seem by some (and perhaps correctly) as a ridiculous 'Touchie-feelie' thing. She hasn't indicated any desire for anything of that sort, so forget the whole stupid impulse!" And then I found myself saying to her (in a somewhat cowardly and indirect expression of what I was feeling): "Michele, if I should tell you I'd like to give you a good *hug,* what would you say?"

163

To my astonishment she quickly replied, "I'd love it." So we stood up and gave each other a strong, close embrace in the middle of the circle. We returned to our places, I feeling definitely embarrassed, but somehow pleased that I had been able to follow an inner feeling, whether right or wrong. Then I was bowled over by her quiet statement, almost an aside: "Maybe I won't fly home tomorrow after all." I could scarcely believe that my intuitive impulse, so scorned by my intellect, had been so much on target. I certainly could not have dreamed that I was acting out, in myself, what was to be a major learning for the whole community.

Days later I checked with Michele. I had doubted whether she had meant what she said. But she told me she hadn't even unpacked her bags for the first days of the workshop, so painful were the old conflicts it aroused, and that she had indeed been on the verge of taking the next plane home.

Even in this fragment of the first two meetings, the power aspects are clear.

The group proceeds at its own pace. It is not manipulated or pressured or pushed.

Risk-taking leads to interpersonal trust. I took the risk of sharing my confused feelings about responsibility and was even more accepted.

Ben took the risk of sharing his philosophy and found the group trustworthy and caring, even though critical.

Michele took the risk of sharing her pain and conflicts and felt accepted and cared for.

I took the risk of acting on an intuition and found both my inner feelings and the reaction of the group worthy of trust.

It is discovered that intimacy is safe. Lessons are learned about personal and group responsibility.

The group realized it is accountable to itself. Each member learns that he must be responsible for expressing himself if the group is to be useful for self-growth.

Thus in important ways the small group helps the person to recognize his potency, ability to influence, capacity for communicating and participating. Power resides definitely in the individual. The possibility of forming a larger unified community of powerful persons is sharply increased.

On Sunday, after everyone had spent two sessions in small groups, there was a second community meeting. For a time everyone sat chattering and conversing. Nervous confusion was evident. I believe the unspoken question was "Who's in charge?" Then Ben—of all people—clapped his hands to begin the meeting. It seemed clear he wished to speak, but someone else wanted to know what people were feeling, and various attitudes toward the small group experience—positive and negative—were expressed. Then Ben told about his experience in our small group. He said, "I finally fell asleep last night somewhere between 3:00 and 4:00 A.M. The feelings that I had denied had gradually come to the surface—confusion, hurt feelings, anxiety, resentment. I doubted the value of *any* theory of personality. The only thing that I knew to be valid was that I have a need for human contact and will do anything to get it, even express negative feelings if I have to. I still feel that it is love that is the force that helps us survive the difficulties in the world, but the view that love is what I *have* to feel, *always,* is now in doubt." He said he had made a very sharp change in his theory and philosophy of living.

After he spoke, many shared the personal experiences they had been having. Others—the more politically oriented—spoke of important social issues, and these were discussed, but not at great length.

The group turned to what it wanted to do at the end of the three-day schedule. It was clear that there were many special interests they wanted to pursue, and the suggestion evolved that

165

at the end of this meeting anyone who wanted to convene a special-interest group write out the topic, his name, and the probable time allotment needed—one two-hour session, two three-hour sessions, etc.—and a place for people to sign up. Joann said she would put up a large piece of paper on the wall of the main lounge for this purpose.

Several people volunteered to serve as a program committee which would schedule these interest groups to avoid overlapping, and arrange other activities as well. This idea was not adequately discussed, and was neither approved nor disapproved, but the program committee set a time for its meeting nonetheless.

Immediately following the breakup of the meeting there was a rush for the main lounge, where several people helped Joann cover a whole wall with butcher paper. Inside of a half hour there were at least thirty special-interest groups listed, and people were busily signing up for those they hoped to attend.

Notice the flow of power and control in this meeting. When it was clear that the staff did not regard itself as being in charge, a member who had urgent business with the group called it to order. Then the community, without conscious intent, began taking care of its needs. First there was personal sharing and a development of greater trust. Then began the planning for the life of the community, and a real consensus was reached about having interest groups and the manner of forming them. The eagerness with which people rushed to do this seemed to indicate how rare it is that they can choose *freely* to follow their own interests, to volunteer what they can contribute, to set their own plans for learning.

As it turned out, the groups that attracted the most serious and continuing involvement were, in no particular order: the couples group, which merged with the men-women relations group; the power group, concerned with political issues of control; the healing group, especially involved in psychic healing; a women's group; a men's group; a group interested in innovative education; a research group, endeavoring to evolve new methods for humanistic research; a group looking into problems of life transitions; an assertiveness training group; a client-centered gestalt therapy group; a group to organize mental health centers staffed by laymen.

The story of the program committee is pertinent here. They were offering to take part in structuring the future life of the community. Their offer had not been refused, but neither had it been accepted. What happened next shows how extremely sensitive persons are to any possible loss of control. By the next morning I had heard a number of rumors about the program committee, stated with such assurance that I wondered if they were true. The committee, it was said, was composed of the power-hungry members of the workshop. They were making plans to alter the whole nature of the conference. They were trying to take over. I did not even know who was on this committee, so I looked forward to discovering the truth on the following day, Tuesday, at the third community meeting, the last event suggested by the staff.

We gathered that morning, and Jane, the spokeswoman for the program committee, began a presentation. She was clear, articulate, considerate of questions and differences. She explained all of the factors they had tried to take into account, so that everyone would have the opportunity to choose what he or she wanted to do, without serious conflicts of interest. She unveiled the schedule they were suggesting. It provided for the interest groups in an excellent way. It gave time for the small groups to continue if they wished. It was the most flexible and complete plan I could have imagined, and presented in a masterful way. I laughed when I thought of the rumors, and felt pride in the trustworthiness of our whole group.

The workshop clearly felt the same way. There were murmurs of "That's great," "It's just what we need." There were a few questions, and then someone said, "Let's adopt it!" and there was a chorus of positive response, and almost every hand, including mine, went up. A group of 136 people had quickly reached consensus on a most difficult issue. The program committee was to be congratulated. It had done something the staff probably could not have done.

Then to my dismay I heard, "Let's not act too rapidly on this. I have some questions." I was really annoyed. I couldn't listen. But then some others spoke up, and I began to hear. They were not objecting to the schedule—they thought it was excellent—but they were questioning the whole idea of *having* a schedule! As John Wood describes that crucial moment: "The intellect, the planner, the schedule-maker, created a schedule—an artifact—which would guarantee that we lived our sixteen days by the *intellect*. . . . The weak voice of intuition was saying collectively, 'This way of doing things, of following a schedule, is not new. It's secure, for sure. But what I would like to do, for a while, *with others in the community,* is to live in a new way, governed by inner feelings and choices. . . .' What was being suggested was 'Let's see if we can all go our own ways *together.* ' The amazing thing, to me, was not so much that these small voices arose, for they are always present, but that they were heard and that *as a group* we responded and acted to test this new way of being in community—by intuition—and we stuck to it."

It was true. The almost complete consensus in favor of the schedule changed to an almost complete consensus for being and coming together in an intuitive way. I had found it very meaningful to act on my intuition in our small group. But what did it mean to act on intuition with 135 other people? The idea was mind-boggling. The meeting broke up with no schedule for the future, not even a time set for the next community meeting. I felt completely adrift. As I walked back to my room I thought about the fact that every time I trust a group to be self-directing I find myself being pushed into frightening new areas of learning. I had thought I knew reasonably well the general directions in which a person-centered workshop would go. But here I was, going along with something far beyond my wildest imagination. It fitted in with my thinking in many ways, but . . . ! I had said, "Man is wiser than his intellect," but it certainly had not occurred to me to put intuition in the driver's seat and relegate intellect to second place in a group of 136 people! I had agreed with John Wood that unless we decrease our emphasis on the intellectual, the scientific, the technological, and give more place to the intuition that allowed so many centuries of "primitive" man, including the American Indian, to live in harmony with his world, we are doomed as a culture. But actually to experience this surrender to intuition was a fearful thing. Would the workshop continue? Would we ever get together again? It was most assuredly an insecure feeling. If this was learning, it was certainly a painful learning.

We *did* come together again. All that I clearly remember is that I had the vague sense, "I think we should be meeting." I had talked to no one about it. When I got to the auditorium at least a hundred people were there, and others kept coming in. Somehow we had done it! Our intuition had not failed us.

It was a good meeting. John Wood meditates on its significance. "The direction taken by this community encourages me to think that it is evidence that perhaps we are beginning to evolve new organs of perception for survival. The undifferentiated silent, intuitive nature of persons is beginning to come to awareness and challenge the control of the intellect. We evidently are becoming willing not only to listen to this inner voice and arrange our individual lives by it but also actually to live in community by it."

After this meeting the workshop moved along constructive lines, following intuition, but using intellect as a planning servant. The small groups continued. There were one or two community meetings, but my memory of them is hazy. Most of the interest groups were exciting places for learning. One person writes, "I spent much time in the interest groups, where I was very impressed by how efficiently they were working. In these and in personal exchanges I learned more about counseling, groups, and psychology than through the last two years of journals and books." All in all the workshop seemed busily in process.

On the ninth day, a large notice appeared on the bulletin board: "Community Meeting Tonight at 7:30." No one seemed to know just who was calling the meeting, but it sounded urgent, and we all gathered. People wanted to know who had called the meeting. The staff? No. Who, then? Finally Mary spoke up to say that the group she belonged to, Group X, had called it, because they were in conflict about some suggested plans for Sunday, the next day. There was a great deal of annoyance that such a meeting had been called without indicating who was calling it. There was even more anger when it was learned that the small group had not itself been unanimous. Gradually the other members of the group spoke up to accept their share of the responsibility for the decision, and to accept the criticism and anger. Finally, Angelina, a member of the group, a shy, sensitive young woman from another country, said, "I was the one who made the sign and put it up." I think no one responded to her statement.

From then on the meeting was a continuous wrangle—about plans, about scheduling, about the options for Sunday, about when to hold the next community meeting. Frustration rose to screaming levels. Three members grabbed a large sheet of paper and some crayons and sat on the floor drawing their feelings of frustration. There was competition for "air time." Someone suggested each speaker summarize the statement of the preceding speaker before making his own statement. Rejected as too "gimmicky." Another suggested that each speaker, when finished, designate the next speaker by choosing one of the up-raised hands. This procedure was followed for a time, until one man abused the privilege when he was chosen by calling on two of his friends to speak before he made use of his own turn to speak. A staff member, Maria, was enraged by his manipulation and blew up at him in an angry outburst. People couldn't agree on *anything.* The group seemed to be falling apart. Wim, who had been skeptical all along about the lack of structure, said vehemently that it was *impossible* to build a community without a leader, a facilitator. He kept looking at me accusingly as he spoke. Others disagreed with this. Several spoke, expressing the theme that *nothing* was happening.

Then Angelina, who had printed the announcement for the meeting, began to weep and moan. She really "freaked out" in an extreme way, beginning to shake and shiver. People hugged her. Natalie came over and held her in her lap, comforting her. Everyone paid complete attention to her for the next half hour —all concerned, some undoubtedly frightened. People put coats and jackets over her to keep her warm. Persons from her own country clustered around, speaking gently to her in her own language and asking questions. Her main response was repeated several times, "I don't know what's going on. I'm frightened of everybody." There was not a sound in the room as we waited for her to express her fears. I tried to respond to some of her fragmentary statements. I remember saying to her, "I can let you have your fear, and own your fear, but for me you are one of us, no matter how you feel. I care for you, no matter what you are feeling." It was a few moments later, as she was calming, that she said, "I feel better, much better." You could feel the sigh of relief in the group.

There followed a discussion of our failure to listen to her, and even more our failure to listen to each other. Someone suggested we meet for a brief community meeting the next morning, and without a word of argument or discussion, consensus was reached. The group was reluctant to break up. We wanted to be together. Finally some started a loud boisterous snake dance—obviously to relieve the tension—and gradually people left.

I have puzzled over Angelina's episode. I suspect that it was due to two factors. Having made and put up the notice for the meeting, she must have felt very vulnerable and guilty in the face of all the attacks. Then, being very sensitive and not especially articulate, she experienced all of the anger and frustration and divisiveness of the meeting in herself, until it became unbearable.

Certainly, without any conscious intent on her part, she became the first person to be listened to with total attention by the whole community. It is probably a natural sequence that it was in the next long community meeting, on the eleventh night of the workshop (described in the beginning of this chapter), that we all began listening to each other. The organism that was the workshop achieved the task it had—without words—set for itself. It became a community.

I can't begin to tell of all that happened except that the group continued to progress, the warmth and liking between members was even more marked, and persons in the small groups went on to make hard, new decisions about actions they were going to take when they returned home.

There was the community meeting where three gay people, two men and a woman who had discovered each other, sat in the middle of the group and said they wanted to make a statement. Each man spoke up, telling of his gay life-style, the problems it had created for him, and the uncertainty he felt as to whether the workshop could accept him. One of them had joined the special-interest men's group, concealing the fact that he was gay. Then that night a horrible nightmare made him realize that he was terrified of "straight" men. He was working on this new insight.

It was with the greatest difficulty that the woman spoke up, with a voice slightly above a whisper, and many tears. She had not revealed her life-style even to her small group, and it took enormous courage for her to tell the workshop. The response to her, and to the men, was very acceptant and supportive. Their statements opened up whole new areas of discussion.

There was the surprising impact of the "silent" group. A sizable number of members got together and decided to spend twenty-four hours without uttering a word, communicating by gestures when communication was necessary. It was an astonishingly powerful experience not only for the participants but for the workshop as a whole.

Then there was what someone called the "mid-life panic" of the group, when people realized there were only a few days left. Some were disappointed in themselves because they had not yet offered or contributed what they wanted to. Others were fearful they were not going to learn some of the things they came to learn. The feeling was, as John Wood says, "That on the day of judgment [the closing day] I would stand lacking in my own eyes, disappointed at lost chances."

Finally there was the unforgettable last morning, when people shared more than ever before what the experience had meant to them. Although the great majority were highly positive, the meeting was open and free enough that those who were disappointed in the lack of structure, and those who were critical of different aspects of what we had done, or angry at our failures, also spoke up. And then there were the tearful farewells of a group which had come to know and care for one another.

The workshop was over.

I should like to give my perspective on the chaotic, frustrating, uneven process by which we became a unity. I suspect many readers must have felt, "What is the sense of this disorderly confusion? No topic gets adequately considered! The waste of time is *enormous!* Why, in God's name, doesn't someone take *charge* and organize the thing so that the participants can at *least* learn *something!?!*" I can assure you there were times when every one of us shared just such feelings, and some like Wim, from Holland, shared them almost to the end. But

I would like to point to several elements which for me are fascinating to contemplate.

This group of 136 people was entirely responsible for itself.

They could at any time have *asked* someone, or some group, to take charge. They did not.

They could, at any time, have decided to do away with community meetings and get together as a whole simply for necessary announcements. They did not.

They could have elected a chairman pro tem and settled issues on a parliamentary basis. They did not.

In some unformulated, intuitive manner they *chose* to struggle together until they developed a process of being together that was satisfying—not always harmonious, but a way that met the collective need.

Certainly this end result was in no way brought about by intellectual means or insights. It was accomplished by gut-level learnings, a "feeling in our bones," a nonverbal sensing of the direction we wished to go. And what were these learnings? It seems to me they were both personal and social, and that in their significance they went far beyond any learning that could have been arranged *for* the group. As one member of the group put it:

"Community meeting . . . a place where I realize my own power. It's up to me. I feel like whatever I need in the group, from the group, it is there for me . . . and I have time to figure out what it is I need or want. There is always room for me. It is a boundary-expanding time. And *ergo,* there is always room for you. Someone else hasn't planned the agenda. No one is going to tell me what to do. It puts me in touch with my power. I take this with me wherever I am. I am—ME."

The social learning is suggested by a participant whose letter I quote. For her, it was an earthshaking learning. "The fact that it was *possible* to establish, at least for a limited time, the type of community we grew into has shattered my whole view of social alternatives and has given me anew a cause to believe in and work for." I tried to state my own experience of discovery in the memo I wrote after the meeting on the eleventh night. "I watch with awe the birth pangs of something new in the world. And my earlier conviction returns. If we can find even one partial truth about the process by which 136 people can live together without destroying one another, can live together with a caring concern for the full development of each person, can live together in the richness of diversity instead of the sterility of conformity, then we may have found a truth with many, many implications."

Let me summarize the politics of the situation in a slightly different way. In a group where control is shared by all, where, by means of a preceding facilitative climate (in the small groups), every person is empowered, a new type of community becomes possible, an organic kind of flow with individuals living together in an ecologically related fashion. Here every individual leads; no one leads. The locus of choice resides in each person, and intuitively the community choice becomes a consensus taking each of these individual choices into account. Power and leadership and control flow easily from one person to another as the differing needs arise. The only analogies which come to mind are from nature. The sap rises or falls in the tree when conditions make one direction or the other appropriate. The bud opens when it is ready—not in an effort to beat competition. The cactus shrinks in the drought and glare, swells to bursting after the rain—in each case the action serving its own survival. And one final analogy which to me fits so many of the persons in our group (in all groups?). The seeds of many plants can lie dormant for years. But when *conditions* are right, they sprout and grow and come into full bloom. For me, that helps to describe our process of community.

Earlier, I told of what happened to Ben, of some risks I had taken, of Michele and her "pull-push" conflict about men. For those who ask, "What happened next?" I add these brief notes.

Ben, the elderly psychiatrist, maintained his new intention of becoming a feelingful person in the group. He told me he no longer needed the answers to his intellectual questions about theories of therapy—he was finding the answers in his own experience. He related to the members of the group in a way astonishingly different from his first impassive manner. He was of great value to the workshop in convening and giving facilitative leadership to the interest group centered around the task of organizing mental health centers staffed by lay paraprofessionals.

As for me, I continued to be a participant in the group in the same fashion as the others—namely, being facilitative to others when that met my need, and exploring my problems in the group when those were uppermost for me.

The most striking example of the latter is one I find myself hesitating to describe. I have mentioned several times the meeting on the eleventh evening of the workshop, and have given the notes I wrote that night. I went to bed elated, feeling very excited and pleased at the way the workshop was going, and about the new spaces into which I was being drawn.

I woke up in the morning quite depressed. It seemed so unreasonable and ridiculous—just when everything was going swimmingly. I took a long walk before breakfast, trying to sort out my feelings. There seemed no doubt about it—I was feeling sorry for myself! How absurd could I get? But I couldn't shake the feeling, and when we met after breakfast it was so urgent for me that I had to share it with the group. As they helped me explore it, two of them with their arms around me, it gradually became clear to me.

I cannot deny that I have had a definitely significant part in initiating the trend toward a person-centered approach to many facets of living. Many, many people are moving in this direction. That is satisfying, of course, but it also constitutes a great burden of responsibility. How do *I* know that this direction is sound? Every movement and trend in history has its unseen flaws and contradictions which tend to bring about its downfall. What are the flaws that I am too stupid to see? To what degree am I *misleading* people through my ideas and my writings? There is absolutely no one to say, and I was feeling the burden of being out in front. Writing this later, I also see the reason why the down feelings hit me at just this time. The whole process of the community, as exemplified in the meeting the night before, was pushing me into unknown areas. I had helped to start a trend that now had a life of its own and was taking me I knew not where. We were "getting better at whatever the hell we're doing." I explored this burdened feeling tearfully with the group—I weep easily—felt guilty at taking so much of their time (just like every other participant) and was temporarily relieved. It was only later in the day that I realized the burden had completely dropped away, and I again had the courage to move with the flow.

As for Michele, I will try to approximate her own words, in a group meeting in the later part of the workshop, as she told of an incident that for me illustrates her own progress. "I've learned so much! I've learned I don't have to try to please men. I can rely on my own feelings. I had a date last night with a man [not a member of the workshop]. I was reluctant to go. I thought we didn't have much in common. On the way to his apartment we stopped at the supermarket to buy things to barbecue. He bought a steak for seven dollars. I thought, 'Buying that seven-dollar steak is not going to get me into your bed!' We got to his place. The talk was superficial. Each time I tried to respond in terms of my own feelings. For instance, he said, 'Don't you want to help me in the kitchen?' and I said, 'No, I'm enjoying listening to this music and reading poetry.' There was more surface talk, and finally he said, 'What is this encountering, anyway?' So I tried to tell him—seriously. We began really to talk. I let him know early on that I was not going to end up in his bed. We had a better and better conversation. We found we had a great deal in common, and I had a fine time. Then I stayed the night in his apartment." [Aha! goes my suspicious mind. So much for intentions! But I was wrong. She *had* slept in his apartment, but she had not slept *with* him.]

She continued: "So often I've spent the whole time on a date being superficial and worrying all the time about how the evening would end. Now I realize I can act from my own feelings. I can enjoy the experience for itself, and rely on what I feel. It felt so *good* to be my own person."

There is nothing that I can add. Michele has empowered herself.

The workshop is only a few months behind us, but already I and other participants and members of the staff have received many letters indicating the impact it has had. Without any claim to completeness, or any attempt at an objective finding, I shall simply quote from a few of these letters. I will first give the most strongly negative reaction I have received. It interests me that the feeling is not at all consistently negative.

"As I look back on the workshop, I have mixed negative and positive feelings, but mostly I feel that it was a very valuable experience." [He quotes from his journal, written at the time, regarding the next-to-the-last community meeting.] "I felt sad that we were already saying good-bye with one half-day still left. I felt angry because I had some negative feelings, mainly disappointment, and was afraid to express it among all the sweetness. I finally said, 'I would like to acknowledge that I feel some negative feelings as well as some positive.' Carl said, 'I would like to hear them and I think the group would.' I said, 'I too often take the naysayer role.' Suzanne said, 'I appreciate your naysayer role.' So finally I said, 'Mainly I wanted more of an ongoing group or organization. I don't feel a part of the community, or rather I feel part of one *now* but didn't this morning, did last night, but not yesterday. I am up and down, in and out.' "

One person tries to express the pervasiveness of the impact.

"I've told you nothing of what has *actually* happened—it's everything, everything I do, everything I say. . . . A good friend tells me I've become quietly but strongly assertive. I feel that all over in my life, but especially at work. I can't believe some of what I said in staff yesterday! I am so in touch with my power, though saying that and seeing it on paper still seems scary—not scary enough to deter me, though."

A mother gives some very positive reactions, ending with this series of statements.

"Somehow a support group right now is less urgent than I expected, because there is so much more of me!" [Tells of new steps she has taken toward getting a graduate degree, which had seemed almost impossible previously.] "I wanted to mention my children to you. I had a long talk with them about the next few months and how hard it might be for all of us. They are so understanding! We are making time to be together over breakfast in the morning, and to meditate together, before their school and my work. Somehow the quality of our relationship is better now than it has ever been. Such unexpected happenings are happening to me!"

Denny, the social crusader, she who said, "I need your bodies to block the roads," wrote me a most moving letter more than two months after the workshop. She tells of the enormous frustration she felt at first. "HARDLY ANYONE WAS SAYING ANYTHING ABOUT SOCIAL CHANGE! I felt alien, lost, unconnected. Compared to the warmth and sensitivity around me, I felt unloving, insensitive, and inadequate. Feelings of political and social concern, mine and others', came to be regularly rejected by the group. I felt hurt and buried the hurt. . . ."

She almost left the community meetings. "I felt increasingly dead and distant at community meetings. Finally I despaired of belonging. I considered giving up the community to devote myself entirely to interest groups, especially the political group. Then I realized that I cared about belonging. In listening to the community I had made, unawares, a deep commitment to process—to staying with what is happening."

Then in the meeting on the eleventh night, as she heard person after person expressing social concerns and being put down, her anger rose to the boiling point and finally, "My anger exploded. They had each been speaking of my concerns. As they had not been heard, so I had not been heard, and I had now to take care of my own feelings. If I did not share my anger, I risked not becoming a member of the community for the rest of the workshop; I would leave behind part of my life unlived, a very sad thing to think about.

"Hearing the ugly sound of my anger, I felt: 'This is it—I'm going to die.' The dreaded thing was happening—I was being revealed. But I did not die. I survived the humiliating shame of my unlovely nakedness, and from that time on felt a member of the community. Had I been fully aware of the hurt and vulnerability behind the anger, I hope I would have tried to communicate that too, instead of concealing it with words about other things."

She tells how, after she returned home, she was involved in three very significant political confrontations. Perhaps the most important was at a public county school-board meeting around the issue of racial integration. "Listening and hearing were not going on at this meeting! I tried unsuccessfully and inappropriately to bring it about. Outwardly, before eight hundred people, I was frustrated, helpless and 'un-together.' Inwardly, I was shaky but absolutely centered on the importance of what I was trying to do. I felt the strength of all 135 people of the workshop backing me up there in that huge room and felt the wonderful release of myself into the larger Other. All the attention focused on my face, my clothes, my body; my communication failure was of no consequence. I felt only slight personal embarrassment. What was happening was so much greater than any of that. I was not diminished. I felt, more fully than ever before, my strength and confidence in my organism. I was told later that my action had had a positive effect on the board's leading, in part, to support of the merger proposal.

"For me, for a while, the conflict I felt at the workshop between political concerns and personal concerns is resolved. The greater knowing of myself that I experience, the more politically effective I will be. It will just come. I 'know' it." For me, her letter is extremely meaningful. It confirms me in my conviction that *lasting* revolutions are brought about not by propaganda or massed demonstrations but by changed people. Denny is a changed person, and hence more—not less—socially effective as a revolutionary.

But for me there is one letter, from a member of our small group, a professional woman in a Latin American country, that seems to encompass beautifully all that I have heard from participants.

During the last session of the workshop three of the research-oriented individuals were making a plea to the participants to be sure to turn in the questionnaires the research group had devised and distributed. Someone asked if the questionnaires were important. A woman said, "The study is important to me because I'm not sure whether this workshop is *really* significant and people have *really* changed, or whether this is just a sophisticated way of spending a vacation." It is this woman who writes the following letter.

August 30, 1975

Carl,

Would you be interested in knowing some of the things happening under the Southern Cross after the workshop?

I had decided to take my time in starting anything new: I've seen them, all those people who return from therapeutic or religious encounters, full of short-lived "touchie-feelie, disgusting" behaviors and sentimental babble about love, peace, and the rest—so I wanted to keep my head. Well, it doesn't seem as if I ever will again; I've already talked to individuals, groups and masses (150 unknown students can be a mass) and, to my extreme surprise, I feel I'm being heard and sometimes even believed. The proposal of a new, unthought-of kind of social

181

form is being perceived as *possible* by tough, scientific minds! I'm rather amazed at my own apparent persuasiveness, as it is indeed not feasible to translate what we lived through into mere words. The only conclusion to be drawn is that people know, at some level, what I'm talking about; it's as if I were only adding to an inner conviction a statement that their beliefs, wishes, or tendencies are in fact not irrational.

Of course, and although such effects are probably very small, I'm scared, which is something nobody knows about but you: am I selling a mirage, misleading starved people by making an unfulfillable promise? The fear is not able to stop me, but leads to an attempt to understate, to voice doubts, and to welcome criticisms against my own too strong faith. It's hard to contain what are like two earthquakes inside me, the community and our group.

The experiences in our Dear Group, and coming so close to you, went so far beyond my most daring previous expectations that they keep echoing inside, like bells that I suddenly hear at the most unexpected moments, and although I'm still not sure of what they will bring to the future, I feel continuous waves taking up every cell of me, transforming me "forever." They come as feelings very pure, without words, as I seem to have forgotten what exactly was said by either you, me, or the others at the most significant moments. What is here, and is incredibly vivid, a thing of now, is what resulted at those moments, how it felt at the instant it was new, the realizing of dumb, obvious things like "I'm free," "I'm a woman," "I don't *have* to be followed by adjectives such as nice, efficient, etc.," "Now I'm angry," "Now I'm soft." Carl, is this the millionth time it's been told? You made me feel you would care to know even so.

September 19

I still want to send this letter because it's so very true in each word almost three weeks later, except I'm surer of it all staying with me. And now, I want to speak very quickly of the second "earthquake" that renewed me in another way. The fact that it was *possible* to establish, at least for a limited time, the type of community we grew into, has shattered my whole view of social alternatives and has given me anew a cause to believe in and work for. There was a former hope, that at a speed of one by one (client or student), some change could be gained for the larger community, but there was also a realization that such limited action had little chance of overcoming present dominant forces and trends. Perhaps we can't do more than light candles in a dark forest, but my own candle seems now much more reliable in showing the way.

In spite of my suspicions regarding overambitious planning, things are happening in every corner—like a weekend community experience on aging I'll hold in October, starting swimming lessons for myself, gathering friends and colleagues every Friday at my home, entering a course on workshops. These are a few concrete innovations but, in a way, no more than natural consequences of how I feel and interact in a qualitatively different manner.

I'm glad you are such an understander, as I could never rely upon words to let you know how very deeply I feel you with me or (will you shudder?) how grateful I am to have you. Although I feel the need here to tell you about myself, I think of you a lot, with love and caring.

In writing this book, it had never occurred to me that I might include a chapter on a workshop. Nor did the thought occur to me while *this* workshop was in progress. But afterward I began to want to write about it—a few pages, I thought. As I got into it I became more and more absorbed, until a lengthy chapter finally wrote itself. For me it has been one of the most rewarding portions of the book, and I wish to explain why.

I realized that of all the ventures in which I have ever been involved, this was the most thoroughly person-centered, from its inception, through its planning, in its initial phases, and in its total process of personal interaction and community building. Consequently it has been, for me, a thoroughgoing test of the value of person-centeredness. It was, in my judgment, successful beyond any reasonable expectation. It was a most important validation of a person-centered way of being.

For one thing it enhanced learning by the whole person—experiential, cognitive, and, now I must add, intuitive learning. It showed the great advantage of a person-centered learning which pushed us beyond what we had ever dreamed of, into areas where we had not expected to go.

I have sometimes thought about what the workshop would have been like if I had been its guru, its leader. Over the years I certainly could have become a guru, with the always ready help of loving admirers. But it is a path I have avoided. When people are too worshipful I remind them of the Zen saying, "If you meet the Buddha, kill the Buddha!" What would have happened if I had accepted the role of the active leader, the authority figure? I could have taken the group to the uttermost limit of my thoughts and feelings—but I could not have taken them beyond those limits. I could have told them—and perhaps partially showed them—how to live in a person-centered way. The results? They would have learned what I know, and the way I am. They would have found in me the answers to some of their questions, and would be ready to turn to me for more answers. Thus there would have been definite limits to their learning, and an encouragement of dependence.

But look at what happened in the person-centered process as it actually occurred. I was less active than ever before in a workshop, content to learn from the process in the large group, and only speaking when I thought I could be facilitative in the small group. So we all became facilitators of learning for each other, taking ourselves into new pathways, learning viscerally, learning intellectually, and in this process learning an independence of thought and being. There was no one to lean on. Each of us became an independent learner.

I like the behavioral outcomes. We didn't learn *a* person-centered way of being. Each person is in process of defining his own way of being himself. The outcome is pluralistic in the very best sense of that word, and yet unified in that each of us is able to say, in a little more confident, a little more sensitive, way, "I am my own person." For one woman this means facing eight hundred people with her convictions on a social issue. For another it means a more open relationship with her children. For one man it means a difficult confrontation with an authoritarian boss. For another it meant initiating a "song fest" on a boring transcontinental plane flight, with passengers and stewardesses actually getting to know one another! For still another it means opening up his life to more love. Another person is trying to change a traditional organization into a community, and then says "and so, in 136 places all over the world this inner power and this trust are at work, spreading out and out, and down, and up to—who knows what limits?" The number 136 is no doubt an exaggeration—not everyone was deeply affected —but the words catch very well the feeling I have. A ferment was started in that group, a yeast, a catalyst, which cannot help but have profound effects in marriages, families, schools, industries, mental health centers, political movements. It has indeed been an exciting, growing experience in which to be involved. Like many of those who have written to me, I treasure it.

Chapter 9 | The power of the powerless

[This chapter is the joint work of Alan Nelson and myself.]

Ordinarily we don't think of children and young people from middle-class families as being an oppressed group. But under certain circumstances they can be exactly that, as this exciting real-life story indicates. Such a group was dictated to and manipulated. Their rights were ignored, their voices unheard. And they were completely powerless—no money, no clout, no part in the *real* decisions. Or were they powerless? The answer that emerges fascinates me.

One thing that, for me, stands out in this account is that freedom is *irreversible*. Once a person—child or adult—has *experienced* responsible freedom, she will continue to strive for it. It may be completely suppressed in behavior by a maximum use of every kind of control including force, but it cannot be eliminated or extinguished.

Another striking element is something I trust is already clear from the preceding chapters. Any person-centered enterprise is, of necessity, extremely threatening to 99 percent of the established institutions in western culture, whether a school, a marriage, or—as in this case—a well-intentioned community center. If you are still in doubt as to the revolutionary character of person-centeredness, perhaps this account will convince you.

I was present when Alan Nelson asked for time to tell this

story. It simply *poured* out of him, as though he had been waiting a long time to present it to a group whose members might understand *fully* what he and the others had been through. I strongly encouraged him to make more public that impassioned account. The printed word can't quite capture the white heat of those moments, but Alan's deep involvement and his equally strong desire to be fair about and understanding of those who in this instance were the "oppressors" come through even on the printed page. I hope you get as much enjoyment out of Alan's account, and as much learning from it, as I have. I will let Alan speak:

I told the following story at an interest group on politics and the client-centered approach at a summer workshop in 1974. At the time we were talking about how the client-centered approach relates to political situations, especially those where there is an imbalance of power—where some persons have and exercise the power to control the lives of others.

My thanks go to Eva Cossack, who taped that meeting and who gave me a copy of her recording from which this material was transcribed. I have rewritten some of what I said then, both to make the story more clear and to insure the anonymity of the community and the other people in the story. But I've tried to leave what Carl called the "urgency and rush of it" as it came out then, so some of the rough edges of story-telling are still intact.

CARL: Alan, the way I feel is that you've given us several things that the client-centered approach is not—in your estimation it's not a strategy or a technique, or that kind of thing. But I feel as though you haven't yet given us your view of what it *is* in the power sphere.

ALAN: Okay. I think it would help if . . . well, I know it was helpful for lots of us when you used a concrete example, so maybe I could.

Could people hang with about a five-minute example? I think it could illustrate some of what I mean by person-centered politics. It will also tell you how I first got involved in trying to understand the way this approach is very immediately political, both in its results and in its process.

OTHERS: Yes, okay.

ALAN: Okay. . . . About four or five years ago, when I was a divinity student considering entering the ministry, I got a summer job directing a day camp in a wealthy suburb of Boston. . . . Let me start by giving you some information about the community—I didn't know all this when I took the job; I learned it during my working and living there.

The community, which I'll call Graceville, is one of the oldest in Massachusetts. A lot of Massachusetts' money is said to be centralized in that community. In fact, it is tied up in one part of the community. Graceville is divided into five political precincts. Most of the wealthy people in the community are in precinct one. The other four precincts are not nearly so wealthy. The disparity is huge—that's the picture I'm trying to give you. But the poor people by this community's standards are not poor by most standards. They are primarily middle-income families.

The community was schizophrenic. The people who had the political power had the least to do with the community itself. Graceville had one of the highest per capita expenditures on garbage collection in Massachusetts—yet the lowest on public education. That was because the rich people sent their kids to private schools.

A number of years ago, in great liberal fashion, the wealthy precinct started the Graceville Community House, and the Community House sponsored the day camp that I was going to direct. I see now that it was a kind of liberal gesture on the part of the community, well motivated and in some ways helpful. The camp was relatively inexpensive, and was used mostly by families in the other four precincts as a place to send their kids during the day for all or part of the summer. There were also a few scholarships for the camp offered to black kids from Roxbury, the ghetto of Boston. There were almost no racial minorities in Graceville.

Control of the Community House resided mostly in the first precinct. Of about fifty members on the board of directors, I think only two were from outside precinct one. And only two were under fifty years of age. All of the people on the executive board of the Community House were from the first precinct. Most precinct-one kids went to another camp nearby—a better-equipped, more expensive, residential camp.

The man who hired me as the day camp director was the executive director of Graceville Community House. I didn't know it at the time, but his hiring me was sort of his parting act. He was too liberal a director for the people in control. He was catching a lot of flak and was leaving for a better job. But he and I talked at length about my directing the day camp, and it was very attractive to me. I was to have full control of the camp, hiring the assistant director and counselors and scheduling activities. We signed my contract in April . . . then he left.

In reaction to him, the board of directors and executive board of the Community House hired a guy who had been eight years in the Air Force directing Air Force day camps as the person to be executive director of the Community House. By the time I met this new director, what he knew was that there was this bearded freak coming from Harvard to direct *his* day camp.

This was the first year I was ensconced in a client-centered approach, and I thought: "All right, I am going to try to do a client-centered day camp." The opportunity to do that, to do what I believed in, was a large part of why I took the job. I looked forward to an exciting summer with a lot of excited kids in camp. I had never done anything quite like this before, but I figured what was most important for me was to really try to hear and understand what others in the camp were concerned with and cared about. I thought most important was my trust-

189

ing others to really be responsive and responsible when given the chance. I trusted that the people would be able to create a good camp. In a way I considered the staff people to be my clients. . . . In some ways I also saw the campers that way.

So I hired an assistant director, Jean, who had worked in the camp for four years . . . a woman who is just really, really fine and knew everyone and was very, very . . . well she was wonderful. We had talked a lot about what was important to us in being with kids and running a camp, and I hired her. Together we interviewed all the applicants for the other staff positions.

The structure of the staff was set and we could not affect it. The staff was divided into two groups, the nonpaid counselors-in-training, aged thirteen to fifteen, and the paid counselors, aged sixteen to twenty-two. The paid group averaged about $35 a week. Most of the people had been on the staff before, and many were turning down better-paying jobs to be a part of the camp because they loved working with kids. Altogether there was a staff of twenty-five, and we anticipated between sixty and one hundred campers each week, ranging in age from six to thirteen.

When Jean and I did the interviews we tried to understand what was important to these people who wanted to be on the staff—to listen and pay attention to them. At a staff meeting later we said: "This is your camp. Nearly all of you have been here before. What shall we do with it? How do you want our camp to be?" We tried to convey to them that we trusted them, we would try to understand them, and we cared about what they wanted.

At first they were a little disbelieving. But gradually we were all just brainstorming about what we wanted to do with the camp, what we wanted it to be. Everyone was talking about what they didn't like about past camps, how they wanted to run this one. It was very, very exciting. The energy was really getting up; people were being creative and responsive to each other.

We decided together that the camp would be more cooperative than competitive. In the past there had been awards each Friday which hardly anyone on the staff liked—a lot of feelings were hurt and the whole spirit of competition seemed to pervade the camp, even to the point where counselors and assistants could hardly get along because they were competing. Separate meetings were often held in the past with the paid counselors at one and the volunteer assistants at another.

When the newly hired executive director for the Community House came from the Air Force, Jean and I went to have our first meeting with him. It was a disaster!

He—call him Kenneth Barnes—came on hostile and aggressive. I guess he was bothered to find *his* day camp being directed by a wild young student from Harvard who, with an assistant director, had already hired the staff. He told us our previous contracts were invalid and that we had to renegotiate our contracts with him, since he was now the director of the Community House. He wanted us to be his assistants and to serve his wishes and commands in running the camp the way he wanted it run—obviously quite differently from the way Jean and I envisioned it. Fortunately for us, it was also quite different from the work for which we had been contracted.

After about an hour, in which hardly a friendly word passed between us, our meeting ended when we said we would not renegotiate our contracts and considered them valid. Jean and I almost pleaded for a more friendly, less authoritarian relationship, and then we left. Outside, we considered resigning, but decided to do the camp as best we could in the face of our obvious difficulties with Mr. Barnes. It was too late to find other jobs, we were really excited about the camp, and we felt some obligation to the staff we had hired.

By the time camp started we, as a staff, were excited about our summer together. Camp began really well. Everyone involved was pleased, from all indications. Enrollment and attendance were higher than ever, parents of both campers and staff expressed pleasant surprise over how well the camp was going and how excited the kids were with it. Perhaps most important, the campers and staff people themselves were happy. Jean and I were pleased. Everyone was working hard and it was great.

The camp felt like an open and free place to be. People were responsive and open with each other. I think partly because Jean and I were and responsive to the folks on the staff, they were more interested in the kids they worked with, and more enthusiastic than anyone could remember. The staff had some freedom to choose and be responsible for what they were doing, and they were being very creative together. It was, all in all, very wonderful.

And the campers—I wish I could show you the campers. They were really fine! Those kids were being so alive and honest. I mean I got tired and cranky sometimes—we all did. But we were really cooperating with each other in being together, having fun and getting to know each other and ourselves.

Meanwhile, problems were getting worse with me and Mr. Barnes (as he preferred to be called, rather than by his first name). From his perspective, the camp was a problem. He kept telling me there was no discipline—which for him meant people standing in straight lines, for a long time. The staff had decided they did not want the whole camp standing in lines saying the pledge of allegiance each morning as the flag rolled up the flagpole. It was boring; it was a hoax. So we didn't do that. We also didn't do it because the way Mr. Barnes had scheduled the camp's use of the swimming pool, one group would hardly get to use the pool at all. The compromise solution to the flag problem was that each morning camp counselors would raise it . . . each evening someone from the camp would take it back down, fold it, and return it to the main office.

There were other changes too. The kids chose more than before what they wanted to do, such as more field trips. Because of the campers and staff involved, we made consensual or compromise decisions; nothing was ramrodded. The major decisions, within the limit established by the budget and the set structure, were made by those most directly affected by them.

That was what was most important to us—how decisions were made and how we related with each other.

Mr. Barnes kept insisting that I take control of things, or else he would. And he did where he could. He set up a bureaucracy of three people so that it took ten days to get chocolate milk for the kids who wanted it—even though milk was delivered daily. The milkman kept saying: "We have lots of chocolate milk, but I can't leave it until I get the order from the people upstairs." Mr. Barnes also changed every lock in the house and kept the only keys. Jean and I couldn't even have a key to the soda room because he thought we would steal some of the soda —someone said he told them this. Every day we had to go to him and get the key to put the day's ration of soda in the cooler for the campers. When he couldn't be found—which was fairly often—the soda was served warm. He even had a lock put on the cabinet that held the instant coffee, and he had the only key to that!

I explained to him that we were trying to develop self-control in the camp. The importance of discipline wasn't being over-looked, but the focus was on *self*-discipline, rather than on a system imposed from above to below.

This didn't impress Mr. Barnes at all, and as camp proceeded, our relations were increasingly strained. As the camp's administrators, Jean and I tried to see that the camp's facilities were used maximally and without schedule conflicts. We also arranged field trips and bought supplies. When we were lucky, we were with the kids, just getting to know them and playing. But we had to spend too much time being buffers between Mr. Barnes and the camp. He would make an occasional appearance to tell us what we were doing wrong—that was the extent of his relating to staff and campers alike. He never commented on what we were doing right. His idea of being educational was to ask people if they knew the right names for things, like: "What do you call the feathers on an arrow?" We found it important to protect the camp from him as much as we could.

I admit that I was poor at empathizing with a man who had

193

come from eight years in the service, and in some ways, early on, I started seeing him as an enemy. And I was pretty stupid. I didn't get to know anybody on the executive board. In retrospect that was poor strategy, and I fault myself on that. But I didn't sense the desperation of this man.

Anyway, from all our feedback, camp was successful. On the first overnight—every other week we had an overnight, in which campers could stay over from Thursday to Friday—we had more than 80 percent of the campers there. In the past, attendance had been about 30 percent.

By the third week, our very success was threatening to Mr. Barnes. He had never seen a camp like this—so open and warm —where people hugged, cried, and talked about what they wanted. That everyone seemed happy with it made it worse for him.

We had another overnight that week which was again very good and attended by nearly the whole camp. But Mr. Barnes came around, yelled at a couple of kids, locked a bunch of doors to which he had the only keys, and left, saying he'd be back later to see how we were doing. Well, he locked us out of the room containing the telephone, so we couldn't even talk to parents who called to see how their kids were doing. And he didn't come back until the next day!

The next afternoon [Friday], Barnes and I had a blowup over some orange peels he'd found under a table. In his frustration over larger issues he'd seized on this tiny infraction. The camp at the time was almost immaculate—since we had all just done a big cleanup—except for those orange peels. I confess I was more concerned about the campers and their parents. After overnights there were always lost clothes to be found, questions to be answered, and parents to be reassured.

Mr. Barnes informed me that he and I would meet on Monday with Mr. Smith, the treasurer of the executive board, to discuss the conflict. I was a little nervous, since I had never talked to Mr. Smith before. But I also looked forward to the meeting as a chance to explain what was going on, to talk about all the difficulties Mr. Barnes was causing for us and for the Community House generally. I spent much of the weekend preparing incident notes on what had happened, so I would have the facts straight when we talked.

I walked into Mr. Barnes' upstairs office on Monday morning of the fourth week of camp and found Mr. Smith there along with Mr. Barnes and some other people I didn't recognize. I was told that *everyone* was not there yet and that they would come and get me when everyone was there and they were ready for me.

"What!" I thought. "This was supposed to be a meeting between three people!" But I went back downstairs to camp, and when everyone was there, they came and got me. I walked into a room full of about eight people.

This, I learned, was most of the executive board of the Community House. The executive director of the board was a sixty-six-year-old woman who could hardly walk, who was a nice person, and who had, in her way, given a lot of her life to doing things for the community—but in a kind of blind liberal way, which was absolutely unresponsive. She knew what people should have and what should be done and nobody should rock her boat and nobody should challenge her because she was an awfully nice lady. And she was. She really was.

When Mr. Barnes was introducing me to the rest of the executive board, he was letting me know how much these people cared about kids legitimately, by telling me who taught Sunday school, how many years, and so on. And I really do not want to leave the impression that these were awful people because they were not. They were concerned about the kids in the camp and they were very concerned about their Community House. They thought I was destroying both.

I learned later that by this time there were some fantastic rumors going around about me: I was a homosexual and was assaulting the men on the staff; I was seducing the women and was caught making love with one of them in the sandbox; I was part of a Communist conspiracy, trained in a camp in Canada to take over this community, starting with the kids—that last one came directly from Mr. Barnes, according to three people. I was seen sort of like a conspiratorial Pied Piper.

They fired me. I walked into this meeting and, after the introductions, I was read my termination notice. I was *blown away*. They said they would give me the money for the rest of the summer, but they wanted me out, gone.

And they didn't want to talk with me about anything. None of them had talked to me before; none of them had ever talked to anyone having anything to do with the camp—campers, staffers, Jean, or, so far as I ever learned, anyone's parents—but they had heard enough.

I was fired at 9:30 in the morning that Monday. It was the biggest morning of the camp, first morning of the week with the largest registration—over a hundred kids. I hung around for about half an hour, gathering some of my stuff together, mentioning to a couple of counselors that I'd been fired, and then I went home. Jean had been called into a meeting with the same people, so I couldn't talk to her. I went home, just hurt and bewildered. I had no idea what to do.

Later I found out that they offered Jean the camp director's title, but she was to take orders from Mr. Barnes. She refused, saying she wanted me rehired.

By 10:30 it was raining and all one hundred campers and twenty-five staff people had to be crowded into the camp's indoor facilities, which were pretty bad—the Community House basement and a small gymnasium. I was home just really, really hurt. My response to being fired was: "I've never been treated so by a community of *adults.*" They had never even spoken with me. I almost couldn't believe this was happening.

By 11:30 that morning the entire camp was on strike, and the Community House was being picketed with signs made in arts and crafts. All but one person on the staff signed a petition saying they wouldn't go back to work until I was rehired.

None of these staff people had ever been involved with anything like this in their lives. They had never been on strike for anything before. And I had nothing to do with the strike. I didn't even know it was happening. Nobody told these people what to do. They knew what they wanted. They had lived in this environment for three weeks—the staff people for some time longer—where they were trusted and dealt with as people, and they were not going to be told what to do by officials who didn't even know what was going on.

What most impressed me was that it wasn't me they were striking for . . . *it was themselves.* In some ways there was maybe charisma or something, or perhaps a style that I possessed that they liked. But I really believe, in my heart of hearts, that most fundamentally it was themselves they were not going to give up. They weren't going to submit to another kind of process for the camp—another way of being, really—once they had experienced an alternative. They had experienced it and that is where they were standing. And I was so proud of them it was incredible. I cried about three times that day. How proud I was of those kids, how much I cared for them. I was amazed, I was just amazed.

Anyway . . . I'm going to try and shorten this story. . . . [Many voices from the group: "Don't shorten it!"]

Okay. . . . By one that afternoon the director was calling to tell me to come down to the Community House. I didn't get the call because I was already on my way. I'd been at home thinking, bewildered, not hearing anything from anyone at camp. I didn't know what to do, and I was afraid that the staff was being talked into compromising away what camp meant to us to get me back.

When I got there the oldest campers were walking around the Community House in the rain carrying signs saying, "We want Al." People ran out to meet me, and I just stood there amazed. I had tears rolling down my cheeks. What a day this was! Absolutely wonderful.

Someone told me that Mr. Barnes had been calling me; he wanted to talk to me. First I went to the gym and the house basement to be with everyone again—that was a joyous reunion —and then I went upstairs to see Mr. Barnes.

He was just in a rage! He blew up at me, saying: "Get this camp back in order." I said, "I can't do anything. I'm fired. I don't work here anymore." And he said, "Okay, you're rehired."

I went downstairs, and the camp re-formed itself into its regular groups very quickly. We were all very happy. Then I went back upstairs and had a two-hour conference with Mr. Barnes. One thing I haven't mentioned yet is that Mr. Barnes still lived with his mother. While we were talking in his office that afternoon she burst through his office door. She was red in the face and screaming at me: "What you need is your bare bottom paddled!" And she yelled about how difficult I was making life for her and her wonderful son, Kenneth, who loved kids so much. I never saw him so embarrassed. He kept saying, "Mother . . . Mother! . . . MOTHER . . . I'll take care of this."

After the campers went home, he and Jean and I and the rest of the staff had a conference. I think Mr. Smith was there too. I was rehired, and the camp would go on as usual. Mr. Barnes and Jean and I decided to meet for an hour every day to keep things straight and clear between us. Mr. Barnes then explained his position to the staff. Unfortunately he lied about events that the staff had been part of, so they knew he was lying. At that time I saw him as stupid, incompetent, and bumbling, rather than as really in trouble and pretty desperate.

After that, camp was better than ever. We had a lot of energy from all that had happened and we felt closer than ever. But the better things went in camp the worse they got with Mr. Barnes. Now, of course, the whole camp knew of our trouble and I think that made it worse for him. He only showed up for one of the scheduled meetings with Jean and me, and in a midweek burst he yelled, "Things are never going to get better between you and me."

During that week I also wrote a letter to the people on the executive board, sharing my wish to be with the camp and the kids for the rest of the summer, saying I hoped we could put the bad feelings of Monday behind us, and offering to talk with any of them if they wanted to. I saw a couple of board members that week and told them directly I would talk to them if they thought that might be helpful. Nothing doing!⁻

The staff had planned a retreat. It was a five-day camp and we were going to spend the weekend at the cabin of the parents of two of the staff people. That, during the course of the fourth week, got incredibly fouled up. Parents of the staff people would call to talk with Jean or me about the weekend, and the upstairs people—Ken Barnes and the assistant director of the Community House—would take the call, saying we were unavailable. We weren't allowed our own phone, and we never even knew these parents had called; nor did we get messages.

They would intercept the calls upstairs and say to the parents, "This is a terrible thing. We don't stand behind it. The camp doesn't have anything to do with it. There is not going to be any adult supervision." Neither Jean nor I were married, so we weren't going to be adult supervisors. I guess they pictured an orgy.

Well, we went, about half of us, after I spent an entire afternoon at home, where I could use the phone, calling parents of staffers and straightening things out. During that week staff persons would go home and their parents would land on them, saying: "You lied to me about this whole thing." Because the parents had talked to the people in the front office. And I would have to call the parents to get the kids out of hot water. "Your kids didn't lie to you," I'd say. "I can't explain to you what is going on, but this is a retreat for the people on the staff who can and want to come, and I am going up there, and Jean is going up there." Fortunately, most of the staff persons' parents had met Jean and me and knew who we were. We were persons to them, and I had some reality besides being the Pied Piper or I don't know what.

Anyway, we went on that weekend, had a wonderful time, and came back for the fifth week of camp. We were looking forward to the last half of our summer together. Monday morning I overslept a bit, rather than getting to camp early as I usually did. While I was rushing to get there I received a phone call from one of the staffers. She said: "Al, you've got to get down here right away! There is a whole new staff here! They're telling us we can't go near the kids and they're herding all of them into the tennis courts with the new staff."

The executive board had met secretly with Mr. Barnes on Tuesday of the fourth week of camp—the day after I was fired the first time—and decided to hire an entirely new staff. When I got to camp I found our staff already there and beside themselves. They were confused and shocked, angry, sad, and afraid. They weren't allowed near the campers, some of whom were crying for them. It was a mess.

Twenty-five staff people were blown away. The campers were blown away. I was blown away.

The executive board called me into a private meeting again and said I was fired and would be arrested if I ever set foot on the property again and to get the hell out of there. I said I would not leave until I knew what was going on with the campers and the staff people. So we had a meeting with Mr. Smith, the treasurer of the executive board, Mr. Barnes, and our staff. Smith and Barnes said: "You all signed this petition saying that you would not work until Alan was rehired. You've resigned and we are just now accepting your resignations."

It was like these kids had no rights! Like they weren't persons worth respecting at all! I pointed out that before the whole staff they had said they'd rehired me. And they said just blatantly, "Well, we lied about that to protect the campers."

I informed them that I was going to sue them for fraudulent contract negotiations. That blew *them* away. They said: "This is the end of this meeting. We are going to talk to our attorney." Not to see what they were going to do; they had to talk to their attorney to figure out what they had done. They told the staff to come back Tuesday to find out what was decided about them.

I couldn't believe these people. They were firing twenty-five kids because they were so uptight about an open, person-centered camp. This *is* a radical idea, and when people see it, it scares the hell out of them.

CARL: I will summarize the final part of Alan's story, following which, he gives some of his learnings.

The "fired" staff decided to meet frequently.

The new director couldn't handle the camp, and she and the whole new staff resigned after one week.

That day the whole situation burst wide open in the local newspapers, with articles and letters on both sides.

Mr. Smith came once, and parents of staff members came often, to the meetings of the "fired staff." He and they began to *hear* the person-centered philosophy that was being implemented. They also saw that Alan "was a human being and that these staff people were not being pulled around by my seductive strings."

When a meeting was called by Mr. Smith, Mr. Barnes failed to show up. There were many indications that he was a thoroughly frightened, insecure person. Mr. Smith—after some dramatic moments of uncertainty—took the responsibility for rehiring Alan and the original staff and reopening camp. All of the preregistered children (and more) showed up and they had a good last two weeks.

ALAN: I think very real changes took place in a lot of people —changes that are subtle and irreversible. People—perhaps especially on the staff—realized, "Oh, this is how I want to live my life." "This is how I am." "This is how I want to relate to others." "I have something to say about my life."

I think a lot of us learned some things that will stay with us. I sure did. And the people I worked with on the staff and in the camp were just amazing to me. I think they amazed a lot of people—including themselves—with what they could do when they were given a chance.

In telling this story I've described the most dramatic events

—those easiest to talk about. What is most important, however, then as well as now as I look back on that very full summer, is harder to talk about. Yet the hard to talk about things are what gave meaning to the events, and I think they are what allowed the spontaneity, courage, and integrity of the people on the staff to emerge.

What is difficult to describe are our feelings for each other, the sense we shared that what we were doing was important to us, and we were doing it fully. It is hard to talk about our caring for each other and the way we cared about the kids in camp. We were relating to each other as whole people, trusting each other, and sharing the energy of our lives in meaningful, honest ways. In the milieu of trust and openness we created, I think we all discovered more capacities in ourselves and in each other than we had thought possible.

Our way of being together turned out to be pretty threatening and, I think, well it should! I see more clearly now the political implications of person-centeredness. It is a far cry from the practiced politics of most institutions and communities, even those so close to the historic origins of our democracy as Graceville, Massachusetts. Yet the spirit of self-determination, freedom, and growth (like life, liberty, and the pursuit of happiness) lives on in people like a fire waiting to be kindled with a spark of trust, understanding, compassion, or awareness.

I think the ideals of democracy are still pretty revolutionary. To me, a person-centered approach is the embodiment of these ideals in the immediacy of human relationships. It cannot be reduced to a strategy or a technique. It is an attitude embodying a respect for the integrity and worth of persons; it is a way of seeing and relating to the world and others. It is a way of being either lived in the present or denied, for person-centered politics is as immediate as people and relationships. A person-centered approach provides a perspective from which it can be clearly seen that democratic traditions and values are neither preserved nor fostered by authoritarian systems.

CARL: This has been a story of what can be seen as a relatively insignificant "tempest in a day camp," but which can also be seen as a microscopic example of arbitrary and impersonal power versus a group of powerless individuals who have tasted the heady experience of responsible freedom.

By a chance incident (the departure of the previous director and his replacement by Mr. Barnes) this experience of the day camp was turned into a clearcut and classic social experiment. A person-centered enterprise was introduced, full blown, into a conventionally organized enterprise. The person-centered approach being revolutionary in the extreme, the two systems absolutely could not coexist, and the quiet (or not so quiet) revolution was inevitable.

There are two contrasting ways of utilizing power. In his dealings with the staff and the children, Alan trusted them, had no desire to control or manipulate them, shared responsibility completely. His primary question was, "How do you want *our* camp to be?" He was met with initial disbelief and distrust. These attitudes rapidly changed to mutual trust, openness, sharing, excitement, creative and self-responsible actions. Cooperation replaced competition. Self-discipline took the place of external discipline. Each person—camper or staff—experienced and freely utilized his own power.

Then comes the authoritative mode of power. Up to the point where Alan was called in to the board meeting and summarily dismissed, there was no "oppression" of anyone, in spite of the emerging realization of enormous differences in "political" beliefs. But the firing represents the exercise of arbitrary impersonal power, with no attempt to investigate, to uncover the facts —simply a surgical operation to eliminate a disturbing presence.

Alan tells of the smarting hurt, the feeling of being "blown away," exterminated, by the injustice of the action. It gives us a tiny view of the destruction of self that has been felt by hundreds of thousands of persons who have been the object of the crushing force of impersonal, arbitrary, blind power. The fact that in this instance—and probably many others—the power was wielded by outstandingly well intentioned people, makes it all the more striking. The politics of power and control can be devastating, even when exercised by those who are only trying to protect and care for the young.

The reaction of the adolescent staff and the still younger campers to the first firing and to the succeeding and escalating events deserves close attention. The reaction to arbitrary authority by persons who have experienced the excitement and responsibility of freedom is entirely predictable, though always astonishing. Leadership, creativity, imagination spring up everywhere as individuals resist this encroachment on their rights as persons. This is true even though in this case they had experienced responsible freedom for only a few weeks, and probably had never experienced anything quite like it before in home, school, or community. The energy that is released seems boundless.

It should be clearly recognized that without Mr. Smith, or even with him, the story could have had a very different ending. Here the outcome is supportive of the persons who wanted to be responsible for their own actions, but it could easily have turned out in a completely different way. As has been stressed before, to be person-centered in your behavior, in any system, involves *risk*.

But the major lesson I glean from all this is that the *powerless have power*. Though things might have turned out badly for Alan, the staff, and the campers, they found and used a power they did not know they had. After the firing of Alan, they learned that even in a situation in which officially they had no voice, no control, no authority, by acting on what they believed in and by accepting and demanding the recognition of themselves as responsible free persons, they were able to have a major impact. They were able to affect the circumstances of their own lives and the lives of others. This is a clue to the politics of the powerless.

Chapter 10 | Without jealousy?

Fred and Trish endeavored to make their marriage a relationship in which primary value is placed on each of them as persons. They have tried to share in decision-making, the desires of each having equal weight. Each seems to have avoided, to an unusual degree, any need to possess or control the other. They have developed a partnership in which their lives are both separate *and* together. They have each developed relationships outside of marriage, and these intimate interactions have often been sexual in nature. They have communicated openly about these relationships and appear to have accepted them as a natural and rewarding part of their individual lives and of their marriage. They like their life-style. Theirs is a marriage both person-centered and far from conventional.

In spite of their openness with each other, communication failed them at a crucial point, and a trauma occurred, which had no obvious connection with their outside relationships. The marriage still continues to be a close one, and still involves outside lovers. This serious flaw, in their lives and in their communication, makes their history even more provocative.

When a partnership is based on growing, evolving choice, when its interpersonal politics is free of a desire to control, it develops in a unique, idiosyncratic way. It shows that when two people are openly and freely endeavoring to be themselves, highly individual patterns emerge. It is not a model, it cannot be copied, but provides much food for thought.

Despite their extramarital relationships, there was very little jealousy. The fact that the green-eyed monster is missing highlights the whole issue of jealousy more sharply than if he were present.

In the autumn of 1973 I received a long letter from a young husband, a graduate student in a Bay Area university, telling of the unusual marriage in which he and his wife were involved. Although it was highly articulate, it was written entirely by him and I wished I knew the wife's reactions. Frankly, the account seemed to me too good to be true.

Three years later I was fortunate in obtaining further information from them and visited them in their community for an interview of several hours.

In appearance, dress, and manner Fred and Trish are not markedly different from other couples their age. They are attractive, the husband somewhat slender, his wife more on the plump side. They dress informally and are quiet in their speech and respectful of each other in conversation. They seem devoted to each other. They do not in any way stand out as "different."

They are a couple with broad, rich interests outside their relationship, and these outside interests are decidedly separate, with only a partial overlap. Trish enjoys outdoors activities; Fred's interests are more aesthetic, and he hopes to devote more time to them as soon as he gets his coveted doctorate. In short they are creative, multifaceted individuals. Here is Fred's first letter:

FRED: I am writing in response to your book *Becoming Partners.* We felt you were too pessimistic about a person's ability to overcome possessiveness and jealousy. Our own experience proves that jealousy is not inherent. We hope that writing this letter will help us—that the process of our having to articulate how we see our relationship will better define our feelings toward it. We hope it will also help you in your study.

I am twenty-five years old and Trish is twenty-four. We've been married three years. We graduated from college and have lived here six years. I'm in my third year of graduate study in [a technical field] and hope to teach upon completion of my Ph.D. Trish is a registered nurse and works in the local hospital.

When we were first married we both felt that our marriage was ideal. At that time we still viewed marriage as a "state" rather than a "process." We both felt some misgivings, however, over what appeared to be the inviolable social law that marital happiness would decline with the passage of time. This feeling was the natural result of the increasing frustration in marriage which was all around us. However, our relationship did seem different from others in that we could communicate with each other. Because of this we talked about Trish being intimate with one of my college friends. At that time it was possible for me to consider such a thing without getting jealous. The reasons are many. I have always been a secure person. My parents were supportive and loving. As a result I've never felt threatened by other people. My marriage was very healthy, with no areas of unresolved frustration. Through our communication we were able to maintain constant contact/feedback with each other and resolve conflicts as they arose. Our relationship is a source of great joy and our point of reference and security in our dealings with the outside world. We've had a satisfying sexual relationship both before and during the marriage. Sex is a great source of emotionally satisfying intimacy and sharing. In this context you can see why, theoretically at least, we didn't feel insecure like many of the couples in your book. I had no real reason to feel that Trish was rejecting me either sexually or as a person.

I feel I've understood Trish from early in our relationship and accepted her needs as a person. I was attracted to her in the first place because she is a physically oriented person—

literally a sensuous woman. She communicates her feeling of concern and love for other persons by physically touching them. Since I too am physically demonstrative this contributes to our compatibility. But the fact that I recognized and loved this trait in Trish was very important. It would have been unreasonable to demand that she have these feelings only when around me and not others. I would have had to deny something in the Trish I loved. Also the fact that I loved and cared for my friends enabled me to see why she could love them also. The main difference was that she could love them sexually, while it was not culturally possible for me to do this.

I have been emphasizing the theoretical nature of our discussions. The opportunity to actualize them never arose during the first two years of our marriage due to the shyness of my friends and our own emotional uncertainty.

Early in our marriage it was difficult for Trish to accept the idea of me having sexual relations outside marriage. We discussed this and decided that her possessiveness came from her lack of confidence in herself as a unique and valuable person. In her upbringing she was not accepted for herself nor was she told that she was attractive. There was a restrictive religious atmosphere and she was expected to live according to an externally imposed moral code.

These circumstances made her unsure of herself. She viewed a hypothetical sexual relation by me outside of marriage as a threat to her security. At that time she still felt that a wife should be able to fulfill all of her husband's needs. If I desired extramarital sex it could only mean that she had failed somewhere.

This all began to change with a period of new growth for our relationship about a year ago. I was in my second year of graduate study and Trish became interested in one of my new friends. I agreed in principle that it would be okay for her to have sex with him if that situation ever arose. The emotional results could only be guessed at, but we decided to forge ahead. With open communication and honesty at each point, we broke new emotional ground. The going was not always easy. I had to reassure my friend that this new dimension would not jeopardize our friendship. As we proceeded we gained more confidence. Soon there were unexpected benefits. Trish began to discover herself as a person. She was forced to relate to this friend as an individual rather than falling back into her comfortable role as my wife. She became aggressive toward life and this new attitude spilled over into our marriage. Her sexual behavior was daring and experimental. We discovered to our delight that our marriage was better than ever.

It was chronologically important to the evolution of our relationship that Trish have this experience first. She saw that loving more people than your spouse doesn't decrease the love in marriage. In fact, her outside experiences have *increased* her love and intimacy with me. With the benefit of this experience it was possible for her to accept my subsequent involvement with other women. Our relationship has grown to the point that we actively encourage each other to seek out other relationships because of the beneficial effects it has on us individually and together. When she has a good time with another man and joyously relates that to me, I share and benefit vicariously. I also benefit directly by having a more interesting, exciting, and self-fulfilled spouse. In this way the energy and growth of the outside involvements are fed into the marriage, keeping it growing and alive.

It is on the basis of this past and ongoing experience that we disagree with the contention that jealousy might have a basic biological foundation. Our only difficulty has come in trying to find time to devote to outside relationships. A few hurt feelings have resulted when one of us has wanted to be with the other partner despite some outside engagement. In nearly all cases, we were able through honest expression of our feelings to distinguish instances of petty unreasonableness from a real emotional need in the other partner. Both of us strongly believe that the spouse must come first when they are experiencing a genuine "emotional down" period. In these instances we would always give emotional support to each other, eliminating any real conflict.

The most successful "extended" relationships we have experienced have been with other couples. It is possible for all four persons to relate simultaneously, either as a foursome or as two separate sets. No conflicts were encountered and a greater sense of parity was achieved by all. Also, having individual relationships with members of another couple made it possible to extend our synergistic interaction with that couple. In other words my relationship with the wife made it possible for me to more intimately relate to the husband and vice versa. Since it is our desire to establish deep, meaningful and multidimensional relations with other people this four-way interaction has proved very rewarding. It is essential, however, that the other couple have a healthy and open relationship with each other in order for this process to work.

I hope I've given you an insight into our relationship as we see it and feel about it. The open and honest reports from the couples in your book have given me considerable motivation. It is not always easy to be candid about oneself. However the warmth and simple "good vibrations" that you show toward the couples in your book made Trish remark, "Let's write to Carl Rogers about our own relationship!" I hope it will be of benefit to you.

CARL: In 1976 I wrote to this couple. "I would like very much to know what has happened in the nearly three years since you wrote me. Whether the news is good or bad, whatever your own relationship is, or your relationship with outside individuals, I would really like very much to hear from you. The one special request I would make this time is that I hope you, Trish, will put down your reactions to the situation in your own terms. Fred gave a very articulate account of your development as a couple and your various relationships, but I should like to get your perspective too, directly in your own words if you are willing." After some months Fred replied:

FRED: Since our relationship has spanned many years' time, as well as ranged through both tragic and ecstatic periods, we hope that it will serve as a learning ground for others. To us it's been an intensely human experience full of growth—we hope we can convey it in that way to you. Our response will be in several parts: A description of ourselves and the relationships we're involved in; an account of a very bad period in my life; Trish's reactions to our relationships; my individual reactions to Trish, and the way we as joint partners *see* our partnership and the way we *feel* about it. Since first writing you, much has happened. In countless ways we have been changed by the experiences we've had in the last three years. New attitudes, fragile and untested when we first corresponded, have now become solidified and strong. Our feelings about the new, expanded directions in our relationship are still good. We are glad about the choices we've made. We're both happy about our partnership and very much in love.

Trish's outside relationship lasted two years. She gained in terms of close companionship, intellectual stimulation, sexual involvement, and emotional growth. When the relationship ended, the emotional toll was heavy. The man was a college friend of mine. He got involved with another girl and things fell apart. His new girl friend was possessive and couldn't share him with Trish. Trish felt emotionally rejected and refused to get involved with anyone else for six months. Gradually she began seeing other people again.

My own outside relationship is still going on. Janet is in her early forties, has been married for twenty years and has two children in high school. Janet and I met in a sense through Trish. Janet's husband is a local dentist and Trish had an appointment with him. They became interested in each other and eventually Trish told him about our open relationship. He said he'd like the same arrangement with his wife, and he invited us both over to meet Janet. I was immediately attracted to her and we soon had a strong, intense involvement. She's older and has a family to look after, but nothing interfered with the development of our relationship. Her marvelous, free-flowing personality and childlike openness, curiosity, and enthusiasm for life make me feel like the older one.

The relationship between Janet's husband and Trish diminished to a casual friendship and they have only occasional contact now. My involvement with Janet has only increased with time. She has opened up whole new avenues of life previously closed to me. Having her family as well as herself to relate to has given me a broad and rich source of contacts/validations. There's been sorrow, too. Five months after we became involved, she fell ill. She has a rare, incurable disease, usually not fatal. There are periodic attacks which cause great pain. I've spent some agonizingly difficult hours with her when she's been in excruciating pain and under drugs while I did what I could to comfort her. Despite all this, she and I look at our relationship as very worthwhile and rewarding.

Trish and Janet have become close friends and confidantes over the last three years. They share their good times and bad times with each other. During periods when either Janet's husband or I were down emotionally, they have given each other support. They are both remarkably open and loving people, free of jealousy.

Now for the current state of our relationship: it involves four people—Trish, myself, Janet, and a new person. His name is Clifford, nicknamed Chip, and he is thirty-eight years old and single.

Trish met Chip a year ago and found him a sensitive, strong, caring person. Trish has similar characteristics which make them very compatible. I look upon Chip as a member of the family; I too am compatible with him. He spends much time with us at our house, but since he has a place of his own he doesn't live full time with us. Next to Trish, who is my best friend, Janet is my best female friend and Chip is easily my best male friend. I can tell him anything. And there is nothing I wouldn't do for him.

There is an equal amount of involvement between Trish, Chip, and myself. While our relationship would be triangular or triad in nature, we wouldn't call our arrangement or living communal since Chip doesn't live exclusively at our house. Also the primary mode of interaction between us is still based on the one-to-one, person-to-person, model. Added to these relationships would be my relationship to Janet.

There is a secondary relationship between Janet's husband, family and myself. On many occasions the three of us, or the four of us—Trish, Janet, Chip, and I—will go out to dinner or have some other joint activity. I should point out that the sexual expressions which arise in our relationships are on a one-to-one level, and are heterosexual.

There are tremendous advantages for growth, support, and community in our present relationships. If one of us gets depressed, there are three others to give him support. Also the potential sources for validation are tripled—a significant emotional benefit in expanded partnerships.

CARL: In the interview with Fred and Trish, I clarified some things that had puzzled me in Fred's description. I wondered how he handled his relationship with Janet when she had adolescent children at home. He said that they get together at his house, and on these occasions Trish usually went over to Chip's home "if we want to see each other in a totally alone time." Sometimes, however, Fred goes to Janet's house.

Janet's visits to their home are known to her children, and it is not unusual for one of them to call Janet there about something, while the next call may be from Janet's son asking Fred's advice about some electronic equipment. The children obviously feel the closeness of the two homes.

I asked about the attitude of Joe, Janet's husband. He has another relationship himself with a single woman—"He's not sitting at home. It's a balanced situation. Like us, they're very open with each other about this relationship." This woman is not, however, closely intermeshed in the foursome of Fred, Trish, Janet, and Chip, although they all know and like her. She is a part, but not such a close part, of the large extended family that has been created.

I wondered if the children of Janet and Joe were aware of the various sexual involvements. Trish said they were not aware; Janet and Joe had chosen to keep it that way. The children are accustomed to the fact that their parents lead separate lives, are often away, and they are accustomed "to seeing lots of physical contact" between the various members of the group. Since the children are adolescent, I wondered about their lack of awareness. Both Fred and Trish thought they probably knew of their parents' sexual involvements and would accept these if they were discussed. "They know there's no danger their parents will break up," and this is their security. "It's never a secret that Janet comes to our house, or that Fred and Janet go on hiking trips together."

Here is Fred's account of a disaster in his life:

FRED: I should tell something of painful and insecure times as well. Last year, we all went through a traumatic event. I realize now I'd set myself up for this emotional crisis. While I'm accepting and free with others, I'm terribly demanding of myself. As a graduate student I always had to be the best and the fastest and I'd set impossible deadlines for myself. Somehow I linked my sense of personal well-being to the achievement of these external goals and I became depressed when nothing happened on schedule. Last summer I took my Ph.D. candidacy examination under great emotional stress. My parents were separating, my grandmother was fatally ill, Chip lost his job, my favorite pet died. To make matters worse, my exam had to be taken early, leaving me only five days to prepare.

I passed it. Emotionally, however, I felt unfinished, as if I'd somehow manipulated the committee into passing me. I was filled with guilt. I looked at my four years of research and it seemed worthless. Could I ever finish my thesis in this state? Then I became depressed over the fear I might get the degree but no job. The state of the world was pretty grim, too, and that only further saddened me. Everything in my environment seemed depressing. Four weeks later my grandmother died. Trish and I went to the funeral and stayed at my parents' house. Somehow I managed to hide my hopeless depression. Back home, I received notice that I was to present my research at a national meeting. Panic and emotional paralysis ensued.

I was in an acute depression. I have never in my life experienced myself as I did then. I was totally unable to function physically or emotionally. The only escape seemed to be death. I waited until I knew Trish would be gone for twenty-four hours. Then I took massive overdoses of two drugs.

How I survived I don't know, but something kept my heart beating and my respiration functioning for those twenty-four hours. Trish and Chip found me and rushed me to the hospital. The doctors couldn't revive me and I was unconscious in an intensive-care unit for seven days. Trish was with me when, over eight days after my overdose, I regained consciousness. I slowly began making my recovery, until one month later tests showed that there was fortunately no detectable mental or physical damage.

Many of our friends, upon hearing of my suicide attempt, naturally assumed that the reason was our unconventional relationship. I can clearly say that this absolutely was not the case. To the contrary, it was the constant support of Trish, Janet, and Chip which kept me going despite the self-imposed pressure I lived under. Trish, Chip, and Janet were the first ones I wanted to see when I regained consciousness.

My altered perception of myself and my world during that period of deep depression did affect my feelings toward our relationship. I became insecure and defensive; I felt threatened by Chip; I felt threatened by Trish, Janet, my university colleagues, and everyone else I came into contact with. I feel now that my temporary insecurity about our relationship then was simply a reflection of my total insecurity about myself as a person.

Here is the suicide note I left for Trish: "I just want you to know that this is something I'm doing totally on my own. It has nothing to do with our chosen life-style. You always have been the best mate/partner/friend and you continue to be even at this moment. Don't let the stresses of society and friends or parents who don't understand what great things we've achieved throughout our relationship wear you down—hang in there.

"Setting yourself up to be an achiever or someone that everyone perceives as always together is a dangerous proposition. You begin to believe that you are capable of anything. The coming down is very hard.

"My greatest fear is hurting those around me. I don't want them to think that they, through something which they did, or in some way which they acted, have contributed to where I am at now.

"My greatest concern, of course, is with you, Trish. With you I've achieved or shared my highest moments. You've seen me at my best. I want you to remember us in that way.

"I love you. Keep tight with your friends, especially Chip. Please reassure my friends, especially Janet, that they have not contributed to my state."

It was a horrible interlude in my life, but there were positive effects too. I feel much better about myself as a total person— more empathic with others in distress. My view of my research was distorted during my depression. At a recent national meeting the reception toward my work was positive and encouraging. The trauma we all went through has for me cemented my bonds to those three people in my relationship. I feel closer to them all now than ever before.

CARL: The first of my many questions about this near-fatal episode had to do with Fred's fantastically high expectations for himself. They had not come from his family, who had not even urged him to attend college. In seven years of university and graduate school, the atmosphere of competition with peers, and his recognition of professional and societal demands and expectations, built up the pressure. "Subtle things made me focused on this *very* high goal. When you've done well, there's no place to go but up. But when I was knocked off of that plateau, it was shattering."

Why hadn't he let Trish know the depth of his depression? When communication was so open between them, why did he hide his deeply disturbed feelings? Fred said, "I felt guilty that I was depressed. Part of me knew this was silly. I felt I had to overcome it myself. During the week I thought of suicide, I was ashamed to speak of it. It seemed incredible. It seemed as though someone else was feeling this. Yes, I have a hard time calling for help." Trish joined in, "Always! He won't even take an aspirin for a headache. He thinks he has to lick it by himself."

Fred continued, "I had a real fear of psychiatric institutionalization. I was afraid that if I told what I was feeling they'd put me in a locked-up place." Trish says, "I knew he was depressed. I couldn't get him to see a psychiatrist. But it was a shock to me. I'm a nurse, and I missed all the classical signs. I guess he didn't talk because he was afraid they'd take him away and lock him up for life." Fred adds, "I hated that part of me. It was horrible. I didn't want to let it out."

Fred had to give up on his first thesis and now is writing one that will be less than world-shaking. "I've shattered my illusions, and I accept me as a person that can fail. Trish, Janet, and my other friends have helped me a lot."

Here is Trish's perception of their relationship and of this crisis:

TRISH: I can't say what the future will bring, I've been through so many changes in the past year—from ecstasy to terror—that now I try to accept each day as it comes. But I feel very good about my present life-style. I cannot imagine myself living a closed, possessive, and jealous existence. I have the freedom to be me; to explore the many facets of my personality with many people without fear of "being caught" or criticized.

I am now seeing a change among some couples where the wife has gone back to school or is involved in some other activities outside the relationship. The general impression is that the husband has allowed the wife these "privileges." Fred and I don't speak of privileges. Rather, we encourage each other to explore new ideas, activities, or feelings; not only with each other but with others as well.

The last three and a half years have been growing, changing years for me. I've learned a lot about myself, met many new people and enjoyed myself immensely. I don't think I would have had these experiences in any other than an open-ended relationship.

How can I explain to you where I am right now? It's very difficult for me. I am in love with two men. I care about them very much. I am married to one—Fred—and we have been close for many years. Chip and I have developed a very close relationship also. Lucky for me they both love me too!

Fred and I have weathered some heavy stress this past year. I'm still feeling the effects. We are still close and communicate freely and openly. But as a result of the depression and suicide attempt nearly a year ago and the manic episode a few months ago, I'm afraid of what the next day will bring. I try to live each day as it comes, but it's hard. It's getting better each day, though. Fred has given me support and not pushed me to act in any particular way. At first I wanted to run; I was scared. But I realized that I didn't want to give up that easily. Fred and I have worked hard to make our relationship work; there is too much love between us to run when the going gets rough. I am very optimistic about our future.

Now, about Chip. The longer I've known him the more important he's become to me. He's gentle, loving, caring—and a realist where I'm a total idealist. We balance each other somewhat. I urge him to be less cynical and he encourages me to be more realistic about the world around me.

When Fred was sick, Chip gave me support and love. I'm not sure I could have gone through that ordeal without him. Aside from all the love between us, I've learned a great deal from him. He shares his past as well as present life with me; both the sad and happy times.

Our present state is just as Fred described. We each have a relationship in addition to our own. I differ from Fred only in that I feel I have two primary relationships: one with Fred and one with Chip. They are both important to me. The most amazing thing is that the three of us care so much for each other. Three years ago I wouldn't have believed this possible yet here we are—I am so happy.

On Thanksgiving last year, Janet and Joe, her husband, invited Fred, Chip, and me to their home for Thanksgiving dinner. It was a warm, beautiful day; happiness among us all—including Janet and Joe's kids—was just as warm and beautiful. It makes me glad to be alive to know that people can be this happy, relating freely without jealousy and possessiveness.

CARL: Trish's mention of a "manic episode" surprised me. Later, they explained that Fred had been helped by lithium after his suicide attempt. The dosage had to be carefully monitored medically. Things went so smoothly he neglected to take it. Then several months after the crisis, he went to Chicago to give a paper on his research. He got caught up in the excitement of the conference, couldn't sleep, got manic, developed delusions, and finally checked into the hospital. Trish found him "so hyper he had to be drugged to get him on the plane."

Trish speaks of "the real trauma" of the suicide attempt, and the eight days of unconsciousness. "Nothing else mattered to me for two weeks." As to her reaction, "I immediately felt guilt. What had I done? Or not done? Now I realize that I just did my best. But there are painful spots like that. Janet wondered, too, 'What didn't I do?' Fred's folks felt guilty. 'What did we do to him while he was a boy?'" Fred adds, "Lots of people thought our life-style was of course the cause of it all. I didn't feel that way."

Trish spoke of another reason why she was vulnerable to guilt feelings at this time. "I was really getting involved with Chip. At such a time you spend a lot of time together, exploring each other—your feelings and reactions, your past and present, and we were just at that stage. So of course I wondered if *that* had something to do with Fred's attempt. It's awful to come home and find your husband sprawled on the carpet."

The manic episode was a further shock to Trish. "I have to be honest. I'm going to be looking. I missed the signs *twice*. So I phone him to ask, 'How are you? What are you doing?' and I make sure he's taking his medicine. It's going to take me a lot of time to get over it." Fred says, "I realize where she is. I don't object to her phoning to find out how I am." It was clear that Trish has been deeply shaken by these experiences, and that Fred recognizes her fears as only natural. They both see that it was a very positive step for Fred to realize, in Chicago, that he *was* sick, and to go to a hospital for help. Still, Trish's fears persist, and she finds herself thinking of him as a patient, as well as relating to him as her husband. She doesn't like this in herself, but she can't help it.

When I received Fred's first letter, three years ago, it seemed clear that Trish was involved in outside relationships because Fred wanted both of them to. I had wondered whether she was now really involved as a person, on her own initiative, in this life-style. Both her letter and the interview left me in no doubt on this point. Though she might have had her first experiences because of Fred, she now enjoys and finds support in these outside relationships, and is happy that they have this openness in their marriage. It was also my impression that up until this past year her outside loves had for her deepened and enriched the marriage. Now, with Fred's attempt to take his life, and her increasingly close and deep love for Chip, her relationship with Fred seemed to me to have perceptibly changed, though her devotion to her husband was also evident.

FRED: I would like to share some of my own personal feelings about Trish and her relationship to me. I have known her intimately now for almost ten years. As the primary person I've loved during those years I've seen some remarkable and beautiful changes come over her. In that time I feel she has steadily grown toward a fuller expression of her own unique personhood. Every day she is exhibiting more of the qualities of the person she has the potential to be. She is a very impressive person; strong, sensitive, capable, a fun-loving child, potent, unsure, powerful, loving, giving. She is someone of great confidence and autonomy. And yet she is related and involved with the people she loves in a very committed, caring way. While most of these qualities were always within her, I feel that some were latent and unexpressed when we first met. It's my belief that the open, facilitative environment of our partnership allowed her to grow into the person she has become.

Another key ingredient has been our commitment to total communication. We felt that we must be able to share the most intimate, painful, or insecure feelings just as freely as we could express the tender, loving, and joyful feelings. As we learned to do this we were able to communicate the growth and development each of us experienced separately as individuals into the experience of our relationship together. In this way I feel we have minimized the possibility of either of us outgrowing the other in our partnership.

CARL: Fred's loving devotion to Trish has been evident in everything he has written about them, and it was clear in the interview. When he speaks about "our commitment to total communication" he is obviously overlooking his failure to tell her of his depressed feelings. As I drew them out on this, it came clearer to me that their commitment to total communication was seen as having to do with everything about their own relationship, or their relationships with others. Fred certainly had not seen that communication of his own deepest private feelings was even more relevant to their partnership than

221

communication about some new attachment he might form.

One other point that stood out in the interview was Fred's total dedication to his work. It was customary for him to spend several nights a week at the lab—in addition to his days—working on his research until one or two in the morning. He seems almost as much wedded to his research as to Trish or Janet. Trish summed this up succinctly in a statement that sheds light not only on her relationship to Fred but to Janet as well. "He's working so hard that both Janet and I are beginning to object to these one-night stands." Chip frequently comes over when Fred is working so late, and this has eased her loneliness. Both Trish and Janet look forward to the time when Fred will be finished with his doctorate and can live a normal life.

Trish's love for Fred is very clear. Yet she makes it plain that for her there are *two* primary loves, Fred and Chip. Also as she makes evident in her statement her love is currently suffused with fear and anxiety about Fred's psychological processes.

Fred and Trish are not swingers, and they never feel they *must* engage in a sexual encounter. "Sexual relations with others evolve from our natural feeling of love, concern and involvement. We value relationships outside marriage as they develop naturally with integrated, holistic persons whose physical feelings are arrayed in a continuous spectrum from the simplest touching to sexual intercourse. The growth which we have encouraged each other to experience has been continuously infused back into our partnership, keeping it strong and alive —a process rather than a fixed entity."

This idealistic description was borne out in our interview. Trish said, "People ask me, 'Do you recommend this for everyone?' and I say, 'Certainly not!'" It has not always been easy, but they like it.

I asked, "If you could start a program of family or marital education for high school or college students, what would you want to stress?" Fred said he would want to expose them to many life-styles. He would also want them to recognize that many things we assume are simply not true—that being jealous of your mate proves love, for example, or that if your spouse can't fill all your needs, there's something wrong with your marriage.

Trish said, "I'd want them always to keep an open mind. When I was in high school, there was always just one way to feel about a thing. I'd want them to observe different couples and see how they are working things out."

They described the uncertainty they felt in the early years. "Are we doing the right thing?" "Is monogamy better?" "Do we know what we are doing, taking these risks?" They felt they were on untrodden ground, "but now we feel we've chosen the path for us."

Their life has narrowed down in that the number of outside relationships is smaller than when they first wrote me. Fred and Trish came to realize that depth and involvement were what they wanted in a relationship, and these qualities can be achieved only in a few instances. Trish said, "I have two deep relationships now, and that's all I can handle."

I had thought they might speak about the possibility of a family, but since they had not, I said, "What about children?" Their answers revealed some fresh issues in their life-style. Fred said, "We're really not sure." Trish explained. "At first we were sure we didn't want children—with Fred in grad school and me working. We were perfectly happy the way we were. Selfish, perhaps, but we were just not willing to give up that amount of time. But now I'm beginning to have little things tug at me, saying that, yes, having children would be a nice thing." Fred commented that he would like to have children and to see a child, a person, develop and grow. Both of them are well aware that children constitute a very long term commitment, and are astonished at young people who think a child will only change their lives for a few years.

But they have special problems. Trish said, "I have two permanent relationships, and a child would have two fathers. I'd have to work that out."

Then they both commented on the problem a child would create with their parents, since their life-style could then hardly be concealed from them. "We would have to deal with our parents. Fred's mother probably realizes how we live, though we haven't discussed it openly with her." "But," said Trish, "my parents have no idea of the way we live." She comes from a very religious, strict home background. "I'm not willing to give up my life-style for them, but it would be a difficult thing to work out."

They have made beginnings in opening up their complex of relationships to the knowledge of others. "Most of our friends already know of our involvements. Recently we took Chip to a big party put on by Fred's sister, and he was accepted and liked by her and her children. It's going to take little steps like that. But it's a beginning."

I invited comments from several colleagues on the experience of Fred and Trish. Here is one from Maureen Miller, authority on human sexuality and the changing aspects of marriage:

MAUREEN: I am delighted that you have chosen to include in your book material related to jealousy. In my own life, my teaching, and counseling, there is no issue in which interpersonal power is so dramatically experienced. It seems to me that there is more interpersonal abuse and crippling coming from either the avoidance of jealousy or the experience of it than almost any other feelings we have about each other.

Because of this and because of my own struggles in living a married life which is not sexually exclusive I am very glad you gave me this opportunity to comment on the story of Fred and Trish.

I responded as I read it on both a "hunch" level and an analytical level. In recent years I have been discovering that often my intuition and my intellect have similar perceptions, so I will give you my reactions as a mixture of hunch and analysis.

My strongest reaction to reading the descriptions by Fred and Trish was like your first response: "It's too good to be true." This was followed by a feeling of self-criticism because I do experience jealousy in myself.

I was disappointed by my reaction because I do believe that nonmonogamous partnerships which are satisfying to those involved are possible, even within a culture which stresses monogamy as the "norm." Fred says that jealousy and possessiveness are not innate. I am inclined, because of personal and professional experience, to agree. What I cannot agree with, however, is the assertion made by Fred that they are evidence of some intrapersonal difficulty, such as a lack of self-confidence. The fact is we know very little about what feelings and behaviors are part of our biological heritage and what are learned from womb to tomb in interaction with the environment, in our battle to survive.

I find that often there seems to be an unwillingness to entertain the possibility that jealousy might be an appropriate response to some interpersonal situations and that in some situations the feeling of it, learned or innate, might have strong survival value, biologically, psychologically, and culturally.

I am drawn repeatedly as I reread the material to the story of Fred's suicide attempt. It plagues me as I try to understand my feelings about this couple and their lives. What is so disturbing is that in the midst of a description of marital and nonmarital bliss, where everything is described in terms like "growth," "richness," "joy," "healthy," "validation," "intimacy," and the like, suddenly comes this disaster. The disaster was so complete that Fred considered his life no longer worth living. I want to believe his suicide note, which exonerates everyone and the relationship, but I can't.

In all the descriptions of the lives of the participants there is heavy emphasis on the lighter elements of human experience. The emphasis is on those characteristics we label as virtuous. What I am aware of, however, is that in each of us, in addition to the angels of faith, hope, charity, wisdom, and loving, are also the angels of doubt, despair, need, passion, and hate. The darker angels are part of us all, I believe. I see no mention of these characteristics in the descriptions of these people. They come across as pre-Raphaelite saints!

Commonly in "nice" families one individual becomes the barometer of these unacknowledged darker elements. The system demands a sponge for this energy if that family is to continue to function at this "light" pole of human interaction. Fred doesn't say what his demons were, although he alludes to recognizing unacceptable impulses and feelings. My guess would be that he was becoming aware of his dark side. In an environment where jealousy, greed, competitiveness, and anger are equated with being imperfect, Fred has no choice but to label himself unacceptable. His culture demands it! Because his feelings don't seem to be experienced by all the other people in his environment he blames himself. My conclusions about the heavy value of positive feelings and the denial of others comes from Fred's inability to share any of his turmoil with those people with whom he has "open and honest communication." I see Fred as the "grief eater," the person who in the face of difficulties convinces everyone else that everything is fine so they are spared anxiety, fear, and grief, whilst at the same time he experiences, deep down, all the collective pain of the system. "Grief eaters" commonly experience themselves on an aware level as stronger than the rest, only to crumble when they themselves have to face problems alone and stoically.

So Fred believes his suicide had nothing to do with his interpersonal situation. I certainly agree that he undoubtedly knows more about this than I do, but accepting that, my doubts remain. The emotions which are missing from these descriptions are the emotions of anger, fear, rivalry, lust, and neediness. All these emotions have enormous survival value. To not allow oneself or others the right to both feel and express these emotions is to hold the person in an emotional strait jacket. When these emotions are allowed to be a legitimate and valued part of interaction, difficulties can be dealt with more flexibly and more humanely than when they are suppressed. It is my guess, and I admit it is a guess, that if Fred had been in touch with his darker energies earlier, and saw them matched and met by the others in his extended family, he might never have tried to end his life, or suffered the mental agonies he describes.

It is important for me to stress that I do not believe it was the nonmonogamous nature of the system that created the stress. I know from my own life that a nonexclusive marriage can be a satisfying way to live. It would be easy for people who value monogamy above any other form of partnership to pounce on my arguments to add to their convictions that such open marriages inevitably result in disaster. This would be a pity because *I* certainly don't believe that. If my interpretation of the imbalance on the side of "lightness" is valid, then the same stress could and does occur in completely exclusive relationships.

This brings me back to jealousy and interpersonal politics. It is common to put jealousy down these days, just as it used to be common to put down anger and sexual feelings. Whether learned or innate, it is deeply felt. My own experience tells me that for many people, along with the intense pain of jealousy, comes a shame at having the feeling at all. That used to be true for me. Instead of experiencing and owning my jealousy I would try to find other rationalizations for my pain, trying to find some way of making sense of my feelings. I guess I don't feel I can make any sense of my jealousy; it comes from a place deeper in me than my "sense" goes. Indeed it has its own sense, and my mind has little understanding of it.

Deeply as I feel it, I find I don't have to be incapacitated by it. My husband and I have found that each other's jealous feelings are important. We care enough about each other to be halted by any pain the other is feeling. We halt to validate the other's feelings, to give whatever care and reassurance are needed by the other; then we decide if we wish to continue doing whatever precipitated the jealousy. We do not try to ensure that jealous feelings never surface; we do not feel obliged to capitulate to them when they do. What we do feel, however, is that the experience of the other is unconditionally valid. We give each other the right to feel our own feelings. We care about them yet we are not willing to respond as though it were always our fault.

What we have discovered in this process is that there are times when jealousy is an important indicator that things are amiss in our relationship. Close as we have been, there are still times when it is easier to establish a relationship with another than to confront problems between us. At these times the one being avoided experiences jealousy. We fear being abandoned because we are being abandoned. In this kind of situation only by exploring the jealousy and its dimensions can the abandonment be discovered and reckoned with. In my experience, jealousy is not always the destructive demon Fred and Trish seem to believe it to be. What has been more of a demon in my life has been *unacknowledged* jealousy disguised as sophisticated put-downs of the other person or of myself.

I admire Fred, Trish, Janet, and Chip for their courage. They are taking on an enormously powerful mythology around marriage and what is possible. I find their courage and openness inspiring, especially when I read that their own parents are so strongly entrenched in a different value system. I feel caution, however. Not only do I agree that their story cannot be a model for others, I wonder if their last year can be a model for their next year.

Any new relationship that matters always brings with it the possibility that it might one day supplant the present one. Trish acknowledges she has two primary relationships and would not want to have to choose between Fred and Chip. The possibility of being left is always in the air, however unlikely it may seem at first. I am wondering for me, and for Trish, Fred, and Chip, what the consequences are. How much depth of intimacy is possible in that state of ambiguity? There is freedom and power in nonexclusivity; is there perhaps another freedom and power in fidelity?

I don't have an answer, Carl, but I am asking the question.

I felt as I wrote that the whole subject of partnership, marriage, love, sex, jealousy, and commitment is a very important one at this time in our culture. I feel that this material opens up the issue in a new and important context. It has generated much thought and discussion in myself and my close friends. I imagine it is going to do the same in many other places!

CARL: I cannot arrive at any solid conclusions from the story of Fred and Trish, but there are provocative questions aplenty. A marriage with a number of satellite relationships, gradually deepening in significance, can exist for years without either partner having more than a twinge of jealousy. Jealousy then may not be an instinctive reaction—not a biological drive that makes a man want to kill his wife's lover, or a wife bitterly jealous of her husband's attachment to another woman. Perhaps one learns to be jealous, and in our culture this is a socially approved lesson. One can also learn *not* to be jealous, as seems to have been the case with Trish.

Social anthropology won't help much here. In many cultures possessiveness is extreme, most often on the part of the man, but frequently on the part of the woman too. There are also a number of cultures—early Hawaiian is one—in which jealousy is infrequent, and sexual freedom is much more accepted.

Biology won't settle the point either. There are species of animals and birds where monogamy and fidelity are the rule. There are others more marked by possessiveness. There are some species where jealousy is unknown. Seals come to mind as a confusing example. The bull seal literally wears himself out, during mating season, willing to fight to the death to keep intruding males away from his harem. By contrast the females are not jealous of each other, and are willingly receptive to the approaches of another male—if the bull is not watchful.

So while the general question remains open, one thing is clear from the story of Fred and Trish. It is possible to love more than one person at a time, sexual love included, without arousing observable jealous or possessive behaviors. Trish not only is not jealous of Janet, but they are clearly close friends. Fred not only shows no jealousy of Chip, but they too are close friends.

The politics of a marriage can be one of equality, shared responsibilities, mutual support, and shared decision-making, as Trish movingly demonstrates when she says that she and Fred do not so much allow each other the "privilege" of freedom as actually encourage it. This is not the irresponsibility of "I'll do my thing, and you do yours." It is in the context of an equal relationship that they go forth to explore and then return to the relationship an enriched person. It has helped to build their independent strengths.

The politics of equality, with primary value attached to the person, extends into the sexual realm. Sexual self-determination is successfully maintained only because communication is wide open. With trusting communication there is, as Trish says, no fear "of 'being caught' or criticized."

There are risks in this as in all innovative living. Trish loses her first lover to another woman and is deeply hurt. Fred has had the pain of dealing with Janet's illness. Both of them have found how complex and time-consuming it is to maintain more than one deep relationship. The greatest risk is that Trish is now involved in two *primary* relationships. If she should ever feel compelled to choose one as more important than the other, which would she choose? I believe neither we nor she can be sure. Fortunately for her the question has not arisen. There is some ambivalence in her statement of her feelings after Fred's suicide attempt—"I wanted to run." Her double tie only emphasizes Maureen Miller's point that "the possibility of being left is always in the air, however unlikely it may seem at first."

Even in a marriage of open communication, you can have feelings so shameful they can't be shared with your partner. There are limits—often unknown limits—to sharing. The kind of feelings Fred had about his depressed state are very familiar to me. The commonest theme in therapy is this: "If you really knew me, my horrible thoughts and feelings, you couldn't accept me, and would confirm my fear that I am insane and/or hopeless." This comes very close to the fears that kept Fred from speaking of his desperation. Here is an attempt to state them schematically. "The feelings arising in me are so wrong, so unbelievable, so shameful that they cannot be a part of me, and I hate and fear them so much that I can't let them out—to anyone. Death is preferable."

What were these horrible feelings? Maureen Miller suggests that they may have been unexpressed anger, competitiveness, jealousy, elements of Fred's "dark side." This is possible in a marriage so free—perhaps suspiciously free—of these emotions. But I feel there is another possibility.

I regard it as somewhat more likely that Fred's deepest horror was a feeling that he was a complete fraud. It is clear that he came to believe he was a fraud professionally. He was not the "hot shot" he thought himself to be. It was a fluke that he had passed his exam. His research was just an attempt to put a good face on a bad reality. The people who believed in him were being duped. And now he would be found out.

To what extent did he feel fraudulent in his personal life? There is just a hint. He says, "Setting yourself up to be an achiever or *someone who is always together* is a dangerous proposition" (italics mine). He had indeed set himself up as a "together person," taking the lead in marriage and moving them toward an unconventional life-style. Everything was great. There is scarcely a hint of self-doubt anywhere. But when the internal gestalt changes from "I am a remarkable person" to "I am a fraud" it must have raised the unspoken feelings of doubt that were always present at some level. "Maybe I'm not so much together. Perhaps I'm not sure at all. Possibly I have been a big fraud in my personal as well as my professional life." Fine distinctions go by the board; from being all positive, you can quite suddenly see nothing but the negative, and since this has never been expressed, its horror is multiplied many times. This is my speculation in regard to his inner world at the time of his deep depression. Fearing that someone may discover the fraud, it is entirely understandable that everyone close to him would seem threatening.

There is one other perspective on Fred's downward emotional spiral which I, and most other humanistic psychologists, are reluctant to admit. This is the possibility that there was a chemical factor in his depression. His positive responses to a correct lithium dosage occurred twice—once in his depression and once when he was manic—and forces me to consider this possibility. There is no way of knowing whether his down feelings brought about a need for lithium, or whether such a need magnified those feelings. But that it was somehow and to some degree a factor seems a reasonable conclusion from his response to the medication. My clinical experience with individuals undergoing a manic-depressive cycle—which is not extensive—has often perplexed me. I have found these situations very difficult to explain in entirely psychological terms. I have regarded it as possible that genetic or chemical factors may play a real part, whereas I do not feel this way about so-called schizophrenia or other "mental disorders."

Fred—and all of us—can be thankful that his very determined attempt at suicide failed and left his mind and body undamaged. Has he learned that it is always better to share horrible feelings than to hide them and let them fester? He has taken a minor step in this direction, seeking help in his manic state. He has made progress in accepting himself as an imperfect person and one capable of harboring "unspeakable" feelings. He could doubtless profit from a more complete exploration of his inner world in a relationship with a therapist who shares his person-centered views. The test of the adequacy of his self-understanding lies in the future.

One thing that I have relearned from my contacts with this pair is the strong underlying desire on the part of every individual for depth and permanence in any close relationship. They have demonstrated in their own lives a wish which I have come to believe is almost universal—a wish for a lasting relationship in which one can know the other as a whole, complex person, and in which the one can *be* known in the same way. As both Trish and Fred are well aware, this does not occur overnight, nor with a large number of people.

Part III Toward a theoretical foundation

Chapter 11 | A political base: the actualizing tendency

Any view of the politics of human relationships must rest basically upon the conception of the human organism and what makes it "tick"—the nature and motivation of that organism. I have, for years, held a more and more sharply defined stance as to these points. I should like to present these views as clearly as I can, drawing on previous formulations, and considering the political implications of my perspective on the nature of human motivation.[1]

I see the actualizing tendency in the human organism as being basic to motivation. Let me begin with a personal experience that made a strong impression, and lead from that into a variety of observations that support my view.

During a vacation weekend some months ago I was standing on a headland overlooking one of the rugged coves that dot the coastline of northern California. Several large rock outcroppings were at the mouth of the cove, and these received the full force of the great Pacific combers, which, beating upon them, broke into mountains of spray before surging in to the cliff-lined shore. As I watched the waves breaking over these large rocks in the distance, I noticed with surprise what appeared to be tiny palm trees on the rocks, no more than two or three feet high, taking the pounding of the breakers. Through my binoculars I saw that these were some type of seaweed, with a slender "trunk" topped off with a head of leaves. As one examined a specimen in the intervals between the waves it seemed clear that this fragile, erect, top-heavy plant would be utterly crushed and broken by the next breaker. When the wave crunched down upon it, the trunk bent almost flat, the leaves were whipped into a straight line by the torrent of the water, yet the moment the wave had passed, here was the plant again, erect, tough, resilient. It seemed incredible that it was able to take this incessant pounding hour after hour, day and night, week after week, perhaps year after year, and all the time nourishing itself, extending its domain, reproducing itself, in short, maintaining and enhancing itself in this process which, in our shorthand, we call growth. Here in this palmlike seaweed was the tenacity of life, the forward thrust of life, the ability to push into an incredibly hostile environment and not only to hold its own but to adapt, develop, become itself.

Now I am very well aware that we can "explain" many aspects of this phenomenon. Thus we can explain that the weed grows on top of the rock rather than on the protected side because it is phototropic. We can even attempt some biochemical explanations of phototropism. We can say that the plant grows where it does because there is an ecological niche that it fills, and that if *this* plant had not developed to fill this niche, the process of evolution would have favored some other organism that would gradually have developed much these same characteristics. I am aware that we can now begin to explain why this plant assumes the form it does, and why, if it is damaged in some storm, it will repair itself in a way consistent with its own basic species form. This will all come about because the DNA molecule—as long as it is a part of, and is interacting with, a living cell—carries within it, like a program for guiding a computer, instructions to each emergent cell as to the form and function it will assume in order to make the whole a functioning organism.

Such knowledge *explains* nothing, in any fundamental sense. Yet it is very valuable as a part of the continuing differentiation, the finer description, the more accurate picture of functional relationships, which our curiosity demands, and which gives us at least a deeper respect for and understanding of the complexities of life.

But my reason for telling this story is to call attention to a more general characteristic. Whether we are speaking of this sea plant or of an oak tree, of an earthworm or a great night-flying moth, of an ape or a man, we will do well to recognize that life is an active process, not a passive one. Whether the stimulus arises from within or without, whether the environment is favorable or unfavorable, the behaviors of an organism can be counted on to be in the direction of maintaining, enhancing, and reproducing itself. This is the very nature of the process we call life. Speaking of the totality of these reactions within an organism, Bertalanffy says, "We find that all parts and processes are so ordered that they guarantee the maintenance, construction, restitution, and reproduction of organic systems."[2] When we speak in any basic way of what "motivates" the behavior of organisms, it is this directional tendency that is fundamental. This tendency is operative at all times, in all organisms. Indeed it is only the presence or absence of this total directional process that enables us to tell whether a given organism is alive or dead.

I am not alone in seeing such an actualizing tendency as the fundamental answer to the question of what makes an organism tick. Goldstein,[3] Maslow,[4] Angyal,[5] and others have held similar views and have influenced my own thinking. I have pointed out that this tendency involves a development toward the differentiation of organs and functions; it involves enhancement through reproduction; it means a trend toward self-regulation and away from control by external forces.

Here, then, at the very heart of the mystery of what makes organisms "tick," is an important foundation stone for our political thinking. The organism is self-controlled. In its normal state it moves toward its own enhancement and toward an independence from external control.

But is this view supported by other evidence? Let me point to some of the work in biology that supports the concept of the actualizing tendency. One example, replicated with different species, is the work of Driesch with sea urchins many years ago. Driesch learned how to tease apart the two cells that are formed after the first division of the fertilized egg. Had they been left to develop normally, it is clear that each of these two cells would have grown into a portion of a sea urchin larva, the contributions of both being needed to form a whole creature. So it seems equally obvious that when the two cells are skillfully separated, each, if it grows, will simply develop into some portion of a sea urchin. But this is overlooking the directional and actualizing tendency characteristic of all organic growth. It is found that each cell, if it can be kept alive, now develops into a whole sea urchin larva—a bit smaller than usual, but normal and complete.

I choose this example because it seems so closely analogous to my experience in dealing with individuals in a therapeutic relationship, my experience in facilitating intensive groups, my experience of providing "freedom to learn" for students in classes. In these situations the most impressive fact about the individual human being seems to be the directional tendency toward wholeness, toward actualization of potentialities. I have not found psychotherapy or group experience effective when I have tried to create in another individual something that is not there, but I have found that if I can provide the conditions that make for growth, then this positive directional tendency brings about constructive results. The scientist with the divided sea urchin egg is in the same situation. He cannot cause the cell to develop in one way or another, he cannot (as yet, at least) shape or control the DNA molecule, but if he focuses his skill on providing the conditions that permit the cell to survive and grow, then the tendency for growth and the direction of growth will be evident, and will come from within the organism. I cannot think of a better analogy for therapy or the group experience, where, if I can supply a psychological amniotic fluid, forward movement of a constructive sort will occur.

Support for the concept of an actualizing tendency comes at times from surprising quarters, as in the simple but unusual experiments that show that rats prefer an environment involving more complex stimuli over an environment involving less complex stimuli. It seems striking that even the lowly laboratory rat, within the range of complexity that he can appreciate, prefers a more richly stimulating setting to a more impoverished one. Dember, Earl, and Paradise state that "a shift in preference, if it occurs, will be unidirectional, toward stimuli of greater complexity."[6] Given the opportunity, a living organism tends to fulfill its more complex potentialities rather than settle for simpler satisfactions.

The work in the field of sensory deprivation underscores even more strongly the fact that tension reduction or the absence of stimulation is a far cry from being the desired state of the organism. Freud could not have been more wrong in his postulate that "the nervous system is . . . an apparatus which would even, if this were feasible, maintain itself in an altogether unstimulated condition."[7] On the contrary, when deprived of external stimuli, the human organism produces a flood of internal stimuli sometimes of the most bizarre sort. John Lilly has told of his experiences when suspended weightless in a soundproof tank of water. He speaks of the trancelike states, the mystical experiences, the sense of being tuned in to communication networks not available to ordinary consciousness, of experiences which can only be called hallucinatory.[8] It is very clear that when you receive an absolute minimum of any external stimuli, you open yourself to a flood of internal experiencing that goes far beyond that of everyday living. You most certainly do not lapse into homeostasis, into a passive equilibrium. This only occurs in diseased organisms.

When it comes to motivation, the organism is an active initiator and exhibits a directional tendency. R.W. White puts this in very appealing terms when he says, "Even when its primary needs are satisfied and its homeostatic chores are done, an organism is alive, active, and up to something."[9]

As a consequence of these and other developments in psychological and biological research, I feel secure in calling attention to the significance of this direction in the human organism which accounts for its maintenance and enhancement.

Sometimes this tendency is spoken of as if it involved the development of all of the potentialities of the organism. This is clearly not true. The organism does not, as someone has pointed out, tend toward developing its capacity for nausea, nor does it actualize its potentiality for self-destruction, nor its ability to bear pain. Only under unusual or perverse circumstances do these potentialities become actualized. It is clear that the actualizing tendency is selective and directional, a constructive tendency, if you will.

The substratum of all human motivation is the organismic tendency toward fulfillment. This tendency may express itself in the widest range of behaviors and in response to a very wide variety of needs. Certain wants of a basic sort must be at least partially met before other needs become urgent. Consequently the tendency of the organism to actualize itself may at one moment lead to the seeking of food or sexual satisfaction, and yet unless these needs are overpoweringly great, even these satisfactions will be sought in ways that enhance rather than diminish self-esteem. And other fulfillments will also be sought in the transactions with the environment: the need for exploration, for producing change in the environment, for play, for self-exploration when that is perceived as an avenue to fulfillment—all of these and many other behaviors are basically "motivated" by the actualizing tendency.

We are, in short, dealing with an organism that is always motivated, is always "up to something," always seeking. So I reaffirm, even more strongly than when I first advanced the notion, my belief that there is one central source of energy in the human organism; that it is a trustworthy function of the whole organism rather than of some portion of it; and that it is perhaps best conceptualized as a tendency toward fulfillment, toward actualization, not only toward the maintenance but also toward the enhancement of the organism.

What I have said thus far pictures a solid, constructive base of human motivation. This is a base that would empower the person, would fit him for a harmonious politics of interpersonal relationships. But I have omitted reference to the great puzzle that faces anyone who delves at all into the dynamics of human behavior. This puzzle has to do with the fact that persons are often at war within themselves, estranged from their own organisms. While the organism may be constructively motivated, certainly the conscious aspects often seem the reverse. What about the all too common rift between the organismic aspect and the conscious self? How do we account for what often appears to be two conflicting motivational systems in the individual?

To take a very simple example, how is it that a woman can consciously be a very submissive and compliant person and then at times blow up in abnormally hostile and resentful behavior that greatly surprises her and that she does not own as a part of herself? Clearly her organism has been experiencing both submission and aggression, and moving toward the expression of both. Yet at the conscious level she has no awareness and no acceptance of one aspect of this process going on within her. This is a simple example of the rift with which every psychologist interested in human behavior must come to terms.

I do not see any clear solution to the problem, but I think perhaps I have come to see the issues in a larger context. In nature, the working out of the actualizing tendency shows a surprising efficiency. The organism makes errors, to be sure, but these are corrected on the basis of feedback. A classic experiment showed that even the human infant eventually does a quite satisfactory job of balancing her diet. She may go on a protein "binge," for a time, or devour too much fat, but soon evens out these errors, showing a "wisdom of the body" in maintaining and enhancing her development. This type of relatively integrated, self-regulating behavior, directed toward maintenance and fulfillment, seems to be the rule in nature rather than the exception. One can, of course, point to serious mistakes over evolutionary time. Evidently the dinosaurs, by becoming very efficiently and rigidly actualized in terms of a given environment, could not adapt, and thus effectively destroyed themselves through the perfection with which they had fulfilled themselves in a given environment. On the whole, however, organisms, through adaptations, mutations, and adjustments, behave in ways that make an awesome degree of directional sense. Life flows into ever more diverse forms, correcting its errors, and moving toward its own enhancement.

In the human being, however—perhaps particularly in our culture—the potentiality for awareness of her functioning can go so persistently awry as to make her truly estranged from her organismic experiencing. She can become self-defeating, as in neurosis; incapable of coping with life, as in psychosis; unhappy and divided, as in the maladjustments that occur in all of us. Why this division? How is it that a person can be consciously struggling toward one goal while her whole organic direction is at cross purposes with this?

In puzzling over this issue, I find myself trying to take a fresh look at the place and function of awareness in life. The ability to focus conscious attention seems to be one of the latest evolutionary developments in our species. It is a tiny peak of awareness, of symbolizing capacity, topping a vast pyramid of nonconscious organismic functioning. Perhaps a better analogy, more indicative of the continual change going on, is to think of the individual's functioning as a large pyramidal fountain. The very tip of the fountain is intermittently illuminated with the flickering light of consciousness, but the constant flow of life goes on in the darkness as well, in nonconscious as well as conscious ways.

In the person who is functioning well, awareness tends to be a reflexive thing, rather than a sharp spotlight of focused attention. Perhaps it is more accurate to say that in such a person awareness is simply a reflection of something of the flow of the organism at that moment. It is only when the functioning is disrupted that a sharply self-conscious awareness arises. Speaking of the different aspects of awareness in this well-functioning person, I have said, "I do not mean that this individual would be self-consciously aware of all that was going on within herself, like the centipede that became aware of all its legs. On the contrary, she would be free to live a feeling subjectively, as well as be aware of it. She might experience love or pain or fear living in this attitude subjectively. Or she might abstract herself from this subjectivity and realize in awareness, 'I am in pain'; 'I am afraid'; 'I do love.' The crucial point is that there would be no barriers, no inhibitions, which would prevent the full experiencing of whatever was organismically present."[10]

In this way, as in various other ways, my thinking is similar to that of Lancelot Whyte, who comes at the same problem from a very different perspective, that of the philosopher of science and historian of ideas. He too feels that in the person who is functioning well "the free play of spontaneous vitality —as in the transitory rhythms of eating, drinking, walking, loving, making things, working well, thinking, and dreaming— evokes no persistent differentiated awareness. We feel right while it is going on, and then forget it, as a rule."[11]

When functioning in this manner the person is whole, integrated, unitary. This appears to be the desirable and efficient human way. Sharpened self-consciousness in such functioning arises, according to Whyte, only as a result of contrast or clash between the organism and its environment, and the function of such self-awareness is to eliminate the clash by modifying the environment or altering the behavior of the individual. His viewpoint is startling but challenging when he says, "The main purpose of conscious thought, its neo-biological function, may be first to identify, and then to eliminate, the factors which evoke it."[12]

It will probably be evident that views such as the foregoing could be held only by individuals who see the nonconscious aspects of our living in a positive light. I have myself stressed the idea that man is wiser than his intellect, and that well-functioning persons come to trust their experiencing as an appropriate guide to their behavior. They find that the meanings discovered in their openness to their experiencing constitute a wise and satisfying means of directing their actions. Whyte places this same idea in a larger context when he says, "Crystals, plants and animals grow without any conscious fuss, and the strangeness of our own history disappears once we assume that the same kind of natural ordering process that guides their growth also guided the development of man and of his mind, and does so still."[13] These views are very remote from Freud's distrust of the unconscious, and his general view that it was antisocial in its direction. Instead, when a person is functioning in an integrated, unified, effective manner, she has confidence in the directions she unconsciously chooses, and trusts her experiencing, of which, even if she is fortunate, she has only partial glimpses in her awareness.

If this is a reasonable description of the functioning of consciousness when all is going well, why does the rift develop in so many of us, to the point that organismically we are moving in one direction and in our conscious lives are struggling in another? My own explanation[14] has to do with the personal dynamics of the individual. Love by the parent or significant other is made conditional. It is given only on the condition that the child introject certain constructs and values as his own. Otherwise he will not be perceived as worthwhile, as worthy of love. Thus, for example, the construct "you love your mother" is made a condition for a child receiving her mother's love. Hence her occasional feelings of rage and hatred toward her mother are denied to awareness, as if they did not exist. Her organism may behave in ways that show her anger, such as spilling her food on the floor, but this is an "accident." She does not permit the real feeling into awareness. Or I think of a young adolescent boy, brought up in a strictly religious home, where it was clear that he was acceptable to his parents only if he believed that sexual thoughts, impulses, and behaviors were evil and awful. When he was caught one night in the home of the next-door neighbor, trying to tear the nightdress off their sleeping daughter, he could say, with a firm belief that he was telling the truth, that *he* had not done it—it was not *his* behavior. Here his organism—with its natural curiosity, fantasies, and impulses in the area of sex—had been so thoroughly denied that he was quite unaware of these aspects of his physical being. So his organism went on endeavoring to meet these needs, while his conscious mind could say quite accurately that his self had not been involved in the behavior.

In this example the introjected beliefs or constructs are rigid and static because they are taken in from outside. They are not subject to the child's normal process of evaluating his experience in a fluid, changing way. The child tends to disregard his own experiencing process wherever it conflicts with these constructs, and thus to this degree cuts himself off from his organic functioning, becoming to this degree dissociated. If the conditions of worth imposed on a child are numerous and significant, then the dissociation can become very great, and the psychological consequences, as we have seen, very serious indeed.

I have gradually come to see this dissociation, rift, estrangement, as something learned, a perverse channeling of some of the actualizing tendency into behaviors that do not actualize. In this respect it would be similar to the situation in which sexual urges can, through learning, be channeled into behaviors far removed from the physiological and evolutionary ends of these impulses. In this respect my thinking has changed. Years ago I saw the rift between self and experience, between conscious goals and organismic directions, as something natural and necessary, albeit unfortunate. Now I believe that individuals are culturally conditioned, rewarded, reinforced, for behaviors that are in fact perversions of the natural directions of the unitary actualizing tendency.

The dissociated person is best described as one *consciously* behaving in terms of introjected static, rigid constructs, and *unconsciously* behaving in terms of the actualizing tendency. This is in sharp contrast to the healthy, well-functioning person who lives in close and confident relationship to her own ongoing organismic processes, nonconscious as well as conscious. I see constructive outcomes in therapy or in groups as possible only in terms of the human individual who has come to trust her own inner directions, and whose awareness is a part of and integrated with the process nature of her organic functioning. I have described the functioning of the psychologically mature individual as being similar in many ways to that of the infant, except that the fluid process of experiencing has more scope and sweep, and that the mature individual, like the child, "trusts and uses the wisdom of her organism, with the difference that she is able to do so knowingly."[15]

The extremely common estrangement of the human being from her directional organismic processes is not a necessary part of our nature. It is instead something learned, and learned to an especially high degree in our Western culture. It is characterized by behaviors that are guided by rigid concepts and constructs, interrupted at times by behaviors guided by the organismic processes. The satisfaction or fulfillment of the actualizing tendency has become bifurcated into incompatible behavioral systems, of which one may be dominant at one moment, and the other dominant at another moment, but at a continual cost of strain and inefficiency. This dissociation that exists in most of us is the pattern and the basis of all psychological pathology in humankind, and the basis of all his social pathology as well.

The natural and efficient mode of living as a human being does not involve this dissociation, this bifurcation. The psychologically mature person exhibits a trust in the directions of inner organismic processes which, with consciousness participating in a coordinated rather than a competitive fashion, carry one forward in a total, unified, integrated, adaptive, and changing encounter with life and its challenges.

The tragic condition of humankind is that it has lost confidence in its own nonconscious inner directions. As Whyte has written: "Western man stands out as a highly developed but bizarre distortion of the human animal."[16] To me the remedy for this situation is the incredibly difficult but not impossible task of permitting the human individual to grow and develop in a continuing confident relationship to the formative actualizing tendency and process in herself. If awareness and conscious thought are seen as a part of life—not its master nor its opponent but an illumination of the developing processes within the individual—then our total life can be the unified and unifying experience that seems characteristic in nature. If our magnificent symbolizing capacity can develop as a part of and be guided by the tendency toward fulfillment that exists in us both at the conscious and nonconscious levels, then the organic harmony is never lost and becomes a human harmony and human wholeness simply because our species is capable of greater richness of experience than any other.

And if the skeptical and natural question is raised, "Yes, but how? How could this possibly come about?" then it seems to me that science suggests an answer. We have already been able to specify and even to measure the attitudinal conditions that bring about growthful effects in both therapy and education. Scientific investigation can help us still further. Having identified the conditions that are associated with the restoration of unity and integration in the individual, we should be able to move ahead and identify empirically those elements that promote dissociation, that bifurcate the actualizing tendency. One testable hypothesis is that dissociation occurs when love and esteem are made conditional. If we can identify the environmental influences that promote a continuing internal harmony in children, without the all too common learning of dissociation, these findings could be put to preventive use. We can prevent the rift from occurring. We can, if we will, use our scientific skills to help us keep the person whole and unified, a creature whose actualizing tendency will be continually forming her in the direction of a richer and more fulfilling relationship to life.

I believe the political significance of this view of human nature and its motivating force is enormous. I have tried to sketch the view that the human species is composed of basically trustworthy organisms, trustworthy persons. I have pointed out that the actualizing tendency, when operating freely, tends toward an integrated wholeness in which behavior is guided as much by the experiencings within as by the consciousness that flutters over these experiencings. But what does this mean from the point of view of the politics of interpersonal relationships?

It leads me to the conclusion that the most trustworthy entity in our uncertain world is an individual who is fully open to the two major sources: the data from internal experiencing, and the data from experiencing of the external world. This person is at the opposite pole from the dissociated individual. Either he or she was fortunate in not developing the internal rift between the experiencing organism and the conscious self or this rift has been eliminated in helping relationships or by healing life experiences.

In such an individual, functioning in a unified way, we have the best possible base for wise action. It is a process base, not a static authority base. It is a trustworthiness that does not rest on static "scientific" knowledge. On the other hand, in its reliance on being fully open to all of the relevant data, it represents the very essence of the scientific approach to life, as science has been understood by its truly great minds. It represents a continual process of testing hypotheses in thought and action, discarding some, but following others. It recognizes that there is no such thing as static truth, only a series of changing approximations to the truth.

Politically, then, if we are in search of a trustworthy base to operate from, our major aim would be to discover and possibly to increase the number of individuals who are coming closer to being whole persons—who are moving toward a knowledge of, and harmony with, their innermost experience, and who sense, with an equal lack of defensiveness, all the data from the persons and objects in their external environment. These persons would constitute an increasing flow of wisdom in action. Their directions would be wiser than the commandments of gods or the directives of governments. They might become the vitalizing stream of a constructive future.

I'm aware that this vision will seem to some hopelessly idealistic, to others a dangerous flouting of sacred authorities, and to others simply bizarre. Yet for me, it is the closest approximation to truth I have been able to achieve, and I find it exciting and hopeful.

Part IV A new political figure

Chapter 12 | The emerging person: spearhead of the quiet revolution

A person-centered approach to many aspects of our life would lead to a desirable, constructive, and viable way of being. I do not, however, deceive myself about the degree of support that this view currently commands in this country. Our nation's future direction now hangs in the balance; we are living in a time of crucial choices—both conscious and unconscious—that will determine our fate. Here are some of the factors weighing *against* valuing the person, against self-direction, against individual responsible power.

The principles of our Constitution, especially the Bill of Rights—both decidedly person-centered in their values—are increasingly questioned. There is a growing disbelief by the average man in the workability of any kind of political democracy, let alone an approach that would diffuse power, control, and decision-making in every area of living. There is evidence that if the Bill of Rights to our Constitution were rewritten in modern language and put to popular vote, it would be rejected. The rights and responsibilities of the citizen are no longer held precious.

The rights to freedom of thought and speech, the right to advocate any point of view in which one believes—these freedoms are not highly regarded today. Even universities, where these freedoms are of the essence, often refuse to permit speakers to appear because their views are opposed by some influential group. And it is not only administrators who limit these freedoms but faculty and students as well.

In government, supposedly the source and protector of personal freedom, the erosion of democratic values is even worse. The average citizen does not trust his elected officials. A cynical and suspicious attitude toward the government and all its members runs deep throughout the citizenry. The attitude is reciprocated: Our government shows a profound distrust of its citizens. The evidence is clear that both the FBI and the CIA—agencies whose function is to protect the nation and its citizens—have been engaged in massive efforts to harass and crush dissent by any means—legal or illegal, ethical or unethical. The means ranged from guns—resulting in the killings at Kent State and at three less-publicized black campuses—to the spread of forged letters and documents to bring about divisiveness in dissenting groups. The Watergate exposure of the federal elite, from the President down, shows an open official contempt for the person and his rights. Lies, deceit, criminal invasion of privacy, flouting of the law, surveillance and imprisonment of dissenters—all these have been tools used to control the populace and to hold power over persons.

It is not in government alone that we see a decline in the valuing of persons. The rot extends further, and shows up in the decay of our institutions. Our public educational system is ossified, failing to meet the needs of society. Innovation is stifled, and innovators squeezed out. In a rapidly changing world, faculty members and their governing boards—whether local school boards or college trustees—cling tenaciously to the past, making only token changes. Our schools are more damaging than helpful to personality development and are a negative influence on creative thinking. They are primarily institutions for incarcerating or taking care of the young, to keep them out of the adult world.

Economically, the picture is bizarre. The wealthiest nation in the world is said to be unable to afford proper health care for its people. The efforts to eliminate poverty are themselves being eliminated, while the top 8 percent of the populace receives more income than the bottom 50 percent. The gap between the rich and poor in this country, and between the rich nations and poor nations in the world, grows steadily wider. Great corporations have an inordinate influence on our government and on our life and even presumptuously interfere in the affairs of foreign countries. High office now goes preponderantly to men of wealth, so that of our one hundred senators, supposedly representing the people, forty are reported to be millionaires. The ordinary person has sensitive and compassionate representation neither in the corporation for which he works nor in the government that rules him.

Our churches are currently lacking in any significant societal influence. What impact they do have is generally opposed to a person-centered point of view. Their politics is either strictly hierarchical, laying down rules for the faithful, or based on a leader-follower relationship, the leader being prized for his charismatic qualities.

The family is in a state of disarray and confusion. In most marriages spouse is alienated from spouse and parent from adolescent. To the extent that it exerts any influence at all, it is generally authority-centered rather than person-centered.

No one can deny the incredibly rapid growth and spread of violence. In our large cities people double- and triple-lock their doors. Walking on the street in the evening ranges from a hazardous to a highly dangerous occupation. The parks, set aside for the enjoyment of the public, are places for ambush and mugging. Senseless stabbings and killings occur every day. In addition to all this there is the development of organized terrorism, with a real or pseudo-political base.

There are many theories as to the causes of all this violence and of the vandalism that accompanies it—the attacks on both persons and property. I do not claim any special expertise in this field, and I will not add to the speculation about causes. I would, however, point out two relationships.

Random violence against persons cannot and does not occur in a culture where each individual feels he is a part of an ongoing, purposeful process. One must be thoroughly alienated from the mainstream of society for impersonal violence to become possible. In China, a culture very different from our own, the impersonal random violence of our cities is, from all reports, virtually unknown. This is not because the Chinese are incapable of violence. There have been fanatic purposeful drives to kill landlords or opponents of the Cultural Revolution and the like. But in day-to-day living the Chinese are organized into local groups with a good deal of self-government. Furthermore they feel, to a surprising degree, a stake in building their country anew. This sense of a unifying purpose seems almost completely lacking in our country today. The purposes that are voiced are mostly to maintain the status quo or to become bigger and better in every technology. These goals do not command the loyalty of our people, nor do they supply a unifying force.

I will leave it to others, more knowledgeable, to explain why such a large part of our population feels no such inclusion in the social enterprise and is thoroughly alien to it, so much so that some of them rob, stab, kill these "others" without any obvious compunctions. The *fact* of their alienation is, however, clear.

The other point I make is that for violence to become possible, any belief in the worth and dignity of each person must first disappear. Unprovoked violence cannot occur where there is a conviction that each individual has an inalienable right to "life, liberty, and the pursuit of happiness." Person-centeredness must have flown out the window before senseless interpersonal attacks can become possible. The victim is not a person to the assailant, or he could not attack.

The disarray in our culture makes it less than surprising that there has been a steady trend toward abandoning personal freedoms and permitting stronger hands to take over. There is a drift toward authoritarian control.

The nation was shocked, not too long ago, by the massive efforts of President Nixon and his colleagues to subvert the Constitution and take control into their own hands. Yet we cannot avoid responsibility for this. It was the will of the people. A steady drift toward increasing the power of the Presidency had been evident for years. Not only that, Mr. Nixon's past record was clear. He believed—and acted on that belief time and again—that any means could and should be used to gather power into his own hands. The use of lies and subtler forms of deceit and the employment of aides who were expert at building an "image" with no resemblance to reality had been the basis of his political life. A large sign in the offices of the Committee to Reelect the President in 1972 summed up the philosophy: "Winning in Politics Isn't Everything. It's the Only Thing!" Yet we elected him with an overwhelming vote. We wanted him. The fact that later we couldn't stomach his lies and forced his resignation is of importance, but it is of no more importance than the fact that we knowingly chose him, not once but twice. And there is no reason to suppose that we have rid ourselves of our desire for a strong, oppressive leader. It is doubtful that our people really desire the participatory democracy that was envisioned by the framers of our Constitution. It seems probable that a majority would vote for a powerful leader who could impose his will on the people. Or if they would not vote for this, the overwhelming apathy and cynicism of the majority indicates their permission for it to happen. In a recent California election 80 percent of the eligible voters age eighteen to twenty-one—the young people whose futures are at stake—failed to vote. Undoubtedly their attitude is "What's the use?" They have no belief that they can participate in government in any meaningful way. This is the perfect soil for developing a dictatorship.

Not only in government is there a trend toward an increasing concentration of authoritarian control. In our great corporations, especially in the mammoth multinational ones, we see a development of power and control that causes the individual to feel impotent. He is simply a pawn at the mercy of faceless groups that determine his life.

Tom Hanna, in his slashing book *The End of Tyranny*, gives a label to this general drift toward dictatorial rule. He calls it "Dysamerica," since it's utterly opposed to the goals, ideals, and political structure embodied in the Constitution. It is "Dysamerican" as opposed to "American."

Many social historians, economists, and forecasters agree that the disillusionment with democracy is growing, and they see it coming to fruition in the future. They say a controlled society is inevitable.[1] The problems will be too complex for democracy to handle. The hard and unpopular decisions that will have to be made to bring an overaffluent society back to a simpler, less wasteful, less polluting way of life can, they believe, only be made by an autocrat or a ruling elite. We will all have to give up our freedom, so the argument goes, in order to survive.

So why not go along with the trend, recognize that the democratic way is dying, that society cannot function if based on the belief in a responsible person who participates in decision-making? Why not relax and enjoy the controls that are or will be exercised by authoritarian government, profit-controlled multinational corporations, a rigidly prescribed educational system, an elitist control of individual behavior? Why fight this supposedly inevitable shift?

I cannot go along with this thinking.

Even under the strictest totalitarian regimes, where government policy, economic organization, personal behavior, and individual thought are all controlled by a central group, *persons* emerge. In Russia, the name of Solzhenitsyn has been but a symbol of a much larger movement. He flourished against incredible oppression and survives. Many others have not survived and will not survive. Yet public opinion the world over admires and rejoices in a man who dares to value his own person and that of others, and from that value base expresses his own thoughts, refuses—to the death—to be controlled, and dares to challenge our system too. Belief in the worth of the free person is not something that can be extinguished even by all the modern technological devices—bugging of conversations, use of "mental hospitals" to recondition behavior, electric torture, and all the rest. Nothing can extinguish the human organism's drive to be itself—to actualize itself in individual and creative ways. We recognize this by applauding a Solzhenitsyn even as we permit our own government to move in the direction of totalitarian control over our own behavior.

There's also the possibility that Americans are choosing a new kind of democracy. A survey made for the People's Bicentennial Commission turned up some surprising attitudes.[2] A representative sample of over twelve hundred individuals from all parts of the country and including all income levels shows that 58 percent believe that America's great corporations tend to dominate and determine the actions of our federal officials. Only 25 percent believe the reverse—that government officials determine the actions of the corporations. A majority—nearly two-thirds—favor *employee* ownership and control of American corporations, with employees owning most of the stock and determining broad policies, including the selection of management. Seventy-four percent favor having consumers in local communities represented on the boards of companies operating in those communities. Fifty-six percent say that they would definitely or probably support a Presidential candidate who stood for employee control of American corporations.

Here is certainly an instance in which the inarticulate groundswell of public opinion has gone far beyond the stand of the political leaders of our country. None of the candidates in 1976 represented any such view. Yet here is evidence that people in general are making a strong statement on two points: they distrust large corporations whose management does not seem accountable to their owners, the competitive marketplace, the government, or their employees; they believe responsible and humane behavior on the part of those companies is more likely if they are owned and controlled by the employees. This would bring about a participatory economic democracy. As John Adams said in 1815, the war was "no part of the Revolution: It was only an effect and consequence of it. The Revolution was in the minds of the people, a change in their sentiments, their duties and obligations. . . . This radical change in the principles, opinions, sentiments, and affections of the people was the real American Revolution."

What the survey is saying is that here, in one segment of public thinking—the economic area—we are seeing a "radical change in the principles, opinions, sentiments and affections of the people" that may be a part of the new revolution. And it's a change from a profit-centered, organization-centered view to a person-centered view. It is closer to the original American view and away from a Dysamerica.

But is this simply an isolated example? Is there sufficient reason to believe that our seemingly declining society has any possibility of saving itself? I wish to explore these questions.

One lesson I have often learned in my garden is that the brown and rotting mess of this year's plant is a mulch in which next year's new shoots may be discovered. So, too, I believe that in our decaying culture we see the dim outlines of new growth, of a new revolution, of a culture of a sharply different sort. I see that revolution as coming not in some great organized movement, not in a gun-carrying army with banners, not in manifestos and declarations, but through the emergence of a new kind of person, thrusting up through the dying, yellowing, putrefying leaves and stalks of our fading institutions.

A number of years ago I gave a short, brash talk on "The Person of Tomorrow." I did not submit it for publication because I felt very unsure of my perceptions of this new person, and whether indeed he was emerging, or whether he was simply a wild fantasy of my own. But since that time my experience has only confirmed what seemed then to be a far-out thesis. Also, encouragingly for me, there has been a spate of books, from widely different sources, each from its own perspective seeing our culture undergoing some sort of drastic change and producing a type of individual, a type of consciousness, a way of being and behaving, that will reshape our world. We have a solid medical scientist, René Dubos,[3] emphasizing that man's very make-up means that the future belongs to the "unique, unprecedented, and unrepeatable person," and that "trend is not destiny." We have a poetic journalist-educator, George B. Leonard,[4] setting forth an almost ecstatic vision of the human species undertaking "an awesome journey into a higher state of being," a transformation he regards as inevitable. From a different vantage point, philanthropist-financier John D. Rockefeller III[5] pictures the second American Revolution already in progress, caused partially by our much sharper and clearer awareness of ourselves and our world, and leading to a humanistic fulfillment of the American dream. A philosopher-psychologist, Thomas Hanna,[6] writes a hymn to the wholeness of the pulsing, growing human soma—body and mind united—and to the new human mutants who are living that realization, leading us toward a new goal. He describes these mutants as the "New American freemen."[7] A noted microbiologist, Jonas Salk,[8] leads us through his biological perspective to see an intellectual and spiritual evolution of man's unfolding potential. The Stanford Research Institute, through its social policy center, has issued an exhaustive report that asks how we may "facilitate the emergence of new images" of man, convinced that we must have a new and more adequate image if we are to survive.[9] Two psychologist-educators, Fred and Anne Richards,[10] state the theme of their book in their one-word title, "Homonovus," the new man. A far-out young medical researcher, Andrew Weil,[11] builds a case for the new man by pointing out the advantages of intuitive thinking—the natural mind—based on unconscious factors and altered states of consciousness, over the conventional rational thinking of the average man and the academic. Provocatively, he says the future will belong to "stoned" rather than to "straight" thinking (though by "stoned" he does not imply drug-induced). A novelist, Joyce Carol Oates,[12] believes we are in a "crisis of transition," between the end of the Renaissance and the "higher humanism" man is evolving toward. She uses the marvelous quotation from Sir James Jeans, the physicist-philosopher, which I have given earlier. It expresses a theme that runs through all of the writers I have mentioned, who seem to be tolling the knell of a narrowly mechanistic view. Jeans says, "The universe begins to look more like a great *thought* than like a great machine."

Such a diversity of strangely convergent perceptions of the future have emboldened me to present with more confidence— and with, I hope, more depth—my view of the radical new budding of persons that may change the fundamental nature of our society. What I say is based on wide personal observation, on interactions with diverse individuals and groups, on my reading. It is an informal speculation, with all the possibility of bias and error that that implies. It is not empirical science, nor is it intended to be, though I hope it may contain some elements of observation that will inspire further study.

It springs primarily from my experiences with what I have come to think of as new persons. Where have I found them? I find them among corporation executives who have given up the gray-flannel rat race, the lure of high salaries and stock options, to live a simpler life in a new way.[13] I find them among simply dressed, long-haired young men and women who have defied most of the values of today's culture and formed a counter culture. I find them among priests and nuns and ministers who have left behind the dogmas of their institutions to live lives of more meaning. I find them among women who are vigorously rising above the limitations that society has placed on their personhood. I find them among blacks and Chicanos and other minority members who are pushing out from generations of passivity into assertive, positive lives. I find them among those who have experienced encounter groups, who are finding a place for feelings as well as thoughts in their lives. I find them among creative school dropouts who are thrusting into higher reaches than their sterile schooling permits. I realize, too, that I saw something of these persons in my ·years as psychotherapist, when clients were choosing freer, richer, more self-directed lives for themselves. The above are a few of the places in which I have glimpsed something of these emerging persons.[14]

Though the sources of my perceptions are incredibly diverse, I find a certain unity in the individuals I am perceiving. The configuration seems similar, even though there are many minor differences. These persons present a new face to the world, a pattern which has not, in my judgment, ever been seen before, except perhaps in rare individuals.

I find these persons first of all to have a deep concern for authenticity. Communication is especially valued as a means of telling it the way it is, with feelings, ideas, gestures, speech, and bodily movement all conveying the same message. They have been brought up in a climate of hypocrisy, deceit, and mixed messages, and are sick to death of double-think and double-talk. They know the falsehoods and guile of Madison Avenue. They have heard consciously deceitful statements from "the highest official sources" in our government. They have observed the word "peace" used to mean "war," and the phrase "law and order" used to mean "repression of dissent by illegal means." They have listened to the double messages of parents and teachers. All of these add up to the admonition, "Don't watch what I am or what I do; listen to what I say." They reject this current hypocritical culture, and long to establish interpersonal relations in which communications are real and complete, rather than phony or partial. Astonishing progress is shown in this respect. They are open, for example, about sexual relationships rather than leading secretive or double lives. Parents, teachers, government officials are confronted with their views, rather than false impressions of agreement being given. They are learning to handle conflict, even in organizations—how to carry on continuing relationships in a climate of trust built on openness, rather than on a basis of façade. These persons are for real.

This desire for straightforwardness is expressed in public and in private ways. There is no doubt that the brutal war in Vietnam was finally brought to a halt by the insistent uncovering, by these new persons, of the hypocrisy of that war. They made it clear that we were not fighting against communist villains to uphold a democracy, but to prop up a corrupt, unpopular, and dictatorial government. It was straight speaking which eventually stopped our massive war machinery.

On the personal side a young woman, Donna Lee Ryan, a senior-class speaker at Sonoma State, says, "This is the time to begin to speak frankly of the things which concern us. . . . This is the time to live the way we talk. This is the time for more action and fewer words. As students we have learned to play the game of intellectualization, and we know that it is a comfortable way to avoid life. But this is the time . . . to stand firmly opposed to that form of compromise which causes us to lose our self-respect."

A highly honored young man, Meldon Levine, in his commencement address to the Harvard Law School, said to the assembled faculty and parents, "You have told us repeatedly that trust and courage were standards to emulate. You have convinced us that equality and justice were inviolable concepts. You have taught us that authority should be guided by reason and tempered by fairness. We have taken you seriously. . . . Now, for attempting to achieve the values which you have taught us to cherish, your response has been astounding." He points out how the efforts of young people to correct injustices and change the system have been met by disapproval, harassment, and oppression. "When this type of violent repression replaces the search for reasonable alternatives Americans are allowing their most fundamental ideals to be compromised." He is challenging our two-faced culture.

One of the deepest antipathies of emerging persons is directed toward institutions. They are opposed to all highly structured, inflexible, bureaucratic institutions. The firm belief is that institutions exist for persons, and not the reverse.

One of the most striking cultural developments of our time is the decline of the power and authority of the institution—in government, the military, the church, the corporation, the school. This is certainly due in part to the attitude of new emerging persons. They will not put up with order for order's sake, form for form's sake, rules for the sake of having rules. Every aspect of formal structure is questioned and discarded unless it serves a human purpose. Every inflexibility of any sort is suspect, for rigidity cannot serve the changing human being.

Beliefs on this score are not idle talk. Emerging persons will leave an institution rather than give in to meaningless dictates. Faculty members drop out of universities, students out of colleges, doctors out of the AMA, priests out of their churches, executives out of corporations, air force pilots out of bombing groups, spies out of the CIA, scientists out of corporations making nuclear power plants.

Many of these actions are taken quietly, without fanfare. The institution of marriage is being deserted by thousands of couples, both young and middle-aged, who have chosen to ignore customs, ritual, and law, to live together as partners without the sanction of marriage. This is done openly, but without defiance. These couples simply believe that a partnership has significance only if it is a mutually enhancing, growing relationship.

In a survey of Catholic wives, of those under the age of thirty, over 75 percent are using methods of birth control of which the church disapproves. To the best of my knowledge there have been no demonstrations against the pope's 1968 encyclical. There is no wave of protest. These women are simply disregarding the institutional pronouncement, and acting in ways that they see as best for persons, not for the structure. It is a striking instance of the new attitude toward institutions.

What will take the place of the institution for this new person? It is too soon to say. One trend that I see is toward small, informal, nonhierarchical groups. Students and faculty have started hundreds of "free schools," "experimental schools," informal, often short-lived, decidedly unstructured, full of excitement and learning. Several graduate schools of high standards permit a student to achieve a doctoral degree through a program of independent study devised by the student. The candidate is advised and aided by a group of faculty and peers who help him make sure that the study is thorough, of sufficient depth and magnitude, and makes a contribution to knowledge. Two such graduate schools known to me personally are Union Graduate School and The Humanistic Psychology Institute. These programs are swamped with applications and attract a high type of independently minded scholars, but all are trying to stay small.

Business executives who have dropped out start personal enterprises, limited in size, where relationships are direct and face to face, rather than at second—or fifth—hand. An ex-navy and Pan Am pilot sets up a pottery shop to sell his own creations. A public relations executive becomes a farmer and freelance writer. A sales manager in a construction company becomes the proprietor of a small wine and cheese shop. Persons of all types join communes, where the relationships are personal, and structure and authority are called into being only to accomplish a specific purpose. Some new professional groups, like the Center to which I am privileged to belong, are bound by a sense of community with no lasting lines of authority and no desire to expand, but carrying on diverse and creative projects.

Another trend is to humanize the institution from inside, simply disregarding meaningless rules. Thus factory assembly-line workers ignore their assigned, routinized jobs and form teams in which they trade off duties, handle two jobs at a time, and in other ways pronounce, by their actions, that they are self-directing persons whose interests come first, not cogs in a great technological wheel.

In government and politics, too—that quagmire in which so

many men have sunk—some are endeavoring to take a human approach. Here is a successful state legislator writing to his constituents to say that "institutions must become life-oriented rather than death-oriented . . . persons in politics [must] be committed to . . . self-realization rather than self-denial. Increasingly I come to realize that the discovery of a new politics for our culture depends upon my living and experiencing and discovering a 'new politics' within myself—getting so much in touch with all the parts of my own being, that out of the resultant oneness within me, I will increasingly live disclosingly so as to expose the institutions and customs of our culture which stand in the way of oneness—within ourselves, between ourselves, between us and the earth."[15] This is indeed a fresh breeze in the political world—an authentic *person* seeking electoral support, getting it, and changing a time-honored institution from the inside.

Emerging persons are indifferent to material comforts and rewards. The machines, comforts, and luxuries of the affluent society are no longer a necessity. Blue jeans, a sleeping bag, and natural food are valued as much as—and sometimes more than —expensive clothing, fine lodging, and gourmet meals. We find corporation men who have become very comfortable as explorers, or ski instructors, because they prefer those lives. We find young people with no interest in accumulating money, but only in using money for constructive personal or social uses. Money and material status symbols are no longer the primary goals of these people.

Emerging persons are neither power-hungry nor achievement-hungry. When they seek power, it is for other than purely selfish purposes. Much has been made of the fact that many of the most visible protesters of the sixties—Tom Hayden, for example—are now working within the establishment. But it is not usually pointed out that this is merely another step in a consistent process. In the sixties they demonstrated, marched, staged sit-ins. They found these tactics effective—to a point. They did alert the public, helped to sharpen the basic issues.

But they were not particularly successful in bringing lasting change. So now many of the individuals are indeed working from within the establishment to bring about change. Whether these efforts are through the machinery of politics, through legal services for the poor, or working on a farm-labor board, the changes they are working for are still in the direction of giving individual persons more power over their lives.

These persons are caring persons. They have a deep desire to be of help to others, to "brothers and sisters," and to society, when its need for help is clear. These persons are, however, definitely suspicious of the "helping professions," where "shrinks," social workers, and drug counselors earn their livelihood by offering help for pay, and too often hide behind a professional façade. They tend to take a more direct route. Young men and women man hot-lines to aid those in crisis, and they do it voluntarily. They share food or lodging without question. When "straight people" are in emergency situations, they respond. In recent river floods, long-haired young men and women have rushed in, sometimes from hundreds of miles away, to fill sandbags, shore up levees, take care of families. And in all of this, financial compensation is a nonexistent or very minor consideration.

The help so freely given by emerging persons is a gentle, subtle, nonmoralistic caring. When a person is helped down from a bad drug trip, the touch is soft and supportive, without overtones of preaching. When an individual is caught in a crime he is helped, not lectured or hassled. These persons are acceptant of the individual in distress, with an awareness that the roles might easily be reversed. They fly in the face of the modes of "helping" most popular in our culture—the diagnostic, evaluative, interpretive, prescriptive, and punitive approaches.

These persons are seeking new forms of community, of closeness, of intimacy, of shared purpose. He and she are seeking new forms of communication in such a community—verbal and nonverbal, feelingful as well as intellectual. There is a recognition that personal life will be transient, mostly in temporary relationships, and that they must be able to establish closeness quickly. In this mobile world persons do not live long in one community. These individuals are not surrounded by family and relatives. They are a part of the temporary society.[16] There is a realization that if they are to live in a human context, there must be an ability to establish intimate, communicative, personal bonds with others in a very short space of time. They must be able to leave these close relationships behind, without excessive conflict or mourning.

One attitude held by emerging persons runs strongly counter to the prevailing view of the current and past decades. It is the deep distrust of a cognitively based science, and a technology that uses that science to conquer the world of nature and the world of people. There is no longer trust in the abstractions of science, or the uses to which they are put. There is an intuitive belief that significant discoveries and learnings involve feelings. These persons were not especially thrilled by the space program; they questioned the littering of space and of the moon with priceless junk. They think that technology should exist for some purpose other than conquest.

One of the manifestations of this distrust of science as we have known it is the interest and belief in the occult, in astrology, in the I-Ching, and in Tarot cards—the sciences of the past. But emerging persons have also been more than willing to engage in modern science and technology when convinced these serve human purposes. Their expertise in electronics as a means of creating and transmitting music is obvious. The eagerness to use biofeedback as a means of enlarging self-awareness, and to bring changes in behavior, is another instance of this willingness.

The general distrust of scientific "progress" should not be misinterpreted. These persons are not dogmatic. They are eager to find truth. These are searching persons, without any neat answers. The only certainty is that we are uncertain. These persons are sharply aware of the fact that each one of us is only a speck of life on a small blue-and-white planet (whose days may be numbered) floating in an enormous universe. Like many previous searchers, they are uncertain as to whether there is a purpose in this universe, or only the purposes we create. The persons of tomorrow are willing to live with this anxious uncertainty as they strive to learn more of the two universes, outer and inner.

For another characteristic of these persons is the clear desire to explore inner space. They are more willing than previous man to be aware of self, of inner feelings, of hang-ups. These individuals are able to communicate with themselves more freely, with less fear. The barriers of repression, which shut off so much of the individual from awareness, are definitely lower than in preceding generations. These are highly aware persons.

The willingness to look within has led these new persons into many new areas—drug-induced states of altered consciousness, a fresh interest in dreams, the use of a variety of types of meditation, a concern with all types of psychic phenomena, an interest in esoteric and transcendental religious views. They are convinced that within themselves lie undiscovered worlds and hidden capacities—that day-dreaming, fantasy, and intuition are but gateways to much more. Cosmic consciousness, thought transmission, and Kirlian auras given off by living things are not nonsensical ravings, but are regarded as within the bounds of possibility, and there is no hesitation to upset a conventional world view by exploring them.

They realize, as I do, that just as the exploding galaxies and "black holes" of outer space have been the focus of much exploration in recent decades, tomorrow is the day of inner space. There will need to be courageous pioneering into the mysterious and currently unfathomable separate realities, which appear to exist, incredibly different from our present objective world. These emerging persons have the daring and the freedom of thought to begin such explorations. They could find support from Einstein's statement: "The supreme task . . . is to arrive at those universal elementary laws from which the cosmos can be built up by pure deduction. There is no logical path to these laws; *only intuition, resting on sympathetic understanding of experience, can reach them*"[17] (italics mine). These new persons already have the intuitive conviction that mysterious laws, operating in the world of the psychic, simply do not fit into the present framework of scientific thinking.

In quite another area these persons feel a closeness to elemental nature. There is a respect for nature and its ways, and a relearning of lessons from ancient tribes on how to live in a balance of man's mutuality with nature, each sustaining the other. In these persons' recreation, the surfboard, the ski, the sailboat, the glider are more symbolic of their interests than the speedboat, the dune buggy, or the racing car. The first cluster bases its excitement on a thrilling *alliance* with natural forces —waves, snow-covered slopes, the wind and its air currents— the second on the determined conquest of nature, with destruction and pollution as results. In this respect for nature the new persons have rediscovered the value of patiently waiting upon the inhabitants of wilderness and desert in order to learn. We have men and women devoting long years of hardship to live with primitive tribes, or with gorillas, lions, chimpanzees, simply to learn from them. It is a new and respectful attitude, a more humble one.

These are persons who are aware that they are continually in process—always changing. In this process they are spontaneous, vitally alive, willing to risk. Likes and dislikes, joys and sorrows are passionate and are passionately expressed. The adventuresomeness has an almost Elizabethan quality—*everything* is possible, *anything* can be tried.

Because these new persons are always in process, they simply will not tolerate fixity. These individuals can see no reason why rigid schools, glaring maldistribution of wealth, depressed ghetto areas, unfair racial or sexual discrimination, unjust wars should remain unchanged. They expect to change these situations, and want to change them in human directions. I believe this person is the first instance in history of man being fully aware that changingness is the one constant in life.

These new persons have a trust in their own experience and a profound distrust of all external authority. Neither pope nor judge nor scholar can convince these individuals of anything that is not borne out by personal experience. So they often decide to obey those laws that are personally regarded as sound and just, and to disobey those that seem unsound and unjust, taking the consequences of their actions. On a minor issue, they smoke marijuana in defiance of laws regarded as unreasonable and unfair, and risk being busted. On major issues they refuse to be drafted when they regard a war as reprehensible; they give out secret government documents when convinced the people should know what has been going on; they refuse to reveal the sources of news reports for the same reason. This is a new phenomenon. We have had a few Thoreaus, but we have never had hundreds and thousands of people, young and old alike, willing to obey some laws and disobey others on the basis of their own personal moral judgment, and living with the consequences of their choice. These persons have a high regard for self, and for their competence to discriminate in issues involving authority.

These are some of the characteristics I see in emerging persons. I am well aware that few individuals possess all of these characteristics, and I know that I am describing a small minority of the population as a whole. Yet these persons appear to me to be having an impact entirely out of proportion to their numbers, and this has, I believe, significance for the future.

The view seems prevalent that while persons of the sort I have been describing were evident in the turbulent and protesting sixties, all is now changed. Students and young people, I am told, are now interested only in security in jobs. They want the big salaries, the big cars, the pensions. They are no longer interested in change—only in stability.

I cannot agree. These emerging persons have never constituted a majority of the young, nor a majority of any age level. So while the majority of young people may be more security-minded than the demonstrators of a decade ago, I find many younger people who still fit the general picture I have given. Perhaps even more significant is the fact that a larger proportion of those who can no longer be classed as youth are becoming process persons. The numbers are larger, not smaller, of those who are deserting the established institutions to live freer, more risky, more uncertain, simpler, and more changing lives.

Another element, often unrecognized, is that most of the causes supported by the radicals of the sixties have now become an accepted part of the mainstream of American life. Students have much more voice in university affairs. The civil rights movement has made great gains. There are now many elected officials of black, Chicano, and other ethnic origins. Affirmative-action programs providing job opportunities for minorities and women are commonplace. Those who suffered in protesting the Vietnam War have lived to see the United States making an agonized search of its past foreign interventions, and an extremely cautious scrutiny of every impulse to intervene in the affairs of another country today. And there are other changes. Homosexuality, bisexuality, and sexual freedom are given far greater social acceptance. One need only mention people's law collectives, free health clinics, radical therapy, alternative schools, the progress toward equal rights for women, to suggest some of the other changes which are in process. Even in minor aspects of life, blue jeans, long hair, beards, mustaches, and the smoking of marijuana no longer cause excited comment. The politics of yesterday's demonstrators is now the politics of a great mass of the population. So perhaps it is not surprising that in a period of recession young people are finding less to protest about. But this by no means indicates that the ferment of change is dying out.

In early 1975 a group including John Vasconcellos, the legislator, began to dream of a new political force—not a new party, but a humanistic network of persons cutting across all party lines, giving a new emphasis to the importance of persons in the process of political action. After a year of groundwork involving seventy-five different groups, a pattern began to emerge and is now taking form as a nonprofit organization termed "Self Determination: A P$_\text{olitical}^\text{ersonal}$ Network." Its sponsors include a half-dozen California legislators—state and national —educators, including two college presidents, several businessmen, some social activists, and a journalist-writer.

The initial statement of Self Determination, Inc.,[18] is so much in accord with the thinking expressed in this book and in this chapter that I read it with some astonishment:

We chose to form a "network" to signify a lateral and largely leader-less process for empowering persons in their own places to live more effectively, in their personal lives and in the realm of "politics." . . . Simply, our network provides a vehicle for people who want to attend simultaneously to their own personal growth and to their concern for humanistic social change. . . .

SELF DETERMINATION is not an organization that's going to do something to you; rather, it's a participatory network through which we will enable each other to do things better for ourselves. . . . It is time we overcome our cynicism and take the risks and responsibility for becoming the authors of our own being and doing. . . .

SELF DETERMINATION proposes a practical and powerful alternative: changing ourselves *and* society, by transforming the most basic myth by which we live—our assumptions about our nature and potential—from negative and self-denying to positive and self-actualizing. . . . Many persons are living a positive vision of self *and* society. We want now to give it vital, public visibility by creating a statewide alliance of such persons. Our purpose is facilitating personal *and* political consciousness-raising, by educating about the political dimension of personal vision, and about the human dimension of political lives and social issues. All this we call humanistic politics. . . .

We realize our proposal is idealistic, but it is time we live our ideals, and make them pragmatic. What began only a year ago as a dream is now a living reality. It's remarkable how far we've come operationally and grown personally, through our shared efforts. That is because we trusted ourselves, trusted each other, and chose to act.

Whether this movement reaches beyond California, whether it succeeds, or whether it falters and fails—these things are to some extent matters of secondary importance. It is the fact that a totally new type of political force is being born that is worthy of note. Even in its process it is person-centered. There is no one person in charge, no big name. It met with more than twenty-five hundred people in small group meetings to try to get grass-roots desires built into the new organization. It did not start with a drive for power, but in a workshop of twenty-one persons from across California, a workshop facilitated by persons with experience in intensive groups and organization development. "During that session, we further clarified our goals, deepened our commitments to SELF DETERMINATION and to each other, and determined the specific services and a timetable for implementing our programs over the next year."

This development comes closer to being an expression of, and an organization for, the persons of tomorrow than anything else I know. It is a strong indication that the emerging individuals I have tried to describe do, in fact, exist and are becoming aware of like-minded others.

Such a fresh and pertinent example should not blind us to the many profound questions that remain unanswered about these new persons. Can these individuals survive in our culture? What kinds of opposition can be expected? To the extent that these persons survive, what will be the influence on our culture? I should like first to look at some of the negative answers to these questions, both from the point of view of history and from the point of view of built-in cultural opposition.

One line of thought which casts doubt upon the survival of these individuals is a consideration of history. These emerging persons bear little resemblance to the types of man who have shown survival qualities. These persons would not be congenial to the practical, disciplined, soldier-ruler produced by the Roman Empire. They bear little resemblance to the dichotomous medieval man—the man of faith and force, of monasteries and crusades. These persons are almost the antithesis of the Puritans who founded our country, with their strict beliefs and strong controls over behavior. These persons are very different from the men who brought about the industrial revolution, with their ambition, productivity, greed, and competitiveness. These persons are deeply opposite to the communist culture, with its controls on individual thought and behavior in the interest of the state. The characteristics and the behavior of these individuals run strongly counter to the orthodoxies and dogmas of the major western religions—Catholicism, Protestantism, and Judaism. These persons certainly do not fit into our present-day culture—its government and military and management bureaucracies, its rigid education. These persons are not at home in our present American society, dominated as it is by computerized technology and the man in uniform—the military, the police, the intelligence agent, and the faceless men in control.

Is there any parallel? During the brief flowering of Greek culture it was believed that the highest form of art and ultimate justification of the community was to create persons of human excellence. Today's emerging persons would be rather congenial to that goal. They would also, I believe, have been more or less at home in the world of Renaissance man, during another painful and exciting period of transformation. But clearly their characteristics have not dominated past history. If they survive, this will be the exception and not the rule.

The emergence of these new persons will be opposed. Let me suggest the opposition by a series of sloganistic statements that may communicate something of the sources of antagonism.

First, "The State above all." The past decade has given us ample evidence that in this country—as well as in others, both communist and free world—the governing elite and the massive bureaucracy which surrounds them have no place for dissenters or those with different values and goals. These new persons have been and will be harassed, denied freedom of expression, accused of conspiracy, imprisoned for unwillingness to conform. It would take a massive—and perhaps unlikely—awakening of the American public to reverse this trend. Acceptance of diversity of values and life-styles and opinions is the heart of the democratic process, but it no longer flourishes well here. So these emerging persons will certainly be repressed, if possible, by government.

Second, "Tradition above all." The institutions of our society —educational, corporate, religious, familial—stand in direct opposition to anyone who defies tradition. Universities and local public schools are the institutions likely to be the most hostile to the persons of tomorrow. They do not fit their tradition and will be ostracized and ejected whenever possible. Corporations, in spite of their conservative image, are somewhat more responsive to public trends. Even so, they will be in opposition to persons who put self-realization ahead of achievement, personal growth above salary or profit, cooperation with nature ahead of its conquest. The church is a less formidable opponent, and family and marital traditions are already in such a state of confusion that the antagonism, though existent, is not likely to be effectively implemented.

Third, "The intellect above all." The fact that these emerging individuals are attempting to be whole persons—body, mind, feelings, spirit, and psychic powers integrated—will be seen as one of their most presumptuous offenses. Not only science and academia, but government as well, are constructed on the assumption that cognitive reasoning is the *only* important function of man. As Halberstam[19] pointed out several years ago, it was the conviction of "the best and the brightest" that intelligence and rational thinking could solve *anything* that led us into the terrible morass of Vietnam. This same conviction is still held by scientists, faculty members, and policy-makers at all levels. They will be the first to pour contempt and scorn on anyone who by word or deed challenges that credo.

Fourth, "The individual should be shaped." As the Stanford report points out, a vision of the individual may logically be extrapolated from our present technological culture. It would involve the application of social and psychological technology to control nonconforming behavior in the interest of a regulated postindustrial society. Such controls would be exercised not by some one institutional force but by what the writers term the "warfare-welfare-industrial-communications-police bureaucracies."[20] One of the first aims of this complex web, if this conforming image prevails, would be to control or eliminate the persons I have been describing.

Such shaping may be brought about not only by subtle coercive control but even by the steady advance of scientific knowledge itself. The biologist and biochemist are learning the possibilities of genetic shaping and of chemically induced alterations in behavior. These advances may, like social and psychological knowledge, be used as controlling or freeing potentialities. The physicists have long since lost their innocence in regard to the uses of their discoveries. The biological and psychological sciences are next. They too may easily become the tools of this massive bureaucratic complex in which movement toward control appears inevitable, with no one person responsible for any given step—a hydra-headed creeping monster that would engulf the sort of persons I have described.

Fifth, "The status quo forever." Change threatens, and its possibility creates frightened, angry people. They are found in their purest essence on the extreme right, but in all of us there is some fear of process, of change. So the vocal attacks on these new persons will come from the highly conservative right, who are understandably terrified as they see their secure world dissolve, but there will be much silent opposition from the whole population. Change is painful and uncertain. Who wants it? The answer is, *few*.

Sixth, "Our truth is *the* truth." The true believer is also the enemy of change and will be found on the left, on the right, and in the middle. This true believer will not be able to tolerate searching, uncertain, gentle persons. Whether young or old, fanatic left wing or rigidly right wing, such individuals must oppose process persons who *search* for truth. Such true believers *possess* the truth, and others must agree.

So, as these persons of tomorrow continue to journey into the light, they will find increasing resistance and hostility from these six important sources. They may very well overwhelm them.

Yet, as history has shown many times, an emergent evolution is not easily stopped. These new persons' arrival on the scene in greater numbers may be delayed by any one or all of the forces mentioned. The quiet revolution of which they are the essence may be slowed. They may be suppressed. Existence may be possible only in an underground. But a potent ferment has been let loose in the world by the qualities these persons exhibit. It will be difficult to put this genie back in the bottle. It will be doubly difficult because here are persons who *live* their values. Such living of a new and divergent value system is the most revolutionary action a person can take, and it is not easily defeated.

Suppose then that there is an outside chance of these persons coming into the light, of gaining influence, of changing our culture. What would the picture be? Is it as threatening or awful as many people might fear?

Emerging persons would not bring Utopia. They would make mistakes, be partially corrupted, go overboard in certain directions. But these new persons would foster a culture that would emphasize certain trends, a culture that would be moving in these directions:

Toward a nondefensive openness in all interpersonal relationships—within the family, the working task force, the system of leadership.

Toward the exploration of self, and the development of the richness of the total, individual, responsible human soma—mind and body.

Toward the prizing of individuals for what they *are,* regardless of sex, race, status, or material possessions.

Toward human-sized groupings in our communities, our educational facilities, our productive units.

Toward a close, respectful, balanced, reciprocal relationship to the natural world.

Toward the perception of material goods as rewarding only when they enhance the quality of personal living.

Toward a more even distribution of material goods.

Toward a society with minimal structure—human needs taking priority over any tentative structure that develops.

Toward leadership as a temporary, shifting function, based on competence for meeting a specific social need.

Toward a more genuine and caring concern for those who need help.

Toward a human conception of science—in its creative phase, the testing of its hypotheses, the valuing of the humanness of its applications.

Toward creativity of all sorts—in thinking and exploring—in the areas of social relationships, the arts, social design, architecture, urban and regional planning, science, and the study of psychic phenomena.

To me these are not frightening trends but exciting ones. In spite of the darkness of the present, our culture may be on the verge of a great evolutionary-revolutionary leap.

Part V Conclusion

Chapter 13 | In a nutshell

Every social revolution is preceded by, or brings with it, a change in the perception of the world or a change in the perception of the possible or both. Just as inevitably, these altered perceptions are first seen as ridiculous nonsense or worse by the collective common sense of the time.

The Copernican revolution is no doubt the prime example. To think that the earth was not the center of the universe, that it orbited the sun and was part of a vast galaxy, was not only absurd, it was a heresy undermining religion and civilization. There are also lesser examples. The thought that invisible organisms, whom no one could see, were the cause of illness, was the most patent nonsense. The belief that slaves were not chattels to be bought and sold like cattle but were persons with full personal rights was not only a mischievous thought that was contrary to history and the Bible, it was economically upsetting and dangerous. The notion that an obscure mathematical formula showed that a most minute form of matter, the atom, could, if split, release incalculable power was clearly just a bizarre offshoot of science fiction.

Yet every one of these "ridiculous" perceptual changes altered the face and the nature of our world. It is the "common sense" that gradually came to be seen as ridiculous.

Let me mention a familiar instance of the way this change comes about. It was a fact perfectly obvious to everyone—and furthermore supported by Holy Writ—that the earth was flat, and those who suggested it was spherical were dangerous heretics. But when Columbus sailed to the New World, without falling off the edge of the earth, this actual experience, this evidence that the previously accepted view was in error, forced a change in the way the earth was perceived. And this change was a change not only in geography. It made for a reevaluation of this new-fangled field termed science. The place of man in the larger scheme of things was brought into question. It even called into question the Bible as an encyclopedia of factual knowledge. It opened the human mind to possibilities hitherto unknown. It led to visions of continents to be discovered and countries to be explored. It altered the whole perceptual framework of life, and men and women were frightened and excited and changed by the prospect. The impossible became possible.

All this was brought about not by the theories concerning the globe. These had been around for a long time. The change was forced by *evidence* that the theories had validity.

In somewhat similar fashion, I believe, it is the *evidence* of the *effectiveness* of a person-centered approach that may turn a very small and quiet revolution into a far more significant change in the way humankind perceives the possible. I am much too close to the situation to know whether this will be a minor or major event, but I believe it represents a radical change. Like every stream that flows around the roots of the culture, threatening to undermine its cherished views and its long established ways, it constitutes a frightening force, a force that is, as usual, met with all the weight of the common sense of the culture.

What I want to do is to contrast various elements of that common sense with the evidence which contradicts it. I do this in very condensed form, since the evidence has already been covered in this book.

It is hopelessly idealistic to think that the human organism is basically trustworthy.

—But—

The research and the actions based on this hypothesis tend to confirm the view—even strongly confirm it.

It is absurd to think that we can know the elements that make human psychological development possible.

—But—

Such elements have been defined, identified as attitudinal conditions, measured, and shown to be effective.

It is nonsensical to think that therapy can be democratized.

—But—

When the therapy relationship is equalitarian, when each takes responsibility for himself in the relationship, independent (and mutual) growth is much more rapid.

It is unreasonable to think that a troubled person can make progress without the guidance and direction of a wise psychotherapist.

—But—

There is ample evidence that in a relationship marked by the facilitative conditions, the troubled person can engage in self-exploration, and become self-directing in profoundly wise ways.

It is dangerous to think that psychotic individuals can be treated as persons.

—But—

The evidence shows that this is the most rapid road to the psychotic's utilizing the breakdown itself as material to be assimilated into personal growth.

It is fuzzy-minded and weak not to take control over persons.

—But—

It is found that when power is left with persons, and when

we are real with them, understanding of them, caring toward them, constructive behavior changes occur, and they exhibit more strength and power and responsibility.

A family or marriage without a recognized strong authority is doomed to failure.
—But—
Where control is shared, where the facilitative conditions are present, it has been demonstrated that vital, sound, enriching relationships occur.

We must assume responsibility for young people, since they are not capable of self-government. It is stupid to think otherwise.
—But—
In a facilitative climate, responsible behavior develops and flowers, in young and old alike.

Teachers must be in control of their students.
—But—
It has been established that where teachers share their power, and trust their students, self-directed learning takes place at a greater rate than in teacher-controlled classrooms.

Teachers must be firm, discipline strict, evaluation tough, if learning is to take place.
—But—
It has been proven that the teacher who empathically understands the meaning of school to the student, who respects the student as a person, who is genuine in relationships, fosters a learning climate definitely superior in its effects to the "commonsense" teacher.

Teachers must teach what students ought to know.
—But—
Significant learning is greater when students choose, from a

wide variety of options and resources, what they need and want to know.

It is obvious that in any organization there has to be one boss. Any other idea is preposterous.
—*But*—
It has been substantiated that leaders who trust organization members, who share and diffuse power, and who maintain open personal communication have better morale, have more productive organizations, and facilitate the development of new leaders.

Oppressed groups must revolt. Violent revolution is the only way for the oppressed to gain power and improve their lives.
—*But*—
History bears out the view that even if successful, this simply leads to a new tyranny replacing the old. A nonviolent revolution, based on a person-centered approach that empowers the oppressed, appears to have far more promise.

Deep religious feuds, cultural and racial bitternesses are hopeless. It is a fantasy to think they can be reconciled.
—*But*—
The fact is that small-scale examples exist in abundance to show that improved communication, reduction in hostility, steps toward resolving the tensions are entirely possible and rest upon tried intensive group approaches.

A conference or a workshop has to be organized and run by one or more leaders who are in charge. Any other view is unrealistic and quixotic.
—*But*—
It has been demonstrated that a large and complex enterprise can be person-centered from start to finish—in its planning, in its operation, in its results—and that such a concentration of persons sensing their own power can move creatively into new

and unexplored areas—a result that could not have been achieved by commonsense methods.

It is obvious that in a strictly controlled situation, with absolute power at the top, the powerless ones can exert no significant influence.

—But—

In an almost perfect laboratory situation, the powerless members of a day camp, who had come to respect their own strength because treated in a person-centered way, showed themselves to be extremely powerful.

In the sixties there was a trend toward basic social change, but that has now died out. Only a dreamer would fail to recognize this.

—But—

More and more people with a person-centered approach to life are infiltrating our schools, our political life, our organizations, as well as setting up alternate life-styles. They are living new values and constitute a continuing and growing ferment of social change.

People don't change.

—But—

A new type of person, with values very different from those of our present culture, is emerging in increasing numbers, and living and being in ways that break with the past.

Our culture is becoming more and more chaotic. We must turn back.

—But—

A quiet revolution is under way in almost every field. It holds promise of moving us forward to a more human, more person-centered world.

References

References

Chapter One

1. R. Farson, 'Carl Rogers, Quiet Revolutionary,' *Education, 95*, No. 2 (Winter 1974), p. 197.
2. *American Heritage Dictionary*, New York: McGraw-Hill, 1969.
3. C.R. Rogers, *Counseling and Psychotherapy*, Boston, Mass.: Houghton Mifflin, 1942, pp. 28-29; London: Constable, 1942.
4. C.R. Rogers, 'In Retrospect: 46 Years,' *American Psychology, 29*, No. 2 (1974), p. 116.
5. C.R. Rogers, *On Becoming a Person*, Boston, Mass.: Houghton Mifflin, 1961, pp. 67-69. London: Constable, 1967 (4th repr. 1974).
6. Available from American Academy of Psychotherapists Tape Library, 1040 Woodcock Road, Orlando, Florida 32803.
7. T. Hanna, *The End of Tyranny*, San Francisco: Freeperson Press, 1975, pp. 162-163.
8. S. Freud, 'My Contact with Josef Popper-Lynkeus,' in *Character and Culture*, from Collier Books edition of *The Collected Papers of Sigmund Freud*, translated by J. Strachey, New York, Crowell-Collier, 1963 (originally published 1932), p. 303.
9. S. Freud, *Outline of Psychoanalysis*, New York: Norton, 1949, pp. 108-109; London: Hogarth Press, 1969.
10. S. Freud, *Moses and Monotheism*, New York: Random House, 1955; London: Hogarth Press, 1951.
11. S. Freud, *Group Psychology and the Analysis of the Ego*, London: Hogarth Press, 1948, pp. 15-21.
12. B.F. Skinner, *Walden II*, New York: Macmillan, 1960; London: Collier-Macmillan, 1962.

References

13. J. McConnell, 'Criminals Can Be Brainwashed—Now,' *Psychology Today* (April 1970). Cited in W. Anderson, 'Politics and the New Humanism,' *Journal of Humanistic Psychology, 14*, No. 4 (Fall 1974), p. 21. (Condensed from his book of the same title, Pacific Palisades, Calif.: Goodyear, 1973.)

14. M.J. Mahoney and C.E. Thorense, *Self-Control: Power to the Person.* Monterey, Calif.: Brooks/Cole, 1974.

15. N. Raskin, 'Studies of Psychotherapeutic Orientation: Ideology and Practice,' *AAP Research Monograph No. 1*, American Academy of Psychotherapists, Orlando, 1974.

16. This general philosophical stance in relation to therapy is expressed not only in my own writings and others of the client-centered group but by R.D. Laing, *The Politics of Experience*, New York: Ballantine Books, 1968 and Harmondsworth: Penguin, 1970; John W. Perry, *The Far Side of Madness*, Englewood Cliffs, NJ: Prentice-Hall, 1974; Thomas S. Szasz, *The Myth of Mental Illness*, rev. ed., New York: Harper & Row, 1974, and St Albans: Paladin, 1972; and other well-known therapists.

17. C.R. Rogers, *Carl Rogers on Encounter Groups*, New York: Harper & Row, 1970; Harmondsworth: Penguin, 1973.

18. M. Brewer, 'Erhard Seminars Training: "We're Going to Tear You Down and Put You Back Together",' *Psychology Today, 9*, No. 3 (August 1975), p. 88.

19. Rogers, *Encounter Groups*, p. 56.

20. J.W. Perry, 'Diabasis II,' unpublished manuscript, 1975.

21. Perry, 'Diabasis II,' p. 5.

22. J.W. Perry, personal communication, 1975, p. 3.

23. B. Heller, personal communication, 1975.

24. Perry, 'Diabasis II,' p. 5.

25. Perry, *The Far Side of Madness*, p. 151.

26. Perry, 'Diabasis II,' p. 5.

27. Perry, *The Far Side of Madness*, p. 151–152.

28. Perry, 'Diabasis II,' p. 5.

Chapter Two

1. F. Leboyer, *Birth Without Violence*, New York: Alfred A. Knopf, 1975; London: Wildwood House, 1975.

2. C.R. Rogers, *Personal Adjustment* (series of ten cassettes), Chicago: Instructional Dynamics, Inc., 450 East Superior Street, Chicago, Ill. 60611, USA. Cassette No. 7, undated.

References

Chapter Three

1. F. Brodie, *Thomas Jefferson: An Intimate Biography*, New York: Norton, 1974; London: Eyre Methuen, 1975.
2. J.W. Ramey, 'Intimate Networks,' *The Futurist*, 9, No. 4 (August 1975), pp. 175–181.
3. Their account of this marriage may be seen in the film *Carl Rogers on Marriage: An Interview with Bob and Carol*, distributed by APGA, 1607 New Hampshire Avenue NW, Washington, D.C. 20009, USA.
4. C.R. Rogers, 'A Theory of Therapy, Personality and Interpersonal Relationships as Developed in the Client-centered Framework,' in S. Koch, ed., *Psychology: A Study of a Science, Vol. III. Formulations of the Person and the Social Context*, New York and London: McGraw-Hill, 1959, p. 198.
5. A. Francoeur and R. Francoeur, *Hot and Cool Sex*, New York and London: Harcourt Brace Jovanovich, 1974 and 1975.
6. R. May, *Power and Innocence. A Search for the Source of Violence*, New York: Norton, 1972.
7. N. O'Neill and G. O'Neill, *Open Marriage*, New York: M. Evans & Co., 1972; London: Peter Owen, 1973.
8. C.R. Rogers, *Becoming Partners: Marriage and Its Alternatives*, New York: Delacorte Press, 1972; London: Constable, 1973.
9. Rogers, *Becoming Partners*, Chapter 9, 'Threads of Permanence'.
10. C.R. Rogers, *Carl Rogers on Encounter Groups*, New York: Harper & Row, 1970; Harmondsworth: Penguin, 1973.

Chapter Four

1. J. Farber, *The Student as Nigger*, North Hollywood: Contact Books, 1969.
2. J.B. Carr, 'Project Freedom,' *The English Journal* (March 1964), pp. 202–204.
3. J. Lipshires, 'Human Relations Training in High School,' School of Education, Rider College, Trenton, NJ, 1974 (mimeo. pamphlet).
4. D. Malcolm, personal correspondence, 1972.
5. J.W. Ramey, 'Intimate Networks,' *The Futurist*, 9, No. 4 (August 1975), p. 176.
6. S. Tenenbaum, 'Carl R. Rogers and Non-directive Teaching,' in C.R. Rogers, *On Becoming a Person*, Boston, Mass.: Houghton Mifflin, 1961, pp. 299–310; London: Constable, repr. 1974.

References

7. D.N. Aspy and F.N. Roebuck, 'From Humane Ideas to Humane Technology and Back Again Many Times,' *Education*, 95, No. 2 (Winter 1974), pp. 163-171; D.N. Aspy and F.N. Roebuck et al., *Interim Reports 1,2,3,4*, National Consortium for Humanizing Education, Washington, D.C., 1974.

Chapter Five

1. C.R. Rogers, 'Some Implications of Client-centered Counseling for College Personnel Work,' in *College and University* (October 1948), p. 64.
2. *Survey Research Center Study No. 6. Selected Findings from a Study of Clerical Workers in the Prudential Insurance Company of America*, Human Relations, University of Michigan, 1948.
3. R. Likert, *New Patterns of Management*, New York: McGraw-Hill, 1961.
4. H.C. Lyon, Jr., *It's Me and I'm Here!*, New York: Delacorte Press, 1974.
5. Lyon, *It's Me*, pp. 165-166.
6. G.W. Cherry, 'The Serendipity of the Fully Functioning Manager,' Sloan School of Management, Massachusetts Institute of Technology, 1975 (unpublished manuscript).

Chapter Six

1. P. Freire, *Pedagogy of the Oppressed*, New York: Seabury Press, 1970; Harmondsworth: Penguin, 1972.
2. C.R. Rogers, *Freedom to Learn: A View of What Education Might Become*, Columbus: Charles E. Merrill Publishing Co., 1969.
3. Freire, *Pedagogy*, p. 102.
4. Freire, *Pedagogy*, p. 111.
5. Freire, *Pedagogy*, pp. 49-50.
6. Freire, *Pedagogy*, p. 110.
7. Freire, *Pedagogy*, p. 49.
8. Freire, *Pedagogy*, p. 14.
9. Freire, *Pedagogy*, p. 67.
10. Freire, *Pedagogy*, p. 118.
11. Freire, *Pedagogy*, p. 74.
12. Freire, *Pedagogy*, p. 14.

References

Chapter Seven

1. D.J. Finlay and T. Hovet, Jr., *7304 International Relations on the Planet Earth*, New York: Harper & Row, 1975.
2. Stockholm Peace Research Institute, June 17, 1976.
3. Finlay and Hovet, *7304 International Relations*, p. 5.
4. C.R. Rogers, *On Becoming a Person*, Boston, Mass.: Houghton Mifflin, 1961; London: Constable, repr. 1974.
5. J. Henderson, 'The Politics of Group Process,' *Rough Times* (Jan./ Feb. 1974), p. 5.
6. Henderson, 'Politics,' p. 5.
7. Henderson, 'Politics,' pp. 4-5.
8. This film, *The Steel Shutter*, is available for rental through Center for Studies of The Person, 1125 Torrey Pines Road, La Jolla, Calif., 92037, USA.
9. B. Kristal-Andersson, 'Intercultural Communication Encounter Groups,' *Invandrar Rapport*, Vol. 3, No. 7 (1975), Stockholm Immigrant Institute.
10. C. Devonshire and A. Auw, 'First Report of Cross-cultural Communications Workshop' (mimeographed report), 1972.

Chapter Eleven

1. In particular, I am using material from 'The Actualizing Tendency in Relation to "Motives" and to Consciousness,' in Marshall Jones, ed., *Nebraska Symposium on Motivation, 1963*, Lincoln: University of Nebraska Press, 1963, pp. 1-24. Used by permission.
2. L. Bertalanffy, *Problems of Life*, New York: Harper Torchbooks, 1960 (first published 1952), p. 13.
3. K. Goldstein, *Human Nature in the Light of Psychopathology*, Cambridge, Mass.: Harvard University Press, 1947.
4. A.H. Maslow, *Motivation and Personality*, New York: Harper & Brothers, 1954; London: Harper & Row, 1970.
5. A. Angyal, *Foundations for a Science of Personality*, Cambridge, Mass.: Harvard UP and New York: Commonwealth Fund, 1941; and *Neurosis and Treatment*, New York: John Wiley & Sons, 1965.
6. W.N. Dember, R.W. Earl and N. Paradise, 'Response by Rats to Differential Stimulus Complexity,' *Journal of Comparative and Physiological Psychology*, 50 (1957), p. 517.
7. S. Freud, 'Instincts and Their Vicissitudes,' *Collected Papers, Vol. 4*, London: Hogarth Press and Institute of Psychoanalysis, 1953, p. 63.

References

8. J.C. Lilly, *The Center of the Cyclone*, New York: Bantam Books, 1973; London: Calder, 1973.

9. R.W. White, 'Motivation Reconsidered: The Concept of Competence,' *Psychology Review*, 66 (1959), p. 315.

10. C.R. Rogers, 'Toward Becoming a Fully Functioning Person,' in *Perceiving, Behaving, Becoming*, 1962 Yearbook, Association for Supervision and Curriculum Development, Washington, D.C.: National Education Association, 1962, p. 25.

11. L.L. Whyte, *The Unconscious Before Freud*, London: Tavistock Publications, 1960, p. 35.

12. Whyte, *Unconscious*, p. 37.

13. Whyte, *Unconscious*, p. 5.

14. C.R. Rogers, 'A Theory of Therapy, Personality, and Interpersonal Relationships,' in S. Koch, ed., *Psychology: A Study of a Science, Vol. III*, New York and London: McGraw-Hill, 1959, pp. 184–256.

15. C.R. Rogers, *Freedom to Learn: A View of What Education Might Become*, Columbus: Charles E. Merrill Publishing Co., 1969, p. 250.

16. L.L. Whyte, *The Next Development in Man*, New York: Mentor Books, 1949, p. 40.

Chapter Twelve

1. R.L. Heilbroner, *An Inquiry into the Human Prospect*, New York: Norton, 1974; London: Calder, 1975.

2. J. O'Toole, 'On Making Capitalism More Accountable,' *Los Angeles Times* (September 18, 1975), part II; J. Rifkin, 'The People Are Passing Us By,' *The Progressive*, 39, No. 10 (October 1975), pp. 13–14.

3. R. Dubos, *The God Within*, New York: Scribners, 1972 and London: Angus and Robertson, 1973; and *Beast or Angel*, New York: Scribners, 1974.

4. G.B. Leonard, *The Transformation: A Guide to the Inevitable Changes in Humankind*, New York: Delacorte Press, 1972.

5. J.D. Rockefeller, III, *The Second American Revolution*, New York: Harper & Row, 1973.

6. T. Hanna, *Bodies in Revolt*, New York: Holt, Rinehart & Winston, 1970.

7. T. Hanna, *The End of Tyranny: An Essay on the Possibility of America*, San Francisco: Freeperson Press, 1975.

8. J. Salk, *Man Unfolding*, New York: Harper & Row, 1972; and *The Survival of the Wisest*, New York: Harper & Row, 1972.

References

9. O.W. Markley and staff, *Changing Images of Man*, Menlo Park, Calif.: Stanford Research Institute—Center for the Study of Social Policy, 1974.
10. F. Richards and A.C. Richards, *Homonovus: The New Man*, Boulder, Col.: Shields Publishing Co., 1973.
11. A. Weil, *The Natural Mind*, Boston, Mass.: Houghton Mifflin, 1972; London: Jonathan Cape, 1973.
12. J.C. Oates, 'New Heaven and Earth,' *Saturday Review* (November 4, 1972), pp. 51–54.
13. D. Biggs, *Breaking Out*, New York: David McKay Co., 1973. Biggs gives a fascinating account of the many corporation and government managers who are transforming themselves by dropping out and developing exciting new life-styles.
14. L.E. Bartlett, *New Work/New Life*, New York: Harper & Row, 1976. Bartlett gives many individual pictures of persons who are already 'living in tomorrow'.
15. J. Vasconcellos, communication to constituents, 1972 (USA).
16. W.G. Bennis and P.E. Slater, *The Temporary Society*, New York and London: Harper & Row, 1968 and 1970.
17. Quoted by R.M. Pirsig, *Zen and the Art of Motorcycle Maintenance*, New York: Bantam Books, 1973, pp. 106–107; London: Bodley Head, 1974.
18. 'Second Report on Self Determination: A Personal/Political Network,' Santa Clara, Calif., PO BOX 126 (December 1975). Written by a group.
19. D. Halberstam, *The Best and the Brightest*, New York: Random House, 1972; London: Barrie & Jenkins, 1973.
20. Markley, *Changing Images*.

Index

intellect, 46, 49, 51, 52, 53, 59, 61, 71, 86, 88, 102, 164, 168–9, 174, 176, 211, 224, 246, 266, 270, 279–80
intensive groups, 3, 21–3, 50, 158, 240, 277, 289
intercultural relationships, 5, 115–40
interest groups, 152, 161, 166, 169, 176, 179, 187
international relationships, 5, 115–16, 134–40
interracial relationships, 5, 111, 115, 116, 118, 120, 122, 127–9, 133, 140, 273, 289
intuition, 168–9, 184, 224, 263, 272–3
I.R.A., 130

jealousy, 53, 54–5, 59, 62, 206–33
Jeans, Sir James, 264
Jefferson, Martha, 42
Jefferson, Thomas, 42–3
job satisfaction, 98, 100, 222
Judaism, 278
Jungians, 18, 20, 23–8

Kent State University, 256
Kristal-Andersson, Binnie, 134–8

La Jolla, California, Center for Studies of the Person, 110–12, 127, 150, 154, 268
Lake Erie, pollution, 117
leadership, 99, 100, 104, 109, 113, 114, 127–9, 133, 136, 138, 139, 184, 204, 257, 282, 289
learning, 71–89, 91, 92, 95, 101, 103, 107–8, 151, 152, 154, 164, 169, 174, 184, 246, 248, 250, 274, 279, 288–9
Leboyer, Frederick, 31–4
Leonard, George B., 263
lesbians, 124–5, 173
Levine, Howard, 23–4
Levine, Meldon, 266
Likert, Rensis, 96–7
Lilly, John, 241
Lipshires, Joann, 78–9
'listening', 123, 126, 133–4, 145, 180
Los Angeles, pollution, 117
Lyon, Harold, 97–8

McConnell, J., 18–19
McMaster University, 88–9
Malcolm, David, 80–1
management, 90–1, 96–104, 261–2, 278
mania, 218–20, 232
marriage, 5, 29, 34, 42–68, 103, 120, 146, 162, 163, 205–33, 267, 279, 288
Marxists, 106
Maslow, A.H., 239

May, Rollo, 54
medical education, 88–9
medication, 25, 27, 219, 220, 232
men; life expectancy, 43; role of, 37–8, 45, 48–9, 51–2, 152
Menninger Clinic, 17
mental health, 167, 176
Mexican-Americans, 110, 111, 127–9
Michael, Jay, 71–2
Miller, Maureen, 224–9, 230, 231
minority groups, 5, 88, 105–14, 127–9, 133, 264, 275
monogamy, 223, 225, 227, 229
mothers see parents and women
motivation, 237–51

National Health Council, 110–12
nature, respect for, 273, 279, 282
Nelson, Alan, 186–204
neurosis, 86, 244
Nixon, Richard, 256, 259
Northern Ireland, 116, 129–33

Oates, Joyce Carol, 264
occultism, 271
On Becoming a Person (Rogers), 120
O'Neill, G., 54
O'Neill, N., 54
operant conditioning, 18
oppression, 105–14, 133, 144, 186–204, 260, 266, 289
overpopulation, 117, 118

Paradise, N., 241
parents, 30–41, 50, 78–80, 103, 119–20, 128, 179, 207, 224, 228, 246–7, 257, 265, 266
partnerships, 29, 42–68, 267
Pedagogy of the Oppressed, The (Freire), 105–9
People's Bicentennial Commission, 261–2
Perry, John W., 23–8
personality: conflict within, 118–22, 162, 164, 175–6; development, 19–28, 51, 104, 152, 185, 218, 221, 256, 276, 279, 280, 287; restructuring, 18–19, 25, 261, theory, 4, 16–18, 165
personal responsibility, 8–21, 25, 26, 29, 30, 39–41, 90, 97, 101, 103, 128, 139, 151–2, 153, 160, 164, 193, 203, 287
perversion, 247
phototropism, 238
pollution, 117, 118, 260
productivity, 96–8, 100
promotion, 90, 94
protest, 269–70, 274, 275
Protestants, 116, 129–33, 135, 278

303

pseudo-control, 76, 96
psychic phenomena, 152, 166, 272–3, 279, 282
psychopaths, 17
psychosis, 7, 23–8, 244, 287
Puerto Ricans, 105

race relations *see* interracial relationships
racial integration, 180
racial prejudice, 111, 116, 118, 127–9, 133, 273
rage, 133–4, 180, 198, 226, 227, 231, 246
'Rap Manual', 123
Raskin, N., 19–20
rational emotive therapists, 18
rats, 241
reason, 49–50
religion, 46, 272, 278, 279, 285–6, 289; *see also* churches
repressions, 31, 266, 272
research groups, 167, 181
resentment, 46–7, 48–9, 94, 134, 147, 165
responsibility, personal *see* personal responsibility
revolution, 109, 112, 114, 125, 144, 181, 203, 262, 263, 281, 282, 285–6, 289–290
Richards, Anne, 263
Richards, Fred, 263
Rockefeller, John D., 263
Roebuck, Flora, 87–8
roles, 55: of men, 37–8, 45, 48–9, 51–2, 152; of teachers, 72, 76, 81–7, 107–9, 288–9; of women, 37–8, 41, 44–5, 48–9, 51–2, 152
Roxbury, Boston, 189
Russia *see* Soviet Union
Ryan, Donna Lee, 266

Salk, Jonas, 263
Sanger, Margaret, 117
satellite relationships, 52–6, 57–68, 205, 206, 208–33
schizophrenics, 23–8, 232
science, 282, 285–6; distrust of, 271–3
seals, 229
sea urchins, 240–1
self-actualization, 98–100, 146, 276, 279
self-confidence, 113, 137–8
self-control, 193, 203
Self-Control: Power to the Person (Mahoney and Thorense), 19
Self-Determination Inc., 276–7
self-direction, 92, 287
self-discipline, 73, 79

self-evaluation, 92
self-exploration, 12–13, 282, 287
self-expression, 17, 24–8
self-knowledge, 72, 77, 78–9
self-respect, 114
sensitivity training groups, 21
sensory awareness groups, 21
sensory deprivation, 241
sensuality, 99
sexual relations, 265, 275; extramarital, 43, 44, 47–8, 51–6, 58–68, 205, 206, 208–33; marital, 49, 51, 57, 61, 64, 65, 207–33; premarital, 43, 44, 56–7, 62–4, 67, 207
shock therapy, 25
Skinner, B.F., 18, 19
social conventions *see* conventions, social
social neurosis, 18
Solzhenitsyn, Aleksandr Isayevich, 260–1
Sonoma State University, 266
South Africa, 116
Soviet Union, 116, 260
Stanford report, 280
Stanford Research Institute, 263
status: symbols, 269, 274; of teachers, 69; of women, 46, 48–9
stimulation, 241
Stockholm, 134
Student as Nigger, The (Farber), 70
students; as an oppressed minority, 105–9; *see also* education
suicide, 215–19, 225–6, 230, 232
super-ego control, 16
support groups, 179
Sweden, 90, 134

teaching *see* education
technology; distrust of, 258, 271
Tenenbaum, Samuel, 82–7
terrorism, 257
T-groups, 21
Thomas Jefferson, an Intimate Biography (Brodie), 42–3
transactional analysis, 18
Twin Oaks, 19

unconscious, 246, 248, 263
Union Graduate School, 268
United Nations, 115
U.S. Bill of Rights, 255
U.S. Constitution, 255, 259
U Thant, 115

vandalism, 257–8
Vasconcellos, John, 71–2, 276
Vietnam war, 57, 266, 275, 280
violence, 257–8

Lightning Source UK Ltd.
Milton Keynes UK
UKOW04f0044230216

268894UK00001B/25/P